To Teresa,
Friend + colleague
for whom I give
great thanks.

Wonder Reborn

WONDER REBORN

Creating Sermons on Hymns,
Music, and Poetry

Thomas H. Troeger

OXFORD
UNIVERSITY PRESS

2010

OXFORD
UNIVERSITY PRESS

Oxford University Press, Inc., publishes works that further
Oxford University's objective of excellence
in research, scholarship, and education.

Oxford   New York
Auckland   Cape Town   Dar es Salaam   Hong Kong   Karachi
Kuala Lumpur   Madrid   Melbourne   Mexico City   Nairobi
New Delhi   Shanghai   Taipei   Toronto

With offices in
Argentina   Austria   Brazil   Chile   Czech Republic   France   Greece
Guatemala   Hungary   Italy   Japan   Poland   Portugal   Singapore
South Korea   Switzerland   Thailand   Turkey   Ukraine   Vietnam

Copyright © 2010 by Oxford University Press, Inc.

Published by Oxford University Press, Inc.
198 Madison Avenue, New York, New York 10016

www.oup.com

Oxford is a registered trademark of Oxford University Press

Library of Congress Cataloging-in-Publication Data
Troeger, Thomas H., 1945–
Wonder reborn : creating sermons on hymns,
music, and poetry/Thomas H. Troeger.
p. cm.
Includes bibliographical references (p.) and index.
ISBN 978-0-19-539888-5
1. Preaching. 2. Hymns—Homiletical use.
3. Music—Religious aspects—Christianity—Sermons.
4. Religion and poetry—Sermons. 5. Sermons, American—21st century.
6. Aesthetics—Religious aspects—Christianity. I. Title.
BV4235.H94T76 2010   251—dc22   2009040350

1 3 5 7 9 8 6 4 2

Printed in the United States of America
on acid-free paper

To my colleagues and students
in the
Yale Institute of Sacred Music

Acknowledgments

A number of institutions, churches, denominational bodies, and schools have invited me to lecture and give workshops on the core themes of this book. Grateful for their hospitality and their lively conversations with me, I am pleased to acknowledge how they have contributed to my work on the place of beauty in preaching and worship. Their critical responses have been the basis for my revising and expanding material that I presented in various forms: lectures on the religious imagination at the Institute for Continuing Ministry Studies of the Claremont Theological Cluster, January 2001; the Brown Lectures on the religious imagination at First Presbyterian Church, Dallas, Texas (February 2001); the Smith Lectures on resurrection at Lexington Theological Seminary (Spring 2001); a workshop and lecture on tracing the church's theology through hymnody for Wake Forest University (September 2001); lectures on the meaning of baptism in a post-Christian age at Virginia Theological Seminary (October 2001); lectures and sermons for a religious arts festival at the Acton United Methodist Church, Acton, Massachusetts (November 2001); Northcutt Lectures on the religious imagination at Baylor University (April 2003); Preaching and Worship Conference at Richmond Baptist Seminary (2004); Parry Lectures at Plymouth Congregational Church, Fort Wayne, Indiana (November 2004); "Refreshing Winds" conference on music and worship at Canadian Mennonite University, Winnipeg (January 2005); lectures and sermons for the Fellowship of United Methodists in Music and Worship Arts (July 2005); lectures on religion, culture, and the arts at the Normal United Methodist Church, Normal, Illinois (September 2005); lectures on music and imagination at the School of Music, University of Iowa (January 2006); Schooler Institute on Preaching at Methodist Theological School in Ohio (October 2006); a lecture on the place of imagination in preaching hope for Societas Homiletica's biannual meeting at the University of Pretoria, Pretoria, South Africa (August 2006); an ecumenical conference on music and worship, Wilmington, North Carolina (November 2006); a lecture for the Forum on Music and Christian Scholarship at Yale Institute of Sacred Music, Yale University (March 2007); lectures on the theological resources offered by great hymns and spirituals for the Association of Presbytery Executives (September 2007); the Saint Mark Lecture at Saint Mark Presbyterian Church, Bethesda, Maryland (November 2007); "Seeing Christ through Music and Poetry" at Cathedral College, Washington, D.C. (November 2007); presentations on the interrelationship of music, theology, and worship for the American Guild of Organists at regional and chapter meetings in Tucson, Arizona (January 2008), Harrisburg, Pennsylvania (September 2008), and Stockbridge, Massachusetts (April 2009); sermons for "Listening Is Performing, Performing Is Listening," a conference on music and worship at the Yale Institute of Sacred Music, Yale University (March 2009); and Preaching Excellence Program of the Episcopal Church (June 2009).

I also am indebted to the following guilds and institutions: the Academy of Homiletics, at whose annual meeting I have given papers for more than thirty years, many of them related to the focus of this book; to the Festival of Homiletics that is sponsored by the journal *Lectionary Homiletics,* where I have lectured and preached for more than a decade; and to the Prince of Peace Chapel, Aspen, Colorado, where I preached on Bach cantatas and arias every summer for fifteen years. I owe a special note of gratitude to Susan Nicholson, the organist at Aspen, for her persistent, visionary efforts to blend great music with the prayers and preaching of the church; to Stephen Finch, a gifted choral conductor and pastoral musician, who conducted the performances; and to Irene Gubrud, who was a vocal coach to many of the young soloists. All three have inspired and encouraged me to write this book.

In addition to these events, I have written extensively for the following journals on topics related to the place of beauty in preaching and worship: *Lectionary Homiletics,* the *Hymn,* and the *American Organist.* Portions of my columns and articles from these journals have been the starting point for some of the sermons and discussions in this book.

I am also indebted to the colleagues and students of the Yale Institute of Sacred Music for their scholarship and support, the inspiration of their music making, their attention to visual and literary arts, their vital contributions to the history and practice of worship, the varied theological perspectives that they bring to their studies, and their mutually enriching conversation with one another. I dedicate this book to the students, faculty and staff as a way of expressing my gratitude and continuing the interdisciplinary work that lies at the heart of the institute's mission.

I owe a special word of thanks to Andrea Burr, my graduate student assistant, who has provided help in checking references, proofreading, preparing an index, and making incisive suggestions and reflections as the work went through many drafts.

Finally, as always, I give thanks for my wife, Merle Marie, for her unceasing patience and encouragement that create a gracious environment for me in which to read, think, and write.

Contents

Introduction

This book had its beginnings long before I wrote the first sentence. As with many of our mature pursuits, the impetus for the work started in childhood, when my capacity for adult thought had not yet emerged. As a small boy I found the world to be overflowing with wonder born of beauty, though at the time I did not have the words to describe my experience. I was in a state of pure amazement at what I saw and heard. I recall before I went to sleep in the summer looking up through the bedroom window into the maple tree in the backyard and being astonished to find that the moonlight made the leaves that had been green all day long silver gray by night. I recall getting up early in the morning and sitting in my mother's lap as she read the King James Version of the Bible or recited to me by heart the psalms she had memorized when she was a child. I grasped only a little of the meaning, but the poetry was music to my ears: "The heavens declare the glory of God; and the firmament showeth his handiwork. Day unto day uttereth speech, and night unto night showeth knowledge." "The earth is the Lord's, and the fullness thereof; the world, and they that dwell therein. For he hath founded it upon the seas, and established it upon the floods." "Lord, thou hast been our dwelling place in all generations. Before the mountains were brought forth, or ever thou hadst formed the earth and the world, even from everlasting to everlasting, thou art God." I recall winter evenings sitting with my father and listening to the symphonies of Haydn and the cantatas of Bach, and then after the last note faded away, I would go to the window and look out at a world of drifted snow giving back the deep blue cast of the night sky, a light that blended with the remembered music still sounding in my head and heart.

As I became an adult, the childhood wonder dissipated, and I started seeing the world with a more calculating eye. And yet the residue of wonder never completely vanished. Beauty kept retrieving wonder again and again in my life. I felt wonder return in a more sophisticated mode when I took a course in physics because there is something beautiful about using equations to plot the path and force of material phenomena. I felt wonder when I was playing the flute because there is something beautiful about my breath turning into melody as it vibrates through a silver tube. I felt wonder when I read lyric poetry with teachers who had a passion for its subtleties and rhythms because there is something beautiful in the visionary powers of the poetic imagination. I felt wonder when I studied philosophers who tried to disentangle the conundrums of existence because there is something beautiful about the mind wrestling with the profoundest matters of life. I felt wonder when I had a deep conversation with my wife or a friend or a stranger because there is something beautiful about catching a glimpse of how the world appears to another human being.

All of these were, however, scattered experiences of wonder, fragmentary intimations that fit no comprehensive constellation of meaning. What finally drew them together was when I worshiped, and the prayers, the reading of scripture, the sermon, the music, and the visual environment were so interwoven that the very Spirit of the Creator breathed through the service. I began to perceive how the wonder of physics and the wonder of music and the wonder of poetry and the wonder of philosophy and the wonder of conversation all flowed from the source of every good and perfect gift, from the wonder of all wonders: God. What I experienced was not the untutored wonder of childhood but the informed wonder of mature faith. I call it "godly wonder," a way of knowing and being in which all the polarities of life complement and enrich one another. In a state of godly wonder, religion and science, feeling and thought, imagination and reason, faith and knowledge dance together, and we gratefully discover that what one lacks the other offers.

Such wonder is related but not confined to the so-called second naïveté that arises from a postcritical reading of scripture in which we "risk allowing the Bible to speak to us again in the power of its appeal to our hearts and imaginations."[1] By godly wonder I mean something larger than a hermeneutical strategy for the reading of sacred texts, though that is one important ingredient. Godly wonder is a state of prayerful astonishment awakened by the Spirit of God through the experience of beauty.

Preachers can help to mend our bitterly fragmented world by reclaiming the place of beauty in preaching and worship in order to renew our sense of godly wonder. This book explores theologically and practically how to create sermons that nurture the godly wonder that keeps us open to dimensions of being and doing that we have yet to imagine or conceive, open to the Spirit whose winds we cannot predict nor control (John 3:8).

Chapter 1 develops the metaphor of musical overtones for understanding the theological significance of beauty and for clarifying how we make judgments about whether or not something is beautiful. Each of the next three chapters takes one art form—hymns, choral works, lyric poems—and explores their theological implications for preaching and worship. The theological discussion serves as a prelude to several sermons that model how preachers can draw upon beauty to feed the godly wonder of listeners. Chapter 5 returns to the themes that were introduced in chapter 1 and expands upon them in light of the sermons and the varied responses they awakened when I preached them to congregations.

Although the seeds of this book began with a child amazed by the silver gray light of moonbeams on a maple tree and his mother reciting the psalms and his father playing great music, its aim is the rebirth of wonder in adults as beauty finds its rightful place in preaching and worship offered to the glory of God.

Wonder Reborn

ONE

The Place of Beauty in Preaching

The standing ovation went on and on and on. The audience members were stomping their feet, clapping as loudly as they could, and shouting, "Bravo! Bravo!" We had just listened to an electrifying performance of Anton Bruckner's Fifth Symphony. As the ovation continued, my wife turned to me and asked, "Can we sing the doxology now?" She was serious.

"Can we sing the doxology now?"

Standing was not enough. Stomping our feet was not enough. Applause was not enough. Shouting "Bravo!" was not enough. Something more than an ovation had been awakened in her soul and in mine. Even though it was a secular concert in a secular setting, her response made perfect sense to me. Bruckner was himself a "devout man" who believed: "God is good. Everything man does should reflect the glory of God. Music should honor him."[1] Bruckner's symphonies have a "repose and unhurried serenity—qualities that so many people today long for. They can live the experience in Bruckner's music."[2] I believe that is what happened on this occasion. My wife's experience of overwhelming beauty awakened her desire to sing the doxology, to respond in gratitude to the source of "every perfect gift" (James 1:17). Langdon Gilkey describes the special quality of such an experience: "When an event that we label art thus stops the heedless flow of time in an enhanced moment, a moment of new awareness or understanding, a moment of intense seeing and of participation in what is seen, then (as the Zen tradition has taught us) the transcendent appears through art, and art and religion approach one another."[3] There is something in the heart, some deep resilience that springs irrepressibly out of us when through music and art we glimpse the transcendent, and we sense, however fleetingly, that life is transfigured by beauty.

Beauty?

At the mention of the word, I can already hear the skeptical voices: What is beauty? "Beauty is in the eye of the beholder." "It's all a matter of taste, and everyone's taste varies." Before we let these tired clichés suppress the urge to sing the doxology, the impulse to give ourselves completely to the praise of God because of what beauty awakens in us, let us acknowledge that in fact beauty is often the medium of grace that breaks through to the most disbelieving and hardened heart.

But what is beauty?

Every attempt to define it seems to falter. Definitions turn out to be too personal or too culturally bound or too historically conditioned. It indeed seems to be the case that "if we could invent a theory to explain beauty, it would spoil the whole thing: it would be like constructing a cage for a butterfly."[4] However, as Aidan Nichols has argued, this does not mean that we ought to eschew all conversation about beauty:

> Familiar it may be, dangerous it certainly is, for the temptation is perennial to use the concept for some specifiable quality defined by a rule of artistic making like the celebrated "Golden Number" in the science of proportion. All such definitions of the beautiful prove otiose because sooner or later they rule out of court artworks which speak powerfully to us while lacking the essential claimed for the beautiful. But this does not mean that the language of the beautiful should be abandoned.[5]

How, then, without "constructing a cage for a butterfly," might we continue to talk in some meaningful way about beauty? Rather than attempt a precise definition of the word, I will identify some of the overtones that sound in my heart and mind when I encounter beauty. They are like the overtones on a musical instrument: when someone plays a fundamental note, a sequence of pitches simultaneously sounds, giving the instrument its unique timbre and voice. We recognize a flute as a flute or a clarinet as a clarinet because of its pattern of overtones. Most of us do not have perfect pitch, and so we cannot name the fundamental note that is played, but we know what instrument is playing from the character of its sound. Likewise, we do not have "perfect pitch" for beauty—we cannot give a fundamental definition that everyone agrees with. But we recognize the overtones, the characteristics that lead us to describe something as "beautiful."

Although he does not use my metaphor of overtones, John Scotus Eriugena, expresses beautifully why analogies drawn from music are one of the most effective ways to talk about beauty:

> The beauty of the whole established universe consists of a marvelous harmony of like and unlike in which the diverse genera and various species and the different orders of substance and accidents are composed into an ineffable unity. For as instrumental melody is made up of a variety of qualities and quantities of sounds which when they are heard individually and separately are distinguished from one another by widely differing proportions of tension or relaxation, but when they are attuned to each other in accordance with the fixed and rational rules of the art of music give forth through each piece of music a natural sweetness, so the harmony of the universe is established in accordance with the uniform will of its Creator out of the diverse subdivisions of its one nature which when regarded individually clash with one another.[6]

Here, then, are some of the major "overtones" that sound when we encounter beauty:

- Beauty is more than prettiness.
- Beauty has a giftlike, gracious quality.
- Beauty can be a vessel of God's creativity.
- Beauty is culturally durable.
- Beauty has room for what is disturbing and difficult.
- Beauty helps us to see honestly what is there.
- Beauty is judged to fill certain standards of value.
- Beauty is best understood by a dialogue between our concepts and experience.

Beauty is not the same as "mere prettiness" because "to be beautiful as opposed to merely pretty, it needs to be associated with other values like truth or integrity."[7] Since beauty is more than prettiness, there is an enduring quality to beauty that is not always instantly detectable. It takes a process of reflection and discernment so that "the church must always be in the midst of sorting out the immediately attractive from the culturally durable."[8]

The process of discerning what is durable is arduous and fraught with all the inevitable complexities of our subjectivity and individual tastes. Nevertheless, I find Nicholas Wolterstorff's distinction between "wants" and "needs" helpful: "Being a responsible artist is not the same as being a pandering artist. The two are in fact incompatible. . . .[The responsible artist] strives to serve the needs and enrichment of his fellows, not necessarily their wants."[9] Wolterstorff's insight reminds me of when I was a teenager, studying to become a professional flutist. I was happily working my way through Handel and Bach when my teacher insisted that I learn the Hindemith sonata. I resisted initially, but my teacher, instead of pandering to my wants, knew that I needed the enrichment of a twentieth-century musical idiom that had its own astringent beauty. In time I came to love the Hindemith as much as the Handel and Bach. I have heard the same story from church musicians about choosing repertoire for their choirs or hymns for a congregation. Music that initially met resistance eventually became part of the beloved repertoire because it had an enduring beauty that served "the needs and enrichment" of the church.

Making such decisions, of course, involves our feelings, but it also involves resisting "an emotion which the will of a man seeks to impose upon me. The artist must be as objective as the man of science, in the sense that he must think of the spectator only in order to present him with the beautiful, or the *well-made,* just as the man of science thinks of his listener only in order to present him with the true."[10] There is no rule book that will guarantee this kind of objectivity, but keeping it in mind can be a part of the process of distinguishing beauty from mere prettiness.

When we encounter beauty, it has the quality of being a gift, something unearned that delights and enhances life at the deepest level of our being. This can be true even for the artists who create beauty. I think of dozens of stories from composers and other artists who sometimes describe how a work "came to them." One of the most famous examples is Handel, who wrote his oratorio *The Messiah* in only twenty-four days, from August 22 to September 14, 1741, and who described his sense of divine inspiration, saying, "I did think I saw all Heaven before me and the great God himself."[11] Handel's experience is a dramatic instance of how "beauty, like grace, is given gratuitously and is transformative. Indeed, perhaps beauty and grace are two varieties of the same thing. . . . many Christian theologians construe the Spirit's work of sanctification in terms of the restoration of spiritual beauty. Thus both sanctification and aesthetic beauty might be subsumed under a wider concept of beauty."[12]

We often sense God's creating spirit reaching toward us through beauty, even when the artist creating the beauty has no awareness of being a vessel of greater powers. "Artistic creativity is a response, whether joyful or painful, whether acknowledged as such or unacknowledged, to that given and discerned in creation and redemption. This links creativity to something far more fundamental than the artist's own imagination and skill, and opens up the possibility that art may be a means of grace."[13] Thus artistic beauty may fill us, as it did Saint Augustine, with a spirit of worship: "But, my God and my glory, for this reason I say a hymn of praise to you and offer praise to him who offered sacrifice for me. For the beautiful objects designed by artists' souls and realized by skilled hands come from that beauty which is higher than souls; after that beauty my soul sighs day and night (Ps. 1: 2)."[14]

Such beauty has ample room to embrace not only what is attractive but also things that are disturbing and difficult for us to confront. Beauty has this capacity because it is "inseparable from truth and goodness. Indeed, beauty is the persuasive power of God's truth and goodness. So beauty is in the end about honesty, about seeing what is actually there and being true to one's own response to it."[15] The beauty of what God has done through Christ includes not only the joy of incarnation and resurrection but also the cruelty of betrayal and torture. As Saint Augustine puts the matter, Christ is "'beautiful' in Heaven, beautiful on earth; beautiful in the womb; beautiful in His parents' hands: beautiful in His miracles; beautiful under the scourge: beautiful when inviting to life; beautiful also when not regarding death: beautiful in 'laying down His life'; beautiful in 'taking it again': beautiful on the Cross; beautiful in the Sepulchre; beautiful in Heaven."[16] Note how Augustine's process of thought circles from heaven back to heaven, thus suggesting the eternal dimension of Christ's incarnate ministry. This is beauty saturated with heaven, with the eternal, with the amplitude of reality that exceeds our mortal comprehension.

As Augustine finds beauty in all that Christ is and all that Christ does, so John Scotus Eriugena finds beauty in the interrelatedness of all things:

> For that which in some part of nature appears to be deformed in itself, considered in nature as a whole is not only beautiful and beautifully ordered, but is the efficient cause of the beauty of the whole: Wisdom is manifested by comparison with foolishness, and knowledge by comparison with ignorance, which is the absence and deprivation of it; life is revealed by comparison with death which is the absence of life, and light is glorified by contrast with darkness which is the deprivation of light: and, in a word, not only is it by contrast with their opposing vices that all virtues are glorified, but without that comparison they would be without glory. . . . For whatsoever is ordained by the dispositions of the Divine Providence is good and beautiful and just.[17]

It is the whole story of Christ that constitutes the beauty of the gospel and that nurtures "honesty about seeing" the human situation as it actually is, including all that we would hide from. John W. de Gruchy describes this as "the alien beauty of the cross." It is "the beauty of the 'suffering servant' (Isaiah 53:2–3), and as such it is a veiled beauty which is not self-evident."[18]

The "veiled beauty" of Christ is especially "not self-evident" in a consumer-driven culture that thrives on an ever-changing parade of products that supposedly make for "the beautiful life." However, the difficulty of grasping the beauty of Christ goes beyond the distortions of contemporary society. One has only to read Saint Paul (1 Corinthians 1:18–25) to realize how difficult it has always been for human beings to expand their "'canon of what beauty is through the Christian beauty of holy saving sorrow.'"[19]

Preaching on works of art that embody an inclusive, holistic under-standing of Christian beauty, one that reaches from joy to "holy saving sorrow," has the potential to awaken a range of varied aesthetic judg-ments in a congregation. Preachers, sensitive to this possibility, may decide it is the better part of pastoral wisdom not to risk the possible conflicts. And yet those conflicts, set in the context of a faithful community, can be a source of rich conversation and growth. For although we disagree about what is beautiful, "the very fact that when such disagreements occur we can talk, put forward reasons for our judgments, be understood and perhaps modify our views somewhat, indicates some shared criteria of judgment. As in the case of disagreement over moral issues, the very fact that we can discourse with those whose views are different from our own indicates the existence of some common ground."[20]

Beauty, then, is not purely in the eye of the beholder. There is some standard of value and assessment that makes possible conversation about beauty, and yet that conversation "is liable to seem only word-spinning unless one has some experience of the beauty in question."[21] Meaningful conversation about beauty involves a dialogue between our concepts and our experiences, a dialogue between our theological thinking about beauty and our services of worship that give us through poetry and music a glimpse of beauty whose amplitude extends beyond the limits of language and sound. Whenever this happens, a congregation comes to realize anew that "the primordial source of all beauty and all honour in heaven and on earth is the glory which God possesses in his own intimate life."[22]

I am not going to join all of beauty's overtones into a single, conclusive definition of the word. That would add up to "only word-spinning," a futile attempt to cage the butterfly. Instead, my method in the chapters that follow is to offer sermons based on culturally durable works of art that are more than pretty and that help us to see honestly the human condition and the glory of God. Then, in a final chapter, we will return to beauty, our conversation fortified by what we have experienced through the beauty of the works that have fed the sermons.

We will discover that beauty sometimes works its way through preachers in ways they never planned and never realized. Thus David Grayson—in an essay that appears to be partly reminiscence, partly fictional—describes an unnamed preacher whose sermons he heard while growing up in late nineteenth-century rural America. The preacher, Grayson recounts, "thought himself the greatest failure,"[23] but in truth the man was a vessel of holy beauty. Although Grayson cannot remember a word of any of the sermons, he remembers the preacher reading "mostly from the Old Testament—those splendid, marching passages, full of oriental imagery. As he read, there would creep into his voice a certain resonance that lifted him and his calling suddenly above his gray surroundings."[24] Grayson acknowledges that he did not understand the meaning of the passages. What gripped him was "the *sound* of them, the roll of them, the beautiful words, and above all, the pictures!"[25]

Some might question if the preaching accomplished anything worthwhile, since all Grayson can remember is the beauty of the sound and the pictures. But Grayson does not doubt its value for a moment. He says of his encounter with the preacher that he is "almost tempted to call [it] a resurrection."[26] One particular Sunday, when the preacher read the Twenty-third Psalm, Grayson found himself coming "out of some formless void, to intense consciousness—a miracle of creation."[27]

Grayson summarizes the impact of the preacher in a single memorable sentence: "Heaven he gave me, unknowing, while he preached an ineffectual hell."[28]

The preacher gave Grayson "resurrection," "a miracle of creation," and "heaven." Not bad for a preacher who counted himself a failure! But, of course, there is the irony that the preacher never realized how the Spirit had moved through him to reach the heart of a child. Grayson reflects that if the preacher had known what happened, he might have rejected it as unworthy of the word of God: "Somewhere, I said, he had a spark within him. I think he never knew it: or if he knew it, he regarded it as a wayward impulse that might lead him from his God. It was a spark of poetry: strange flower in such a husk. In times of emotion it bloomed, but in daily life it emitted no fragrance."[29]

There is a sadness to Grayson's story that goes deeper than his regret that he never told the preacher how much the minister had touched him. It is the sadness of a religious faith that fails to embrace the role of beauty in giving witness to God through music and poetry. It is the sadness of a church that fears beauty will be "a wayward impulse," leading us astray from God. Such fear has shaped the belief and practice of many Christians through the centuries. As Don Saliers observes: "Christian theology has shown a long and studied ambivalence toward human aesthetic capacities, especially toward relationships between art and religious faith."[30]

This ambivalence stretches across the centuries from Augustine, who oscillates between his love of music and his fear that its beauty will entice him from God, to Aquinas, who insists that preachers and teachers "should not be involved in singing lest they neglect greater things,"[31] to the influential contemporary homiletician David Buttrick, who counsels preachers:

> *Be concerned for craft.* Not art, but craft. There have been books on "the art of preaching." Skip them. Preaching is a craft to be learned like carpentry or cooking. Ego-driven self-expression is not what's wanted. We can live without polished sermons, the kind that draw admiration from listeners. A good sermon moves in the minds of listeners like their own thoughts. They are not aware of your sermon as separate from their hearing. They certainly don't give a hoot for aesthetic considerations; neither should you. Instead, you will study homiletic craft.[32]

The distinction between "art" and "craft" is a modern one, and Buttrick sets them too sharply against one another when in fact they are closely related. *The Oxford English Dictionary* points out that "*art* and *craft* were formerly synonymous and had a nearly parallel sense-development, though they diverge in their leading modern senses."[33] Hence an earlier writer on homiletics implores preachers to perfect their art: "It is just such art as this that we ask of the preacher . . . that he shall take diligent heed to do what he has to do as well as he can."[34] In insisting on the craft of preaching rather than the art of preaching, Buttrick risks choking the impulses of beauty whose origins are not fed by "ego-driven self-expression," but rather by the Spirit, who calls preachers to craft their sermons as art that gives glory to God. Preaching that is artful is congruent with the Bible. The artfulness and rhapsodic beauty of scripture, what Grayson describes as "those splendid, marching passages," demonstrate that art is often an integral part of disclosing the divine to the human heart and mind. "Since Scripture is counted by most Christians as in some way revealed, and since a significant portion of Scripture is artistic, then it follows that art can play a part in divine revelation."[35]

Buttrick's contention that preaching is a "craft" rather than an "art" is but one more manifestation of the church's persistent anxiety about the allure of the aesthetic, the suspicion that it will draw us away from God. To understand this fear, it is helpful to consider three distinct but interrelated terms that are frequently used in discussions of art: "beauty," "aesthetics," and "wonder." Although I have eschewed giving beauty a comprehensive definition, I have already named some of beauty's characteristic qualities by considering its "overtones."

The term "aesthetics" was first used by Alexander Baumgarten in 1735. Inspired by Descartes's famous statement, "I think, therefore I am," Baumgarten, "fully aware of the difference between the scientific and the artistic mind," was eager to find some criteria for evaluation that would fit the less logically precise nature of music, poetry, painting, and sculpture.[36] The work of Immanuel Kant and others broadened the meaning of aesthetics to include the critical study of how we receive things through the senses, particularly through artistic creations, and the ways we respond to and assess our experience of artistic work. Although this historical definition and development of aesthetics has informed much of my thinking, as a preacher I am also working with a much broader understanding of the term so that it includes not only our systematic understanding of sensory apprehension but also our emotional responses to art.

Alejandro García-Rivera provides this broader perspective on aesthetics when he asks:

> *What moves the human heart?* Put in this way, aesthetics has existed since the first human heart was moved by the influence of the beautiful. The cave paintings of Lascaux or Altamira, for example, still manage to affect the modern heart after thousands and thousands of years. As Jean Clottes, France's foremost expert on prehistoric rock art, confessed: "I remember standing in front of the paintings of the horses facing the rhinos and being profoundly moved by the artistry. Tears were running down my cheeks. I was witnessing one of the world's great masterpieces." Asking the question, *what moves the human heart?* I believe, brings us closer to the mysterious experience of the truly beautiful, an experience that transcends geological space and prehistoric time, an experience that holds the most persuasive claim to being what has become an *aporia* in our day, the real universal. Moreover, the tears of Msr Clottes, like the tears shed by St Ignatius in his mystical trances, speak as well of a religious experience.[37]

Although aesthetics is not restricted to the study of the beautiful, beauty has often been one of its chief concerns. In this book "aesthetic" refers to a theologically informed way of studying how we respond to and assess our experience of artistic work, including attention to what moves the human heart. It is, for example, the theological meaning of the cross that leads me to claim that beauty has ample room for what is disturbing and difficult, and that beauty helps us to see honestly what is there, including what we might otherwise hide or avoid. I name these as overtones of beauty because my aesthetic is shaped by the birth, life, ministry, passion, death, and resurrection of Christ, by the continuing ministry of Christ through the church, by the life of the Spirit in the world, and by the cosmic dimensions of Christ as the one in whom all things were created and all things hold together (Colossians 1:15–20). Someone else's aesthetic might begin from entirely different assumptions, and might conclude that what is disturbing and difficult can never be beautiful. It is important to be clear about these differences because religious people sometimes reject aesthetics, assuming that the term implies "art for art's sake." It has meant this for some artists and critics, but "art for art's sake" is not an automatic corollary of the term. For me, theological convictions about the character of God shape the aesthetic that I use in creating sermons based on works of art.

The third term interrelated to our discussion of art is "wonder." By wonder I mean the kind of experience with which I opened this chapter: my wife's being so moved by the beauty of a musical performance that while the audience roared and clapped their delight she wanted to sing the doxology. At such a moment our hearts leap upward. We sense irrepressible gratitude and vitality. We understand in the core of our being Bernard Lonergan's observation that "'there exists in man [and woman] an exuberance above and beyond the biological account-books of purposeful pleasure and pain.'"[38] Art fills us with wonder, stirs within us a resilient, joyful, vital exuberance. This is why "art should not and cannot be reduced to matters of 'practical concern.' Ultimately art has to do with the awakening of a sense of wonder, and it is in and through that awakening that aesthetic existence becomes possible and transformation begins to take place."[39]

Preaching on works of art inevitably engages the interrelationship of all three terms: "beauty," "aesthetics," and "wonder." I hope to show preachers how they can use a theologically informed aesthetic to preach on works of artistic beauty that renew a congregation's sense of wonder. Because that wonder is experienced in the context of corporate worship, it is more than a generalized feeling of awe and astonishment. It is an encounter with the numinous, the holy, the deep, dear core of things, the One who has created and redeemed us and in whose presence we are "lost in wonder, love, and praise."[40]

However, before turning to the work of creating sermons based on art, we need to consider some of the reasons that preachers and congregations may initially be skeptical of such preaching. Identifying the basis of their fear will help us develop a theologically informed aesthetic that can disarm the resistance that preaching on works of art might otherwise awaken. Perhaps the greatest and historically most persistent fear is that beauty will displace God, that it will become an idol, and religion will be reduced to what brings pleasure to the senses. Not having a theologically informed aesthetic amplifies this fear:

> The lack of a theology of beauty, both of beauty in general and of divine beauty in particular, follows in part from fear and suspicion of the question, expressed in pejorative terms like "aestheticism" and "elitism." . . . Even those who have widened their concept of beauty to include moral and spiritual beauty have often failed to relate these to natural and artistic beauty, and so have tended to depreciate the latter as being transitory or as restricted to what is bodily.[41]

The fear that artistic beauty might entice us from the true worship of God is not entirely unreasonable. Beauty can become a substitute for religion. But such "aestheticism is a disruption of the correct order of things or a corruption, and not an essential aspect of interest in the arts as such."[42] Yes, we have the potential to abuse the gift of artistic beauty, but that is equally true of all the gifts that God has given us. We are as capable of abusing the hunger for truth and goodness as we are the hunger for beauty. Sin can warp anything, even the noblest gifts God has given us, and if we dismiss a gift on the basis that it might lead us to sin, then we will be paralyzed and unable to use any gift.

As Patrick Sherry observes, "Human creative capacities may, of course, be ignored, suppressed, abused, or exercised in a repetitive and humdrum way."[43] But they also can be used to the glory of God. The first and most important reason preachers need to employ works of artistic beauty in their preaching is because they can draw us along with the psalmist "to behold the beauty of the Lord" (Psalm 27:4). But the church often suppresses the very beauty to which the psalmist gives witness: "The fact is that God is beautiful and the Church is hiding this. . . . For without a positive theological evaluation of beauty there is no motive to delight in God and no compelling reason to love him."[44]

There are also pastoral and ethical reasons for using artistic beauty to draw us to the beauty of God. We live in an age where beauty has been commercialized and degraded. I think here of "the beautiful people" or "the beautiful life." Beauty is reduced to being young, fit, rich and glamorous. It is a lifestyle of extravagant consumption that is environmentally disastrous and often personally destructive. In light of this culturally diminished vision of beauty, the eternal beauty of self-giving love that pours from the heart of God needs compelling expression to awaken the holiest and healthiest capacities of the human creature. Using the beauty of art to draw us to the beauty of God thus supplies a countercultural vision of what it means to be beautiful people and to lead a beautiful life.

The countercultural vision of beauty includes a prophetic perspective that employs beauty in nurturing justice and peace: "The beautiful serves transformation by supplying images that contradict the inhuman, and thus provide alternative transforming images to those of oppression. We are, in a profound sense, redeemed by such beauty, for art does not simply mirror reality but challenges its destructive and alienating tendencies, making up what is lacking and anticipating future possibilities."[45] Some people are skeptical of such transformation. They fear that a concern for beauty will blunt the church's moral judgment and its capacity to work for a more equitable, peaceful human community. Aesthetics will displace ethics. Although that could happen, it is not inevitable. Furthermore, there is potential for the equally serious distortion of a grim moralism whose "focus is too much on naked duty," so that it "does not take seriously enough the sphere of the beautiful" and "tends to deprive the good of its attractive power and of its giftedness which generate gratitude, the very energy-source of a morality under the law of grace."[46]

As Fred Craddock has reminded us:

The power of a revolution resides in the spirit that approaches life aesthetically. The great champions of the Social Gospel application of the message of Jesus and the prophets to the industrial, social, and economic problems of America were people who looked at those problems with aesthetic sensitivity. The poetic spirit of Washington Gladden was violated by injustice and economic imbalance; the ugliness and stench of poverty and disease stirred to action beauty-loving Walter Rauschenbusch. And those now involved in the church's struggle against injustice would do well not to permit the aesthetic dimensions of the problems to be dismissed in the name of "stark realism." The social crises of our time are, among other things, conflicts of harmony and noise, symmetry and distortion, poetry and prose, beauty and ugliness, fragrance and stench.[47]

The dynamic that Craddock describes between aesthetics and social action can be traced back to the psalms. Those beloved ancient poems often present a vision of beauty and justice feeding one another. Consider the opening verses of Psalm 33 in which music, righteousness, and the artistry of the Creator are interwoven as one coherent act of praise:

> Rejoice in the LORD, O you righteous.
> Praise befits the upright.
> Praise the LORD with the lyre;
> make melody to him with the harp of ten strings.
> Sing to him a new song;
> play skillfully on the strings, with loud shouts.
>
> For the word of the LORD is upright,
> and all his work is done in faithfulness.
> He loves righteousness and justice;
> the earth is full of the steadfast love of the LORD.
>
> By the word of the LORD the heavens were made,
> and all their host by the breath of his mouth.
> He gathered the waters of the sea as in a bottle;
> he put the deeps in storehouses.

Instead of separating ethics and aesthetics, the psalmist presents doing justice and performing "skillfully on the strings" as actions that flow together in a single stream of faithful living that in turn points to the creative artistry of God. By placing the values of righteousness and justice between the descriptions of human and divine artistry, the psalmist suggests that morality and aesthetics are seamlessly connected in the divine ordering of things. The movement from musical artistry to ethical principles to the creative work of God reveals that "the morality of beauty is something much deeper than that of 'must' and 'ought.' Its experience is inescapably personal, a loving and grateful approach to life itself. The fullness of being is experienced as a beautifying gift, an attractive appeal that solicits a loving response. Anyone who allows the beautiful, in all its dimensions, to bring its message home, knows that life is meaningful, a wonderful gift and opportunity."[48] Instead of making art an idol that entices us from what is good and true, the psalmist demonstrates how "virtue is more convincing and imitable when it is embodied concretely in art than when it is commanded or expounded theoretically."[49]

I have sometimes seen the psalmist's integrated vision embodied in the ministry of the church. On a study trip to the Balkans in May 2008, I encountered a witness to the power of beauty in healing a world broken by war. Ivo Markovic is a Franciscan priest, professor, musician, and activist who suffered through the violence that tore the Balkans apart in the early 1990s. He recalls his captors telling "'how they had killed Muslim women, even children, people who couldn't get out of bed.'"[50] This was in early 1991. Two years later his own father and several family members were killed by Muslims: "Days after receiving the news of his father's death, Ivo learned of an event taking place at the Zagreb mosque. He called the students from the choir he worked with to accompany him to the mosque, to sing for peace. The students were Croat Catholics from Bosnia who had fled their homes."[51]

Singing at the mosque became the prelude to a much more extended effort at reconciliation. Markovic and a choral conductor named Josip Katavic founded a choir to which they invited "Orthodox Christians, Muslims, Jews, atheists or anything else. . . . 'The basic goal was to create a symphony of religions, to bring together through song the three springs of monotheistic religion: Judaism, Christianity, and Islam. That was the fundamental idea, and also to create a community of people who would sing together, socialize, become a community.'"[52]

The group created its name, Pontanima, from two Latin words: *pons,* meaning "bridge," and *anima,* meaning "soul." The choir is building bridges between living souls as members from the various conflicted groups come together to sing each other's music for audiences that are as diverse as themselves. Markovic reflects on this arduous but reconciling work: "'I think that acts are most important, witnessing, living the things that we talk about rather than remaining within some internal hedonism, enjoying beautiful ideas. Ideas aren't beautiful in themselves—beautiful ideas are real. Beautiful ideas have to be lived.'"[53]

Hearing Pontanima sing, seeing their diverse faces, and listening to their wide-ranging repertoire, an audience experiences the transformative power of beauty in the service of a reconciling spirit. This is not something that happens automatically or easily. It is a process that unfolds as people persist in singing and listening to the beauty of each other's music: "When we start singing, when people hear the power of beauty, the power of soul, people become a little embarrassed and surprised and become more respectful."[54]

Like Ivo Markovic, preachers can employ the beauty of creative art in their sermons to remind congregations that God gave us the gift of creativity to use in ways that reflect rather than distort the image of our Creator. The creation and performance of poetry, music, and other arts are a means of continually renewing our awareness of being made in the image of God. When the church forgets this, it risks "what Claudel called 'the tragedy of a starved imagination,'"[55] and consequently diminishes the vitality of its spiritual life. This is doubly tragic when people live in a world that is already brutalizing them with ugliness. Although the following passage by D. H. Lawrence describes an earlier era, it could as easily be written of today's world: "The great crime which the money-eyed classes and promoters of industry committed in the palmy Victorian days was the condemning of the workers to ugliness, ugliness, ugliness: meanness and formless and ugly surroundings, ugly ideals, ugly religion, ugly hope, ugly love, ugly furniture, ugly houses, ugly relationship between workers and employers. The human soul needs actual beauty even more than bread."[56] When our sermons use the enduring beauty of excellent art, we are doing something far greater than prettifying our preaching. We are meeting an essential need of the human soul. We are reaffirming Christ's magnificent retort to the tempter: "'One does not live by bread alone, but by every word that comes from the mouth of God'" (Matthew 4:4, citing Deuteronomy 8:3).

P. T. Forsyth uses the image of "drought" to describe the spiritual barrenness of a church that is without art. He is "insistent that faith without a sense of beauty, or a religion severed from imagination and 'over-engrossment with public and practical affairs,' leaves us with 'a drought in our own souls.' It no longer evokes a sense of wonder. Art, in fact, is 'not a luxury' but a necessity of human nature."[57]

The necessity of art is manifest in a myriad of ways in varied contexts and cultures:

> Humans in their struggle for survival have never been so reduced that their privations snuff out aesthetic life. Put them in the simplest cabins and they will plant petunias about the doors; drive them into a cave and they will play the artist on the wall; leave them nothing but sticks and they will devise flutes; bind them in chains and they will drag them to some remembered cadence; imprison them and they will sing hymns at midnight.[58]

No wonder, then, that the starved imagination of the church and the resultant drought in the soul have driven many people from the community of faith. They do not find the church to be an environment hospitable to the divine gift of creativity that is self-evident in their common life "If the preaching of the church would address the whole person, then let the imagination play over the facts and awaken tired spirits. Many of the parishioners are not so much evil as they are bored, and their entire Christian experience has never provided them a chair in which to sit for an hour in the heavenly places with Christ."[59]

Richard Harries recounts a story that confirms the boredom and disillusionment that can result when the church neglects the creative work of the imagination. He tells of the great English poet Wilfred Owen (1893–1918), who worked for a while as a lay assistant in a parish and then left the position. A note found after his death on the battlefield in World War I said "'To Vicar . . . the Christian life affords no imagination, physical sensation, aesthetic philosophy.'" Many of Owen's powerful poems would later be set to music by Benjamin Britten in the *War Requiem*. Harris reflects: "The experience of Wilfred Owen can be paralleled many times over, from both Protestant and Catholic sources. People have found the Christian faith too narrow in its sympathies, inimical to the feelings and stifling to the imagination. . . . This is a disaster. For without an affirmation of beauty there can in the end be no faith and no God worth our love."[60]

An unimaginative and aesthetically starved faith not only diminishes God but also diminishes us. We are no longer all that God made us
to be: "Extract from a person's life a healthy portion of songs and flowers
and you have reduced to something less than human 'the creature the
Lord God has made to have dominion over land and sea.' This issue
involved here is no less than the nature of humanity."[61]

This book is part of my lifelong ministry to preach sermons that
widen the church's narrow sympathies, that draw upon enduring beauty
to give witness to a "God worth our love," to reclaim the fullness of our
humanity, and to nurture a hospitable ecclesial environment for the
artistic and creative imagination. I do this not to make the church artsy
but because I have experienced again and again what Patrick Sherry
predicts will happen when the church attends to beauty: "Now if the
responses of wonder, awe, and delight in beauty could be drawn together
into worship, and if thereby a sense of vision could be communicated,
this might produce a radical change in the life of many churches."[62]

Sherry grounds his hope for the revitalization of worship in the
witness of the Psalms. As we saw in our examination of the opening
verses of Psalm 33, "The sense of God's holiness, too, is often associated
closely with a sense of His glory, beauty, and majesty, and with the responses I have mentioned. When these responses are muted or the sense
of God's splendour and loveliness is lacking, then, as Moltman points
out, Christian existence gets subjected to judicial and moral categories.
Perhaps this explains a lack of joy, not just in worship, but in much
Christian practice."[63] How different such joyless worship is from the
intensity of holy desire that drives the psalmist to exclaim:

> One thing I asked of the Lord,
>   that will I seek after:
> to live in the house of the Lord
>   all the days of my life,
> to behold the beauty of the Lord,
>   and to inquire in his temple. (Psalm 27:4)

Many of the lines that precede and follow this prayer are verses of
lament about surrounding enemies. The psalmist's desire "to behold the
beauty of the Lord" lifts him above his somber situation and ultimately
sustains his hope so that he concludes: "I believe that I shall see the
goodness of the Lord in the land of the living" (Psalm 27:13).

In a world filled with terrors, the heart longs for a vision of divine beauty, and when the church fails to attend to beauty, the life of faith often becomes grim and onerous. We distort the image of God in ourselves and in our understanding of God's character, often concentrating on the power and might of God to the neglect of other divine attributes. Brian Wren offers a striking example of this phenomenon by analyzing an ecumenical hymnal published in 1983. Wren counts the number of times various names for the first person of the Trinity occur. He finds that there are "only 4 Loves, 6 Makers, and 7 Shepherds, but 12 Almightys, 34 Kings, 91 Fathers, and 87 Lords."[64] There is not one reference to God as Beauty. Wren's research is a detailed analysis of a single hymnal, but it is representative of a larger historical pattern. Patrick Sherry summarizes what Wren so vividly illustrates: "Western Christianity has given more attention to God's power than to His beauty."[65]

I wonder what would have happened if things were reversed, if the church had followed in the footsteps of its Jewish forebears who were "penetrated through and through with the delirium of Beauty. It is that which inspires the psalmists."[66] What if the church had given more attention to God's beauty than God's power? Would it have been more difficult over the centuries to sanction war in the name of Beauty than in the name of Power? Possibly not, since we human beings are capable of distorting any gift God has given us. Nevertheless, the question suggests why it is so important not to let power squeeze beauty out of the image of God. Without the counterbalance of beauty, our imaginations may warp our vision of what it means to be made in the image of God and to be the body of Christ in the world: "The emphasis on power in much of Western theology has been associated with ecclesiastical and dogmatic triumphalism rather than the 'glory of the Lord.' Or, better, the glory of the Lord has implied the glorification of divine power exercised by God's representatives (hierarchy; elect people), rather than the redemptive beauty of God as the power to save and restore humanity and creation."[67]

The roots of the problem lie not only in the church's truncated theology and its fear of the aesthetic but also in the way that art itself has been understood. Frank Burch Brown observes: "The predominant assumption in *modern* (as opposed to *postmodern*) aesthetics and criticism was that, if one wanted to get at what was truly artistic and aesthetic about a work of art or music or literature, one needed to bracket, or at least render inert, the actively religious stuff. . . . It was typically kept distant from religious commitments or actual worship, or indeed from any serious engagement with religious ideas or ritual themselves."[68]

In short, there have been forces outside as well as inside the church that have worked to separate beauty from its spiritual and religious roots. But that situation is now changing. Burch Brown's essay explores an increasing openness to the spiritual dimension of art: "Happily, as I say, we have set aside much of that modernist tendency to isolate art artificially and aesthetically. In the 1970s and early 1980s . . . one could witness the beginnings of a recovery of the realization that, after all, a spiritually and socially deprived art is not necessarily *more* satisfying aesthetically, and is often *less* satisfying."[69] While I am writing this book, I have attended or seen advertisements for concerts and art exhibitions that specifically invoke the spirituality or spiritual life of particular composers and visual artists. Something is stirring in our culture and the arts: "A quiet renaissance is occurring in pockets of the art world. In place of the modernists' battle cry 'art for art's sake,' other voices are rising that speak of art and music as expressions of . . . spirituality."[70] I believe these voices are a manifestation of the restlessness of the human heart that can never find enduring fulfillment in anything less than the ultimate source of our life and being.

Robert Wuthnow has done an extensive national study of the phenomenon, using statistical surveys, spiritual-journey interviews, elite interviews, focus groups and clergy interviews. On the basis of his research Wuthnow concludes "that the arts hold potential as a source of religious revitalization, at least insofar as artistic activities help to nurture interest in spiritual growth. This potential is evident in the fact that people with greater involvement in artistic activities are also more likely than those with less involvement to say that their interest in religion has been increasing, to attend religious services regularly, and to say that these services are important to their spiritual growth."[71]

Contrary to the opinion that an appeal to the arts is elitist or highbrow or of little interest to most worshipers,

> the data reveal that the vast majority of church members in all three traditions [evangelicals, mainline Protestants, Catholics] consider the arts (here, referring to painting, sculpture, music of all kinds, dance, theater, and creative literature) to be important in their personal lives. Among evangelicals, three-quarters do,

and among mainline Protestants and Catholics, more than four in five do. This means that the typical pastor, looking out at his or her flock on a given Sunday morning, can be pretty sure that most of the congregation has some appreciation of the arts.[72]

Wuthnow's research suggests that "religious leaders need to understand the profound cultural shift that the current interest in the arts represents. It is a move away from cognition and thus from knowledge and belief, a move toward experience and toward a more complete integration of the senses into the spiritual life. It is uncharted territory. Few clergy have learned anything in seminary that will help them to address it."[73]

Although Wuthnow's final observation about the clergy is largely true, there are growing numbers of happy exceptions. Some theological schools have developed programs in religion and the arts, a movement that is documented and succinctly described in the title of a work I have already quoted from: *Arts, Theology and the Church: New Intersections.* I celebrate these new intersections and the way they are giving future clergy the knowledge and creative understanding they will need if the church is to realize the spiritual renewal that Wuthnow describes. I teach in an institute whose mission is to be a "crossroads" where theology, music, and the arts meet,[74] and I am writing this book to add to the intersections between arts, theology, and the church by considering how preachers can give witness to the glory of God through music and poetry.

Generations of preachers have drawn upon hymnody, music, and poetry, but I will present a particular way of using these arts as a resource for the very substance of what a preacher says. Usually when preachers quote hymns or poems or refer to music in the course of the sermon, they do so for purposes of illustration. It is a sound homiletical practice, and I do not discourage it. But I want to do something more: I want to demonstrate how hymns, musical compositions, and poems can serve as the "text" for a sermon in the same way that preachers regularly use a passage or theme from the Bible. The method I present here is not a pattern to be used every Sunday but one that will often open the preacher and the congregation to the glory of God moving through the beauty of a work of art. It is a method that belongs in a preacher's repertoire of varied homiletical strategies. Far from being "unbiblical," it helps people to intuit and experience anew the divine realities to which the Bible gives witness.

My goal is to model how preachers can use the tools of literary and musical analysis to create sermons that explore in depth spirituals, hymns, cantatas, anthems, and poems that are subsequently offered to God in the service following the sermon. These are methods that seminary students and pastors can learn just as they learn the tools of biblical exegesis and historical analysis. The sermons that result are *not* art lectures. They are sermons. They proclaim the glory of God, the wonder of the risen Christ, and the presence of the Spirit. They draw their liveliness and organization from careful study of the artistic, theological, and spiritual dimensions of the work on which they are based. As a result, when the members of the congregation sing or hear the artistic work, they are drawn more completely into its theological substance and spiritual vitality. The preacher's sermon has prepared their imaginations so that they receive the work with their hearts and minds fully engaged. The preacher's words and the artistic work thus become one seamless witness to the Word of God, through whom "All things came into being" and without whom "not one thing came into being" (John 1:3).

Such sermons fit well into the context of worship because "after all, liturgy at its best is a creative work of art in and through which we are enabled to discern the redemptive beauty of God."[75] The sermons use a theologically informed aesthetic to draw upon works of art whose beauty can deepen the wonder that a congregation also experiences through sacrament and prayer.

Wuthnow's research documents that "nationally, 65 percent of the public agree that churches should do more to encourage their members' creativity and imagination."[76] The homiletical methods that I develop here demonstrate one practical way that preachers can faithfully engage the creativity and imagination of their congregations. This is a down-to-earth, "that-will-preach" homiletic that I have used for more than thirty years in scores of different church, university, and seminary settings with dedicated pastoral musicians and volunteer choirs. There is no need to be scared off by the artfulness of the selections on which my sermons are based. In my earlier work, I have written about ways preachers can create sermons that draw upon the electronic media and popular culture,[77] but here I am deliberately using what some may call "high culture." I, however, do not find the term helpful. It often feeds the fear that we will be seen as "elitist," so that rather than risk such criticism, we forgo using art that could have provided the congregation a "disclosure of truth,"[78] a transforming revelation about life and faith. I have discovered again and again that it is groundless and condescending to assume that "people won't go for that high art stuff." What they will not go for is stuffiness and snobbery. They will go for beauty that transfigures life by revealing the glory of God. Their hearts hunger for it.

When I was a young pastor, I was initially reluctant to share with the congregation my passion for great English poetry because I feared it might be considered elitist or snobbish. Then one year, I decided I would venture basing a Lenten study series on a number of poems by John Donne (1572–1631), a complex but profound poet. I was astonished at the number of people not only who attended but also became absorbed in the man's poems. At the final session, an individual who had the least education in the group borrowed my collection of the poems because he wanted to continue to read them. Then and there I tossed to the winds my fear that church people would be put off by my using great art. I had discovered the truth of Marilynne Robinson's observation that "there is no snobbery in saying things differ by the measure of their courage and their honesty and their largeness of spirit, and that the difference is profoundly one of value."[79]

The church is a treasure house of Christian art that is characterized by "courage," "honesty," and "largeness of spirit." It is art that gives vivid witness to God and that constitutes an extraordinary homiletical resource for preachers. Donald Whittle suggests the virtually boundless store of creative work that is available to us by distinguishing three different ways of understanding the phrase "Christian art":

1. Christian art is an historical category referring to those works whose themes are explicitly Christian.
2. Christian art is a way of describing works that share a Christian vision though they make no explicitly Christian reference.
3. Christian art is "a re-enactment of creation" so that all works of art manifest to Christians "the conviction that God created man to be, in his own turn, a creator."[80]

Although I am interested in all three understandings, this book deals specifically with works that fall under the first definition: they all are explicitly Christian. Preachers can certainly use works of art that fall

under the other two definitions. But I have chosen to focus on the first
definition for several reasons.

First of all, preachers who have never tried these homiletical
methods will find themselves most comfortable starting with explicitly
Christian works. There they will encounter symbols, stories, biblical
allusions, and theological meanings that resonate with their faith. They
can thus focus on the challenge of developing the requisite skills of
theological and artistic interpretation. As they gain greater assurance in
preaching this way, I encourage them to move on to Whittle's other
classifications of Christian art.

Second, generations of Christians have found in these works the
overtones of beauty that I discussed at the start of this chapter, especially
the overtone of being culturally durable. They are classics: "works of
exceptional quality that deeply and repeatedly reward attention and
that can be valued similarly over a long period of time by a wide range
of perceptive and receptive people."[81] The judgment of their excellence
is based on something far greater than our narrow slice of historical
existence.

Third, I am eager that the church realize how it too often ignores
its own treasure house of great artworks that are inspired by the gospel
and alive with the Spirit. Not only the church but the culture at large
seems to have amnesia about this historical legacy. A few years ago
someone wrote in the newspaper that religion kills the imagination. A
reader, much wiser and more knowledgeable, responded in a letter to
the editor with a litany of great names: Michelangelo, J. S. Bach, John
Donne, and more. I wondered if the first writer might have been influ-
enced by the church's neglect of its storehouse of imaginative, creative
art. How are people outside the church to know that the Christian faith
is highly imaginative if the church fails to use effectively the imaginative
treasures that it has?

I fully agree with Whittle that contemporary secular works can be
"profoundly religious" and "far nearer to the faith which the New
Testament sets forth than the many works which are placed firmly in
Biblical or ecclesiastical settings of the first century."[82] I consider his
point indisputable, but it must not be allowed to overshadow that much
of the profoundest art we have—enduring the test of centuries—is
Christian art, and it is irresponsible of the church to ignore this resource.
To do so is to admit tacitly that faith does kill the imagination and

creativity, when history is filled with a vast store of splendid imaginative creations inspired by faith in God.

Finally, I employ these particular works of art because "certainly, in our multicultural world, it is vital to explain and interpret one's own tradition in terms intelligible to others. It may, however, be equally vital for us to interpret our traditions to ourselves."[83] There is keen wisdom in this succinct observation. It suggests that we will not be effective citizens in a multicultural world unless we have a strong sense of our own tradition. I think of individuals I have seen who go searching for spirituality in multiple traditions without knowing their own in depth. They become spiritual tourists, collecting souvenirs from here and there but never making a commitment that lasts long enough for them to probe the depths of any one tradition. By preaching on Christian works of great musical and poetic beauty that give witness to the glory of God, we help our people mature in their faith. Such maturity equips them to live graciously in a multicultural world by making them secure in their own Christian identity while heightening their ability to understand why the riches of other traditions mean so much to their adherents.

I have limited myself in this volume to what John de Gruchy calls "the chief contribution" of the Protestant Reformation to Western art, namely, "music, hymnody and poetry, that is the arts that appeal to the ear and add enrichment to the Word."[84] In no way do I mean to imply that these arts or the culture that produced them are preeminent. They are the arts that I have practiced, studied, and been immersed in from my childhood to the present moment. My hope is that readers more conversant in other art forms and more knowledgeable than I about their cultures will draw upon the work that they know best. They will preach sermons that are faithful to the Spirit's creative movement in their particular context. I have been present in services where preachers have offered sermons on paintings or sculpture or movies or dance, often originating in a culture different from my own. These sermons moved me. They strengthened my faith and illumined my life, but they were not sermons I would have been competent to create and preach. What they shared with the sermons I offer here was a theologically informed aesthetic that drew upon the beauty of an artistic work to awaken wonder in the congregation. It was the wonder of profound worship, the wonder that inspires people with the living presence of God and empowers them for ministry in the world. Preachers can help us experience such wonder through a wide range of varied arts and cultures.

David Grayson, whose childhood memories of church we discussed earlier, writes that his pastor regarded the spark of beauty "as a wayward impulse that might lead him from his God."[85] We have now seen that the preacher's fear was not something he dreamed up on his own. It arose from a suspicion of art and beauty that has sadly afflicted many persons of faith who fail to see that "without the language and experience of Beauty and the beautiful, the Church will find difficult the expression of her faith, much less her conviction of the dignity of the human person, and, even less, be a sacrament to the world."[86]

The necessity of beauty becomes even more apparent when we place it in the context of the whole human community coming to terms with a global economy, a pluralism of cultures, and an ecological crisis. We are engaged in "a battle between vast destructive systems which feed on sameness, uniformity and power, and the fragile diversity of the human species as we struggle to evolve, not according to some evolutionary myth of progress, but according to that innate desire within our species to make meaning, to imagine worlds, to create beauty, even in the midst of violence and destruction."[87] We need preaching that contributes to the strenuous work of making meaning, imagining worlds, and creating beauty. This book is about one major way to realize that goal. It demonstrates how the spark of beauty that shines through music and poetry can flame up to the glory of God in our preaching and renew our lives with holy wonder.

TWO

To Make the Wounded Whole

Preaching on Hymns

I can now see that my mother planted the seeds of my preaching on hymns during my childhood, when she sat at the piano and played hymns we never sang in church.[1] I was raised in the northeastern United States. My mother had come north from South Carolina after she married. Opening a tattered old hymnal to play her favorites, she would often remark: "They don't sing the hymns I know, and they don't sing with the warmth we used to sing in our little church at home." The difference she was referring to was typified by the contrast between "In the Garden," which she played with substantial rubato, and "O God of Bethel by Whose Hand," which we sang in my upstate New York childhood church to "Dundee" with a steady beat.

As a child I recognized immediately the difference in the sound, and with a child's way of knowing, I sensed two different musical characterizations of God in the contrasting tunes and rhythms. The words of "In the Garden" always made me picture my great-aunt's flower garden where I used to weed with her in the early morning when I visited my mother's childhood home. And the words of "O God of Bethel by Whose Hand" always brought to mind a picture in my history textbook of the Pilgrims in New England simply because the first verse speaks of "this weary pilgrimage."

I recall being fascinated by these contrasts, especially because my mother also read the Bible to me every morning, and I could not quite figure out how to fit these different songs together with the pictures I imagined of the biblical stories.

In reading Robert Wuthnow's sociological study of how American churchgoers search for a vital spirituality through the arts, I discovered that the importance of my childhood experience with hymns is not in the slightest unique. Wuthnow presents a statistical chart demonstrating those factors that shape the degree of interest various people take in their spiritual growth. He divides these into four groups: "highest," "high," "low," and "lowest." Sixty-six percent of those with the "highest" degree of interest in spiritual growth mentioned a favorite hymn from childhood as a significant factor, and 55 percent of those in the "high" group also mentioned the importance of hymns.[2] Looking at the data, Wuthnow observes: "The childhood experience that matters most is not attendance at services but the subliminal contact with the holy that comes through hymns and other religious music, pictures, Bibles, crosses, candles, and other sacred objects."[3]

These are significant data for preachers because they indicate the use of hymns in sermons can be an effective way of connecting with people's spiritual commitments and energies. At the same time, hymns usually grow out of efforts to interpret scripture and theology in poetically beautiful, easily accessible, and pastorally empowering ways.

As an adult who has ended up spending his life in the study of preaching and worship, I had long wanted to find some way of understanding hymns that would help preachers more effectively draw upon them as a primary spiritual and theological resource for sermons, not merely quoting them to add a poetic flourish or end on a familiar note. I sought a concept that would build a bridge between the spiritual energies that hymns awaken in our congregations and the larger story of biblical faith. Such a concept would aid in developing a positive appreciation for the vast range of biblical interpretation and theological perspective that is represented by the multiple traditions of hymnody.

Several years ago I discovered the concept I had been looking for in a splendid anthology of poems based on texts from the Hebrew Bible.[4] The editor, David Curzon, provides an introduction in which he presents the poems as a collection of midrashim. The word "midrash," the singular form, comes from the Hebrew, meaning "to inquire, investigate." The term is used twice in the Bible: in 2 Chronicles 13:22 and 24:27. The New Revised Standard Version (NRSV) translates "midrash" as "story" in the first of these references, but in 24:27 "midrash" is rendered as a "Commentary on the book of Kings."

One of the basic functions of midrash is to interpret a scriptural text so that it is relevant and meaningful to the contemporary situation of its readers. James Sanders, however, warns against too constricted an understanding of the term and defines midrash in its broadest sense as an interpretive process: "When one studies how an ancient tradition functions in relation to the needs of the community, he is studying midrash."[5]

Many biblical scholars have found the origins of midrash in the Bible, particularly how later books provide commentary on passages of scripture written many centuries earlier, such as the way the apostle Paul recollects and interprets passages from the Torah. Compare, for instance, Genesis 16 and Galatians 4:21–5:1, and Deuteronomy 30:11–14 and Romans 10:5–10. It may be, as Richard Hays has argued, that these reinterpretations are more accurately described by the term "intertexuality" rather than midrashim.[6] Whatever terminology we use, the dialogue of ancient authoritative text and contemporary situation is clearly alive in Paul, "who, while undergoing a profound disjuncture with his own religious tradition, grappled his way through to a vigorous and theologically generative reappropriation of Israel's Scriptures."[7]

There are forms of postbiblical rabbinic midrash that are clearly more than intertexuality. They embroider the scriptural account with added details, explanations, and rearrangements of the material, and they focus on interpreting the Torah, the first five books of the Hebrew scripture. Because the Torah was the most sacred of writings, and because it was believed to contain all that was essential to know about God and humanity, heaven and earth, the rabbis brought a passionate intensity to its study and their commentary on it. But since the rabbis also realized that the Bible speaks to people in different ways, they accepted multiple interpretations of the text. Thus the same passage or word from the Torah could give birth to many different and even contradictory midrashim.

Just as the history of hymnody is filled with shifts in subject matter and theological focus, so too midrashim develop and focus on different topics in different ages. For example, the early period of highly developed postbiblical midrashim (400 to 640 C.E.) includes apocalyptic and eschatological interpretation, but as the form develops over the centuries, it becomes more homiletical.[8] And to this day we might accurately say that a great deal of preaching is midrash: preachers use their theologically informed imaginations to provide an interpretation of a biblical text that will help make sense of the congregation's life and empower people to live their faith.

Midrash is, then, a concept rooted in the history of biblical interpretation that allows for multiple readings of scripture in light of contemporary life. This sounds remarkably like the function of hymnody as it has flowed into new times and places and branched into many different streams. I had known about midrash through my studies in homiletics, but it did not occur to me to apply it to hymnody until I read Curzon's revealing introduction in which he describes how "some poets manage to retain a contemporary sensibility while writing of biblical material, so that their poems on sacrifice and murder, and love and the lack of love, *combine modernity with the resonance and depth of the ancient texts.*"[9] We can take that last phrase and easily rewrite it to understand the midrashic character of hymnody: "Hymn writers combine the spirit and concerns of their culture with the resonance and depth of the ancient texts." The hymn "In the Garden" worked powerfully upon my mother's early faith because it fuses echoes from the biblical stories of Eden and Gethsemane with her being raised by an aunt who throughout her active years tended a large flower garden. In a similar way, "O God of Bethel by Whose Hand" worked well in the northern Presbyterian congregation that had many people of Scotch and Welsh descent. Each hymn was an effective midrash. It was an interpretation of biblical images and stories that made sense of the experience and faith of the congregations that sang them. But it is clear from my mother's remark—"They don't sing the hymns I know"—that our favorite midrashim are often the ones we sang as children or that we first came to know when we found God later in our lives. The heart, if not the head, considers them to be the most faithful interpretation of scripture and tradition.

While the concept of midrash awakens a positive appreciation for what the past has supplied us, it also reminds us of the task of reinterpretation: "For the sake of maintaining the continued vitality of the text, new interpretations have been needed every generation or so."[10] The unceasing nature of the process of reinterpretation arises from the scriptures themselves, for the Bible . . . is artfully contrived . . . to open up a dense swarm of variously compelling possibilities, leading us to ponder the imponderables of individual character, human nature, historical causation, revelation, election, and man's encounters with the divine. If all literary texts are open-ended, the Bible, certainly in its narrative aspect, is willfully, provocatively open-ended: that indeed, is why there is always room for more commentary.[11]

Despite his being a superb anthologist, Curzon is apparently unaware of the work of hymn writers throughout history coming to terms with changing theologies and cultural conditions: "The scarcity of midrashic poems in existing anthologies of religious poetry forced me to realize how far modern midrash is from conventional notions of the religious."[12] Although I owe to Curzon the idea of considering hymns as midrashim, this is evidently not an understanding that he himself holds. However, I can hardly imagine a sounder theological reason for preaching on hymns than Curzon's description of what happens through the genre of poetic midrashim: "This engagement with biblical material, like all living traditions, assists the free imagination to avoid solipsism. It permits the type of seriousness and wit possible only in relation to known stories and propositions, the fundamental wit of variance from what is established, of originality grounded in the familiar."[13] Hymns leave the imagination "free" but engage it with the Bible in order to avoid "solipsism," the reduction of everything to the self and its feelings. Hymns strive for an "originality grounded in the familiar." In great hymns we encounter God anew, but at the same time the poetry resonates with what we know from scripture.

The principles for preaching on hymns that I have derived from Curzon sound much like Haggadah (huh-gah'-duh), a form of midrash that interprets passages of Hebrew scripture that are not of a legal character: "Unlike the strict logic of legal interpretation, Haggadah could give free play to the imagination. Haggadic expositions are not bound to the previous tradition. However, the story had to remain within the bounds of what was *acceptable to the religious community.*"[14]

Sometimes the bounds of the religious community are narrow, and sometimes they are broadly expansive, embracing a number of very different images of the same biblical story. Hymns as midrashim perform a crucial theological task: they help to save the church from bibliolatry, the turning of scripture into an idol. We do not worship the Bible. The Gospel of John does not open, "In the beginning was the Bible and the Bible was God … and the Bible became flesh and dwelt among us." It uses the much more dynamic word "Logos," which is rich with meanings far greater than our more constricted English translation "word." "Logos," for example, carries associations with the feminine figure of Wisdom and her role in creation.[15] Hymns as midrashim keep the gathered church mindful that what matters is not simply the literal page but the encounter with the living God, who, like the wise rabbis, allows multiple and even conflicting interpretations of the same biblical passage.

Although some traditions claim to be strictly biblical, their hymnody often reveals a diversity and creativity that their dogmatic theologies discourage. Traditions that have eschewed or minimized the elaborations of symbol, image, and ritual have found an outlet for the impulse of the religious imagination in hymnody. It is as if the eye, having been starved of beauty, is fed intravenously through imaginative language. It is the imaginative, midrashic quality of hymns that has empowered communities of faith to endure terrible suffering, to dream dreams, to claim anew the hope of the gospel, and to reach toward a fuller realization of the reign of God in their congregations and in the larger world around them.

The regular metrical forms that characterize the vast majority of hymns are a means by which the poet "channels strong feelings into deep designs."[16] For the faithful those "deep designs" extend beyond the fixed meters and rhyme schemes to the pattern of a life that has been warmed by the Spirit. George Herbert captures this pattern in his poem "Love (2)," as he describes how we respond when we have been attracted to the "Immortal Heat" of God:

> Then shall our hearts pant thee; then shall our brain
> All her invention on thine Altar lay,
> And there in hymns send back thy fire again.[17]

Although humans write and sing hymns as an expression of their creative power, their "invention," hymns are also a medium through which the divine "fire" is returned to its source. Singing hymns is a way of enacting our desire to respond to the "greater flame" that attracts us by first kindling our hearts. Because hymns are a point of conjunction between divine initiative and human response, they give us access to the vital nerve of lived faith, supplying preachers with a vision of the heart's holiest perceptions and yearnings.

The act of singing hymns also puts us in touch with the act of creating hymns. Members of the congregation recapitulate the mystery of finite creatures seeking to praise the Creator. They give expression to the overflowing impulses of their hearts, while at the same time they are aware of the inadequacy of their song. How can our limited constellation of organic cells ever rightly sing the wonder of the one who created and redeemed us? Tukaram, an Indian peasant mystic, gives words to the conundrum of existence that finds articulation in our hymnody:

> Ah, Lord, the torment of this task that Thou hast laid on me
> To tell the splendour of Thy love!
>
> I sing, and sing,
> Yet all the while the truth evadeth telling:
>
> No words there are, no words,
> To show Thee as Thou art:
>
> These songs of mine are chaff,
> No spark of living truth hath ever lit my lips:
> Ah Lord, the torment of this task that Thou hast laid
>   on me![18]

In preparation for preaching on hymns, it is helpful to consider the conditions that gave rise to their creation and to identify some frameworks for interpreting them as a particular kind of midrashim, as a genre that fuses theological, liturgical, and poetic qualities. Preachers can think of this interpretive work as a form of exegesis. Just as they identify the genre of a biblical passage, investigate its historical context, and analyze its images and rhetoric, so too they can do the same with hymns.

Erik Routley, a renowned historian of Western hymnody, summarizes a lifetime of tracing the origin and theology of hymns with this observation:

> Periods when somebody somewhere is tearing up the turf and
> asking questions and organizing rebellions and reconstructing
> disciplines produce hymns: when the steam goes out of such

movements, or they become part of an expanded main stream, hymn writing goes on in a more tranquil way, but never for very long. Another colour is added to the picture by another "movement," and that movement brings new hymns and new kinds of hymn into the repertory.[19]

When we sing hymns from different historical periods and cultures, we encounter strikingly different theological understandings of the gospel, of Christ, the Spirit, and the Word of God. The way hymn writers present these realities, the character of their piety, their diverse theologies, and the varied responses that they seek to awaken in the faithful—all these are shaped by different periods of "tearing up the turf," different periods of "organizing rebellions and reconstructing disciplines."

The process of creating hymns is dialogical because the poet's imaginative work oscillates between tradition and the emergence of new needs and insights. The tradition reinterprets the present, and the present reinterprets tradition. Earlier we considered how the process results in hymns as a form of midrash, an original retelling of something ancient and familiar. Amos Wilder describes what emerges from this dynamic as the "theopoetic" of the church: "In each new age and climate the theopoetic of the church is reshaped in inseparable relation to the general imagination of the time."[20] The history of preaching the gospel through hymns stretches all the way from the first century C.E.—see, for example, Philippians 2 and Colossians 1—to the current day. During those twenty centuries "the general imagination of the time" has seen extraordinary upheavals and transformations. The history of our hymnody preserves for the church the record of all those changes. To study the hymns of different eras is like boring into the earth's crust to recover geologic history. We discover the shifting contours of faith through the ages and come to a deeper appreciation of the processes that have shaped the landscape of faith that we inhabit.

The theopoetic is not limited to words alone. Although I am presenting this material in print and, therefore, tend to focus on the poetic texts, it is important to remember that the imagination of any particular era is shaped not only by language but also by the sum total of the ways a culture engages and uses the senses. Different eras and cultures teach people to visualize, hear, and organize sensate reality in distinctive modes and patterns of response. Walter Ong calls this phenomenon the "sensorium": "By the sensorium we mean here the entire sensory apparatus as an operational complex. The difference in cultures . . . can be thought of as differences in the sensorium, the organization of which is in part determined by culture while at the same time it makes culture."[21]

Those differences in the sensorium include what Stephen H. Webb has termed the "soundscape" of Christian theology.[22] Thus even as we read these texts we need to remember how varied the soundscapes of different traditions are. Sometimes the soundscape is all voices in unison with no instrument, sometimes it is voices accompanied by pipes or strings, sometimes it is while the body moves, and sometimes it is while the body is still.

In summary, hymns and how we respond to them arise from the conjunction of many factors:

- poets creating midrashim, creative retellings of familiar stories
- people "organizing rebellions and reconstructing disciplines"
- a dialogue between culture and tradition that results in an ever-changing theopoetic
- a sensorium that uses the senses in particular ways to shape the imagination of the community at prayer.

The Bible itself often employs hymns for homiletical purposes. Paul the apostle uses a hymn to develop his sermonic point in Philippians 2, and the author of Colossians quotes a Christ hymn that "is the cornerstone of the author's argument"(Colossians 1:15–20).[23] A close study of the Colossian hymn and the forces that gave birth to it reveal that the dynamic interaction of faith and culture that characterizes the entire history of Christian hymnody begins in the New Testament.

The hymn in Colossians describes Christ in cosmological terms:

> He is the image of the unseen God,
> and the firstborn of all creation,
> for in him were created,
> all things in heaven and on earth:
> everything visible and everything invisible,
> Thrones, Dominations, Sovereignties, Powers–
> all things were created through him and for him.
> Before anything was created, he existed,

and he holds all things in unity.
Now the church is his body,
he is its head.

As he is the Beginning,
he was first to be born from the dead,
so that he should be first in every way;
because God wanted all perfection
to be found in him
and all things to be reconciled through him and for him,
everything in heaven and everything on earth,
when he made peace
by his death on the cross. (Colossians 1:15–20, Jerusalem
    Bible)[24]

Colossae was a pluralistic city, home to many different religions.
Raymond Brown observes that Colossae was located in an area
where "religious observances reflected a mixture of native Phrygian
cults, Eastern imports (Isis, Mithras), Greco-Roman deities, and
Judaism with its insistence on one God."[25] Thus the letter to Colossae gives us a perspective on the stress and strain of being Christian
amid multiple religious and philosophical views. Since hymns are
one of the most important ways that worshiping communities incul-
cate their beliefs and understandings, the Colossian hymn gives us a
feeling for how early Christian faith was taught and practiced in a
cosmopolitan, pluralistic city. Although the text was possibly modi-
fied to make it more congruent with the writer's argument,[26] the
author of the letter grants substantial authority to the hymn. He
appeals to it as the basis of his theological admonitions to the
Colossians.

The hymn is marked by a confluence of Greek and Hebraic cultures.
The descriptions of God and Christ resonate with overtones from Hellenistic writings, while the role of Christ in creation seems to echo claims
about Wisdom in the book of Proverbs. This cultural confluence is significant: it tells us that while our ancestors drew their unique identity from
Christ, they also drew upon the idiom of their era to express their faith.
When the materials of the surrounding culture enriched the expression
of belief, our ancestors were willing to interfuse them in Christian

worship, even into the language of their hymns and thereby into their understanding of the faith and how it was to be interpreted to others.

But at the same time, our ancestors in the faith balanced their use of the surrounding culture with an ability to critique that culture. The author of Colossians employs language familiar to his readers and hearers in a way that simultaneously relates to their world and criticizes their world. The rhetorical, theological balance of Colossians and particularly its hymn has implications for understanding the subsequent history of hymnody and for figuring out how we are to live faithfully in our own time and culture. The hymn and its Greek cultural accretions suggest that we need not be automatically hostile to the culture or the era in which we find ourselves. Instead, we are to think critically not only about what is distorted and wrong in our culture but also what it has to offer faith that is valuable, usable, and worth singing about!

There is in the Colossian hymn an even profounder confluence than the confluence between cultures. It is the confluence between the divine and the mortal, between the eternal and the transitory, between the ineffable and the tangible, between heaven and earth. The confluence of these realities sounds in the paradoxes and juxtapositions of the poem: "the *image* of the *invisible* God," "things in *heaven* and on *earth*," "all things have been created *through* him and *for* him." This is the work of a skilled hymn writer who awakens wonder through poetic and rhetorical beauty.

The confluence of two different realities, two different domains of being, becomes even more dramatically evident in the closing verse: "Through [Christ] God was pleased to reconcile to himself all things, whether on earth or in heaven, by making peace through the blood of his cross." After the poetic splendor of the opening verses, the hymn ends with "the blood of his cross." Whatever Hellenistic, supernal piety the Colossian congregation found in the grand rhetorical flourishes that open the hymn, that religious sentiment is transfigured by the final phrase, "making peace through the blood of the cross." To worship in a community that sings a hymn marked by the confluence of splendor and blood is to be given a vision of reality that spans from the brutality of human violence to the sublimity of the One who has created us. Only by a vision this expansive can we face the truth of our human situation as it actually is. If the Colossian hymn had only the grandeur of God, and "no blood of [Christ's] cross," then belief would devolve into escapism: we would be related to a sublime deity who has no interest in our violent, bleeding world. Or if the Colossian hymn had only the blood, and no grandeur, then belief would devolve into despair. We would be related to a God who has no power to lift our vision beyond the brutal life we suffer here and now. But this great hymn has both splendor and blood, and it locates their interconnection in the very nature of God and God's action in Christ. The hymn overflows with overtones of beauty that we named in chapter 1. It is more than merely pretty, it has ample room for what is disturbing, it is culturally enduring, it helps us see honestly what is there.

The hymn models how to interpret the gospel in a pluralistic world. It affirms and celebrates that Christian faith stands at the confluence of human need and divine extravagance in responding to that need. The human need is for some way of glimpsing the reality of God. The divine extravagance is Christ who "is the image of the invisible God." The human need is for some assurance of meaning in a fragmented world. The divine extravagance is Christ, the one "in whom all things hold together." The human need is to know that the alienation between humanity and God is overcome. The divine extravagance is Christ through whom "God was pleased to reconcile to himself all things." The human need is for the solace of knowing that God is with us in our pain and death. The divine extravagance is Christ who has made peace "through the blood of the cross."

Because the author of Colossians was writing only some thirty years after the earthly ministry of Jesus, he had a limited repertoire of Christian art for expressing the confluence of divine extravagance and human need. But now, nearly 2,000 years after he posted his letter, there is an endless treasury of hymnody, visual art, music, and poetry that give witness to the confluence of human need and divine extravagance. Although the hymns from subsequent Christian history that we are about to explore do not directly refer to the Colossian hymn, their images and metaphors are a witness to the confluence of human need and divine extravagance that has continued to find expression through the centuries. To preach on these hymns is to continue the theopoetical process that is so vitally manifest in the Colossian hymn.

I offer now four examples of preaching on hymns. The first three are sermons in which a single hymn is the primary text for the preacher. Each sermon draws upon the scriptures, but it is the hymn text that inspired the sermon and carries the sermon to its climax. The fourth way suggests how to draw on a number of hymn texts to develop a series of sermons based on a theological theme or a season of the liturgical year.

The first sermon that I present explores an African American spiritual. I am using the word "hymn" here in its broadest sense: any poetic text that is set to music and sung by the congregation as an integral part of a service of worship. I have chosen for illustration hymns that are deeply beloved and familiar to most English-speaking congregations in the United States. All three are found in every major hymnal I have on my bookshelves. I can trust that most readers will be able to hear the music in their minds, and many will be able to sing some of the verses from memory. It would not be an exaggeration to consider these hymns "canonical." They have an authority that nearly equals the authority of scripture for those who regularly sing them.

Like beloved passages of scripture, we have heard them again and again. Their familiarity is both a blessing and a liability: a blessing because in times of need they often bring comfort, a liability because we sometimes assume we have exhausted their meaning when in fact their greatest depths remain unplumbed. One of the gifts of preaching on a beloved hymn is that the congregation often remembers the sermon whenever they sing the hymn again in future services. The sermon is thus a way of deepening the congregation's life of corporate prayer and making it an even more effective vessel of pastoral care in times of pain and need.

There Is a Balm in Gilead

Sometimes I feel discouraged and think my work's in vain,
But then the Holy Spirit revives my soul again.
There is a balm in Gilead to make the wounded whole;
There is a balm in Gilead to heal the sin sick soul.

If you cannot preach like Peter, if you cannot pray like Paul,
You can tell the love of Jesus and say, "He died for all."
There is a balm in Gilead to make the wounded whole;
There is a balm in Gilead to heal the sin sick soul.

Don't ever feel discouraged, for Jesus is your friend;
And if you lack for knowledge, He'll never refuse to lend.
There is a balm in Gilead to make the wounded whole;
There is a balm in Gilead to heal the sin sick soul.

Sermon: Jeremiah 8:22–9:1

Sorrow.[27] *There are so many things that can awaken sorrow: the sorrow of chronic illness, the sorrow of broken relationships, the sorrow of death, the sorrow of letting someone down whom we love, the sorrow of hunger, the sorrow of war. The sorrow, the sorrow of it all.*

But today I want to look at one particular sorrow. Only one. However, it is a sorrow so deep and so pervasive that it has come to influence every aspect of our ministry.

The sorrow I have in mind is the misuse of religion, the misuse of the name of God to repress and exclude various people by following a narrow and rigid reading of the Christian tradition. I weep to think that the body of Christ spends its precious resources debating who is in and who is out, instead of focusing our energies exactly where Christ tells us to: on feeding the hungry, on clothing the naked, on visiting the imprisoned, on God's wounded, bleeding creation.

What is the place of sorrow in living a life of faith in an age of religious violence and spiritual hunger? Note the adjectives describing our age: religious and spiritual. The two words are not synonymous, and in many people's minds, they are not even interrelated. I can think of scores of people—including many theological students—who tell me they are spiritual but not religious. In their minds spirituality is good and religion is bad. For such people spirituality means being in touch with the deep, dear core of things, while religion means being narrowly dogmatic to the point of violence: physical violence and rhetorical violence.

Have you ever been to a public meeting in which every voice was so shrill and angry you became less concerned about the topic under discussion and more concerned about whether people would start shooting each other? Perhaps it was a school board or a legislative hearing or a zoning commission or a church vote on a social issue. Or perhaps you were not there, but you saw it on television or heard the aftershock on a talk show or a blog, or a friend told you about it and your friend's voice was still trembling with the fright of the conflict. Whatever the case, the experience gripped your heart with the realization that the tissue of human community can easily be ripped and shredded. What you experienced is rhetorical violence.

What can we as religious people do to stop the ripping and shredding of the human community that feeds the sorrow of the world?

Historically, religion has sometimes nurtured a sense of our interrelationship with one another. Religion has provided a structure of belief and practice that sustains a community of shared conviction, empowering people for the work of love, and finding an enduring purpose for life even in the face of death.

The word "religion" itself comes from the Latin religare *meaning "to bind together." Think of a time in your life when you were a member of a community of shared conviction that bound your heart to other hearts, that empowered you to do justice and show compassion, and that gave you a sense of deep meaning and purpose. Think about the most positive qualities of the experience. My hunch is that in many cases you will discover spirituality and religion were not at all opposites. Religion was the environment, the context in which your spirituality flourished.*

But what happens when a community of shared conviction begins to fragment, each faction claiming that it more faithfully represents the core values of its tradition? And then, to make things even more complex, what happens when that same community becomes aware of a pluralistic world filled with competing and conflicted values and practices? In short, what happens when there is neither external nor internal coherence?

There is a wide range of possible responses, from hospitality and conversation with the strange new perspectives to violence, and by violence I mean not only physical violence but also the rhetorical violence that rips and shreds the tissue of human interconnectivity. In recent times, as I follow the news I sometimes feel as if we are living in an exhausting public meeting where nearly every voice is shrill and angry, and religious voices are among the shrillest and the angriest.

How will we find our way in an age of religious violence?

One very contemporary answer is to turn to forms of spirituality that are free of the structures of belief and practice that characterize religious communities. Articles in the popular press report increasingly large numbers of people who identify themselves as spiritual but not religious. Thus an age of religious violence has spawned an age of spiritual hunger, and the two exist side by side.

But what about those of us who continue to be active in religious communities? How will we live faith? How will we minister together as a corporate body in an age of religious violence and spiritual hunger? We cannot ignore the spiritual hunger that has been intensified by religious violence, but neither can we escape to our inner selves. For better or for worse, we all live together on this whirling, watered stone that hurls through the immensities of space.

Of course, we are not the first age to be characterized by religious violence and spiritual hunger. I think of Jeremiah, the fiery prophet who was born sometime between 645 and 640 b.c.e. Jeremiah lived through a time of devastating violence and intense desire for spiritual reassurance. Although Jeremiah was often called to announce the judgment of God, the violence and destruction of his times brought him to tears, brought him to the kind of sorrow that enables

us to claim more fully our humanity and our human connection to others. Listen
to Jeremiah lament:

> *"Is there no balm in Gilead?*
> *Is there no physician there?*
> *Why then has the health of my poor people*
> *not been restored?*
> *O that my head were a spring of water,*
> *and my eyes a fountain of tears,*
> *so that I might weep day and night*
> *for the slain of my poor people!" (Jeremiah 8:22–9:1)*

The prophet asks: Is there no balm in Gilead? Gilead was located in the
Transjordan, basically where modern-day Jordan is. "Gilead" in Hebrew means
"rugged," which describes well the region's densely wooded, mountainous terrain.
Its slopes were covered with balsam trees that exuded an aromatic resin. The
ancient inhabitants prized the resin because they could mix it with certain vola-
tile oils to make a balm, an ointment to nurture the healing of wounds.

There are three things to note about a balm. First, it is not a single pure
substance but a mixture of resin and oils. Second, a balm is not an elixir, it is not
a miracle drug, it is not a quick cure, it is not an instant fix. Upon application a
balm is soothing. It brings some relief, but it does not erase the wound overnight.
A balm does not relieve sorrow all at once. Third, the balm nurtures the process
of healing, but that process is a function of something greater than the balm alone.
The restoration of skin and flesh comes from the body itself, from its own energies
for wholeness and health.

The ancients lacked our modern medical technology, but they were as
bright and as observant as any of us. They would have known a balm is a
mixture of elements, a balm soothes but is not a quick fix, a balm encourages
the health-restoring processes of the body. Thus, when Jeremiah asks, "Is there
no balm in Gilead?" his question is rich with metaphoric, theological implications: "Is there no balm in Gilead?" means: Is there no mixture of elements
that might help bring healing to our age of religious violence and spiritual hunger? "Is there no balm in Gilead?" means: Is there nothing to soothe the rawness of our divisions even if it will not provide a quick fix for our brokenness?
"Is there no balm in Gilead?" means: Is there not some way to draw forth the
energies for wholeness and health that are part of our varied religious traditions
and spiritual practices?

Our English translations of this passage from the book of Jeremiah usually print the words as though it is the prophet who asks, "Is there no balm in Gilead?" Some exegetes, however, believe it may be a more faithful reading of the Hebrew text to understand that the speaker is God. God is the one who asks: "Is there no balm in Gilead?" God is the one who says: "O that my head were a spring of water, and my eyes a fountain of tears, so that I might weep day and night for the slain of my poor people!"

The Hebrew Bible scholar Patrick Miller believes that the most important thing is not to settle whether Jeremiah or God is the speaker. What matters most is to realize: "There is no separation between the anguish and pathos of the prophet over what is happening to the people and the anguish and pathos of God."[28] No matter how we translate the passage, it is clear that God is in anguish and pathos over the violence that destroys Jerusalem and sends the people into exile.

I believe God is now in our own time once again in anguish and pathos. God grieves. God is in sorrow for how religion misuses the name of God. To ask how we should live the faith in an age of religious violence and spiritual hunger involves asking: How do we respond to a weeping God? Think for a moment of how we respond to people who are mourning the death of someone they loved. Even if in the past we have been in total disagreement, we do not take advantage of their grief to continue the conflict while they mourn. Instead, their tears awaken in us a sense of our shared humanity. Their sorrow connects them to us in a way that was never possible when we treated them as alien and strange. If human tears have the power to broaden the sympathetic reach of our hearts, what do the tears of God mean for an age of religious violence and spiritual hunger? What does a weeping God awaken in us?

The most obvious answer is that we do not invoke the name of God to prove we are right and others are wrong, any more than we use the occasion of human grief to take advantage of those who mourn. When God weeps, the most important question is not, Whose side is God on? but instead, How do we tend to the sorrow of God? How do we live faith, how do we minister in a way that would bring comfort to God who is weeping over the misuse of God's own name? How do we answer the sorrowing God who asks: Is there no balm in Gilead? Is there no mixture of elements that might help bring healing to our age of religious violence and spiritual hunger? "Is there no balm in Gilead?" Is there nothing to soothe the rawness of our divisions even if it will not provide a quick fix to our brokenness? "Is there no balm in Gilead?" Is there not some way to draw forth the energies for wholeness and health that are part of our varied religious traditions?

African American slaves took this profound question and applied it to their own Gilead, to their own rugged, ragged life as human chattel, abused and denigrated by their masters. The slaves' oppression and abuse were a form of religious violence, for their masters appealed to the Bible to sanction slavery in the name of God. Nevertheless, an astounding thing happened in the process of creating one of their greatest spirituals. Instead of asking "Is there no balm in Gilead?" the poet/ composer of the spiritual declares: "There is a balm in Gilead to make the wounded whole." As Howard Thurman puts the matter, the enslaved poet/theologian "straightened the question mark in Jeremiah's sentence into an exclamation point: 'There is a balm in Gilead!' Here is a note of creative triumph."[29]

Given the terrors of slavery, one might expect that the spiritual would have started with the anguished question that arises from the prophet, from the very heart of God: "Is there no balm in Gilead?" How did the slave move from question to declaration, from discouragement to hope, from sorrow to assurance? How did this transformation take place?

Understanding the forces that shaped the spiritual can help us find the balm that our religiously conflicted world desperately needs. Arthur C. Jones, a clinical psychologist who teaches at the University of Denver, is one of the great scholars and interpreters of African American spirituals. Jones writes:

> *"Balm in Gilead" is an especially important song in the spirituals tradition, expressing the ability of enslaved Africans to transform sorrow into joy, to make a way where no way seemed possible. That ultimate message of hope and healing . . . is the product of a creative tension between awareness of painful oppressive circumstances and the simultaneous envisioning of a hopeful future. This is not a naïve optimism, but rather a genuine inner transformation.*[30]

The slaves found balm in their Gilead by honoring the full range of their reality. They looked unflinchingly at the terror that beset them, and with an equally stubborn gaze they beheld the hope that sustained the holiest and highest dreams of their hearts:

> *Sometimes I feel discouraged,*
> *And think my work's in vain,*
> *But then the Holy Spirit*
> *Revives my soul again.*

The slaves lived in a world of religious violence and spiritual hunger. Slavery was religiously sanctioned violence. Masters justified the institution by appealing to the Bible and Christian belief. The abuse of the slaves, the breaking up of their families, the suppression of their cultural inheritance—all worked together to create in them an intense spiritual hunger for freedom, for respect, for some larger meaning that could redeem their suffering. The spirituals arose, then, in an age of religious violence and spiritual hunger.

The three qualities of a balm are all present in these profound songs of sorrow and hope. First, there is the mixture of elements that flowed from "a creative blend of African traditions and Christianity, creating a new, transformed religion different in form and substance from the religion of the slave holder."[31] It was a Christianity that with daring and creativity eschewed a narrow Biblicism for a broader, more integrative, visionary faith.

Second, there is the balmlike power to soothe without offering an instant cure. For the spirituals provided "a means of combating the potentially destructive internal psychological damage that could be inflicted by the experience of prolonged enslavement."[32]

Finally, like a balm, the spirituals drew forth religious energies for wholeness and health as they helped to empower "the freedom movement led by the Rev. Martin Luther King, Jr., and his African American tribesfolk."[33]

The balm in Gilead was the spiritual itself: the mixing of diverse elements, the finding solace in the midst of suffering, the drawing forth of wholeness and healing. When the slaves sang the spiritual, they felt the balm in their hearts. The act of singing confirmed what the words declare: "There is a balm in Gilead to make the wounded whole."

At this point in the sermon, have a single instrument play or a single voice hum the melody of the spiritual. This should be done with simplicity and feeling, not loud and not hurried.

What about us, living in our Gilead, our own rugged, ragged landscape of religious violence and spiritual hunger? Are we, like the poet/composer of the spiritual, able to move from the question—Is there no balm in our Gilead?—to the affirmative declaration: "There is a balm in Gilead to make the wounded whole."

Yes, I believe we can. In this age of religious violence and spiritual hunger, there is a balm in Gilead. I have sometimes received that balm through congregations, through individual believers, and through religious leaders who lived the same qualities that we saw in Jeremiah and that we saw in the spiritual: the mixing of diverse elements, the finding solace in the midst of suffering, the drawing forth of wholeness and healing. They did not know the answer to every religious conflict.

But they had the wisdom to know they did not know. They did not provide food for every religious hunger. But they had the wisdom to know it is not possible for any one community to feed every religious hunger. But over time they were a balm because they invited and welcomed diverse people with diverse commitments, and diverse practices to join together as a religious/spiritual community.

Note that last adjective: not a religious community, not a spiritual community—but a religious/spiritual community. I am using religious/spiritual as one continuous word. A religious/spiritual community fuses together realities that are meant to be complementary, not oppositional.

It is a religious community because it understands the necessity of institutions. We need governing boards and forms of polity and budgets and agendas and buildings and dependable rituals. For without these institutional realities, who will offer the corporate worship that empowers the community to raise the money to put in the time and the energy to provide week after week, year after year, century after century a continuing ministry of service and transformation to this wounded, bleeding world?

Spirituality without religion and without its institutional structures easily becomes narcissism and self-illusion.

But a religious/spiritual community is also a spiritual community. It is alive to the startling presence of God, alive to the profoundest thirst of the soul, alive to the glimpses of beauty and wonder that awaken and nurture faith and hope and love. Religion without spirituality easily buries the deepest hungers of the heart beneath institutional operations.

In an age of religious violence and spiritual hunger, the church is a balm whenever it truly becomes a religious/spiritual community. Remember: a balm is not an elixir, not a quick fix, not a miracle drug. But over time, a balm brings healing. It sets off a process of thought and action, of prayer and art, of belief and practice, of conversation and community. Over time it will bring healing and wholeness to a world of religious violence and spiritual hunger.

Yes, there is a balm in Gilead to make the wounded whole.

Have the whole congregation sing the spiritual.

Christ, the Lord, Is Risen Today!

Christ, the Lord, is risen today, Alleluia!
Sons of men and angels say, Alleluia!

Raise your joys and triumphs high, Alleluia!
Sing, ye heavens, and earth, reply, Alleluia!

Love's redeeming work is done, Alleluia!
Fought the fight, the battle won, Alleluia!
Lo! the Sun's eclipse is over, Alleluia!
Lo! He sets in blood no more, Alleluia!

Vain the stone, the watch, the seal, Alleluia!
Christ hath burst the gates of hell, Alleluia!
Death in vain forbids His rise, Alleluia!
Christ hath opened paradise, Alleluia!

Lives again our glorious King, Alleluia!
Where, O death, is now thy sting? Alleluia!
Once He died our souls to save, Alleluia!
Where thy victory, O grave? Alleluia!

Soar we now where Christ hath led, Alleluia!
Following our exalted Head, Alleluia!
Made like Him, like Him we rise, Alleluia!
Ours the cross, the grave, the skies, Alleluia!

Hail, the Lord of earth and heaven, Alleluia!
Praise to Thee by both be given, Alleluia!
Thee we greet triumphant now, Alleluia!
Hail, the resurrection day, Alleluia!

King of glory, Soul of bliss, Alleluia!
Everlasting life is this, Alleluia!
Thee to know, Thy power to prove, Alleluia!
Thus to sing and thus to love, Alleluia

Hymns of praise then let us sing, Alleluia!
Unto Christ, our heavenly King, Alleluia!
Who endured the cross and grave, Alleluia!
Sinners to redeem and save. Alleluia!

But the pains that He endured, Alleluia!
Our salvation have procured, Alleluia!
Now above the sky He's King, Alleluia!
Where the angels ever sing. Alleluia!

Jesus Christ is risen today, Alleluia!
Our triumphant holy day, Alleluia!
Who did once upon the cross, Alleluia!
Suffer to redeem our loss. Alleluia![34]

Sermon: Luke 24:13–35

I have a picture gallery in my mind to which I return again and again to contemplate certain favorite images. Some of them are works of great art. Some of them are family photographs. Some of them are horrifying news scenes. Some of them are cartoons. I keep returning to this picture gallery because when I behold the image in my mind's eye, I call up a web of memories and associations. The picture gallery in my mind is charged with meaning, and it is therefore a place that often inspires sermons.

Today I am standing in that picture gallery and contemplating a cartoon that I must have used in a dozen or more sermons over the last forty years. Before I describe the image, let me describe when I first saw the cartoon. It was at the end of the sixties maybe in 1970 or 1971. Many of you remember the sixties. And if you are too young to remember, you probably have heard about that decade from your parents or your grandparents.

It was in the sixties that President John F. Kennedy was assassinated. It was in the sixties that Martin Luther King Jr. was assassinated. It was in the sixties that Robert Kennedy was assassinated. It was in the sixties that the civil rights movement gathered to a mighty force for change. It was in the sixties that we became embroiled in the war in Vietnam. It was in the sixties that the nation divided into hawks and doves, and there were massive antiwar protests on campuses and in the streets. As the seventies began, a single question was repeated again and again on the news, in interviews, and on talk shows: "Is there any light at the end of the tunnel?"

It was in the midst of all this conflict that I first saw the cartoon that I am viewing in the picture gallery of my mind. A lone human figure is sitting in a waiting room with two doors. One bears a sign saying: no exit. The other door says: no entrance. No exit. No entrance. The words leapt off the page and landed on my heart with the force of a massive weight. No exit. No entrance. In one simple drawing the artist had given expression to the spirit of the times.

No exit, no entrance is more than an image. It is a posture of the soul. It is a state of being. It is a perception of the world that debilitates our energies to hope and to act in ways that can transform life. A large part of ministry is dealing with people who live in a state of no exit, no entrance: people who are addicted, people who are trapped in abusive families and relationships, people who are in devastating grief, people who suffer chronic depression, who feel they live in a world where there is no exit, no entrance. No way out of their oppressive situation. No way in to a new way of being and living.

And it is not just true of individuals. It is true of institutions and organizations, societies and nations. No exit, no entrance. That is what it must have felt like to be a Jew living in Palestine 2,000 years ago under the iron fist of the Roman Empire. Try to get free of Caesar's reach and they would nail you to a cross, and erect that instrument of torture on a garbage heap where they already had crucified scores of others before you. No exit, no entrance.

Consider how that feeling would only have intensified if you had once foolishly hoped that an exit, an entrance was being opened to you, only to find it slammed shut in your face. You might well be like those two disciples on the road to Emmaus who told the stranger walking with them about the one whom they had followed because they hoped that he would be the one "to set Israel free."[35] The devastation of losing such hope could be enough to blind you with sorrow so intense you could not even recognize your closest friend, even if that friend were walking at your side.

If you put the resurrection stories from the Gospels side by side, you will discover that nearly all of them share a similar pattern: grieving followers do not recognize the risen Christ. In our eagerness to get to the joy of Easter, we may skim over the pattern and as a result fail to see the extraordinary relevance of the resurrection stories to the current state of our church and the world.

Each story opens with Christ's followers in a state of no exit, no entrance. When they awake on the first Sunday after Good Friday, the one thing they know with absolute certainty is that the world is sealed shut to hope. There is no exit from the despotic power of the Roman Empire and its collusion with repressive religion, and there is no entrance to a better future. It is a world of solid meaning, and the solid meaning is this: there is no exit out, there is no entrance into a new creation.

Not a single one of the resurrection stories begins with the words: "Alleluia! the Lord is risen!" "The Lord is risen indeed. Alleluia!" Despite variations about this or that detail, the resurrection stories share a somber, sorrowful opening. In Mark, the women carry spices to anoint the cadaver of Jesus, and they wonder while they walk, who will roll the stone away. In Luke, the disciples on the road to Emmaus lament to a stranger their loss of hope. In John, Mary Magdalene weeps outside the tomb, assuming the body has been stolen. In each case the character or characters carry with them an assumptive world of solid meaning in which there is no door or window or crack for other possibilities to shine through.

No wonder the women in Mark ask: "Who will roll away the stone?" No wonder the disciples going to Emmaus lament: "We had hoped he was the one to set Israel free." No wonder Mary, in the garden, assumes that the person speaking to her must be a gardener who has moved the body to another location. In every case their assumptive world adds up to a state of no exit, no entrance. It is not unreasonable to speculate that this repeated pattern represents what first-century Christians may have often felt in light of Rome's continuing tyranny and their rejection by the established religious authorities.

But in every story of the first Easter the world of no exit, no entrance crumbles. The women in Mark discover the stone is rolled away. The two disciples invite the stranger in for a meal, and when he breaks bread, their eyes are opened and they recognize him. Mary hears the supposed gardener call her by name, and she realizes it is her beloved teacher. The resurrection of Christ opens a way out where there was no exit, it opens a way in where there was no entrance. We come to realize that the way we see the world is not the final word on reality.

At any moment we may be as surprised by resurrection as the women carrying the spices to the tomb and wondering who will roll away the stone. We may be as surprised as the disciples in Emmaus when their eyes are opened by the one who blesses and breaks bread with them. We may be as surprised as Mary when she hears her name pronounced by the voice of the one she mourns.

To the world, it looks as though there is no exit, no entrance. But faith in the resurrection reveals the world is wrong. Reality has possibilities we never dreamed of, including that new life can spring from death. The risen Christ discloses the irrepressible resilience of the divine vitalities that set the atoms spinning, the creation breathing, and the human heart sighing and sensing how love and grace persist beyond every human effort to kill and bury them.

Christ teaches about the resilience of the divine vitalities before his death and resurrection. On Palm Sunday, the beginning of Passion Week, Christ rides into town, and when the crowds in the street begin to sing his praises, the religious authorities, according to Luke, tell him to order his disciples to stop. Christ responds that if his followers were silent, "the stones would shout out" (Luke 19:40).

The idea that the stones would shout is not original with Jesus or with Luke, who ascribes these words to him. Some of the psalms are filled with verses that exhort sun and moon and stars, earth and sea monsters, hills and trees to praise God. The psalms suggest that the natural order itself gives witness to the irrepressible resilience of the divine vitalities that set the whole creation humming and buzzing in the first place.

In the presence of the Christ through whom all things were made, it is not possible to kill or to muffle the praise and gratitude that arise from the human heart and even from the rocks. That is why we cannot refrain from the worship of God and from living a life of hope. If we failed to make such a witness, the rocks would drown us out. Like them, like the sun and moon and stars, like the depths of the ocean and the sea monsters, we are alive with the irrepressible resilience of the divine vitalities that move through the cells and tissue of our human bodies. We feel that resilience every day when we awake, knowing that "each breath is borrowed air/not ours to keep and own,"[36] and we trust that after our final breath the irrepressible resilience of the divine vitalities will transform us in ways that are in complete harmony with the grace and love of the risen Christ. For as the most beloved Easter hymn in English affirms: resurrection is not a one-time-only event. "Christ the Lord Is Risen Today"[37] does not put resurrection in the past or future tense but in the present tense, suggesting that Christ is risen at the very moment of its singing, and that here and now the world of no exit, no entrance is broken open again and again.

The hymn is not entirely original with Charles Wesley. It is based on a fourteenth-century Latin carol from Bohemia: "Surrexit Christus hodie." The first English translation appeared in London in 1708 in Lyra Davidica. *Wesley's version was first published in 1739, but given the joy and conviction with which most congregations sing the hymn, a newcomer to the faith might conclude that it was sung on the very first Easter.*

I went online to find the original text of "Christ the Lord Is Risen Today" and found a ten-stanza version. Although the poem uses the past tense in a few stanzas, whenever the past tense occurs, it is about Christ's death, not about the resurrection. We do not sing, "Christ the Lord was risen that Day," but rather, "Christ the Lord is risen today." This proclamation of resurrection in the present is immediately followed by an exhortation to the natural order to sing, an exhortation that resonates with the psalms and with Christ's declaration that the rocks will shout if his followers are silenced:

> *Earth and heaven in chorus say, Alleluia!*
> *Raise your joys and triumphs high, Alleluia!*
> *Sing, ye heavens, and earth reply, Alleluia!*

The hymn throbs with the irrepressible resilience of the divine vitalities. The hymn raises us out of a state of no exit, no entrance. I went through the ten-stanza version and wrote down every present-tense declaration about the resurrection. Here they are in the order in which they appear in the original:

> Christ the Lord is risen today,
> Love's redeeming work is done.
> Lives again our glorious king.
> Soar we now where Christ has led,
> Made like him, like him we rise.
> Thee we greet triumphant now,
> Everlasting life is this,
> Jesus Christ is risen today.

Wesley's insistence on using the present tense for resurrection represents a profound theological insight. It rescues us from one of the church's chief afflictions: our propensity to turn faith into archaeology. Becoming a Christian means taking an excursion back to ancient Palestine, where we revisit Jesus as though he were fixed in the past. But Christ is not bound by the past. "Christ the Lord is risen today."

When I quoted all the present-tense verbs from the hymn, I left out the "Alleluias" so your ear could easily catch the present tense in each line. But it is theologically significant that every single line of the hymn ends in "Alleluia." When resurrection happens in the present moment, the irrepressible resilience of the divine vitalities bursts forth in us. We cannot sing more than seven syllables without breaking into an alleluia, for resurrection faith dances with praise:

> Everlasting life is this, Alleluia!
> Thee to know, Thy power to prove, Alleluia!
> Thus to sing and thus to love, Alleluia!

When Christ the Lord is risen today, a new way of being and acting—everlasting life—comes alive in us here and now. Instead of being paralyzed in a state of no exit, no entrance, we give witness to what the rocks would shout if we kept still.

And what would the rocks shout? The rocks would tell the world there is an exit, there is a way out of the wounded, bloody, chaotic mess we have made of God's creation. The rocks would tell the world: there is an entrance into a new way of living and being, there is an entrance to a mode of existence that will stop the religious violence and feed our spiritual hunger. The rocks would tell the world: follow Christ and you will find the exit and the entrance. Follow Christ and tend to the broken, the hungry, the ill, the imprisoned, the despairing. Follow Christ and your whole life will turn into an Alleluia!

But I am not going to let the rocks have the last word. Are you? Not if you believe, and not if you sing, "Christ the Lord is risen today! Alleluia!"

Sing the hymn. It might be effective to do all the stanzas, especially if you have varied instruments to accompany different stanzas. Even if you do not sing all the stanzas, it would be good to print the full text of the hymn on the bulletin cover or as an insert.

Love Divine, All Loves Excelling

Love divine, all loves excelling,
Joy of heaven, to earth come down;
fix in us thy humble dwelling;
all thy faithful mercies crown!
Jesus thou art all compassion,
pure, unbounded love thou art;
visit us with thy salvation;
enter every trembling heart.

Breathe, O breathe thy loving Spirit
into every troubled breast!
Let us all in thee inherit;
let us find that second rest.
Take away our bent to sinning;
Alpha and Omega be;
end of faith, as its beginning,
set our hearts at liberty.

Come, Almighty to deliver,
let us all thy life receive;
suddenly return and never,
nevermore thy temples leave.
Thee we would be always blessing,
serve thee as thy hosts above,
pray and praise thee without ceasing,
glory in thy perfect love.

Finish, then, thy new creation;
pure and spotless let us be.

Let us see thy great salvation
perfectly restored in thee;
changed from glory into glory,
till in heaven we take our place,
till we cast our crowns before thee,
lost in wonder, love, and praise.

Fairest Isle, All Isles Excelling

Fairest isle, all isles excelling,
Seat of pleasure and of love
Venus here will choose her dwelling,
And forsake her Cyprian grove.
Cupid from his fav'rite nation
Care and envy will remove;
Jealousy, that poisons passion,
And despair, that dies for love.

Gentle murmurs, sweet complaining,
Sighs that blow the fire of love
Soft repulses, kind disdaining,
Shall be all the pains you prove.
Ev'ry swain shall pay his duty,
Grateful ev'ry nymph shall prove;
And as these excel in beauty,
Those shall be renown'd for love.[38]

Sermon

As someone who has taught preaching for more than thirty years, I often tell my students: avoid big words. Do not think you will impress a congregation by using complex terminology that points to how knowledgeable you are. The deepest truths are available in plain, accessible, everyday language.

But there is an exception to every rule. Sometimes there is a big word, an unusual term worth our learning in order to explore something profound about faith and life. So today I offer you one such word. The word is "contrafactum." It means substituting one poetic text for another without changing the meter so that the new version echoes the original. If the original words were sung to a particular musical setting, the new set of words sing as easily to the same music. For example, Charles Wesley's beloved hymn text "Love Divine, All Loves Excelling" is a contrafactum based on an earlier poem by John Dryden, "Fairest Isle, All Isles Excelling," a patriotic aria in praise of England that was set to music by Henry Purcell in his opera King Arthur *(1691). Here are the opening lines of the aria:*

> *Fairest Isle, all isles Excelling*
> *Seat of Pleasures, and of Loves;*
> *Venus here will chuse her Dwelling,*
> *And forsake her Cyprian Groves.*[39]

The language may seem antiquated to third-millennium ears. We no longer live in a culture where allusions to the classical poetic traditions of Greece and Rome are part of our regular thought processes. However, in Dryden's day this was a poetic convention that engaged people's imaginations and patriotic sympathies.

Through his contrafactum Charles Wesley offered an alternative to the nationalism of eighteenth-century England. Compare the first four lines of his hymn to what Dryden wrote:

> *Love divine, all loves excelling,*
> *Joy of heaven, to earth come down,*
> *fix in us thy humble dwelling,*
> *all thy faithful mercies crown.*

Every line transforms the praise of the nation into an awareness of humanity's deeper need. While Dryden lauds England as the "Fairest Isle, all isles excelling," Wesley addresses a reality that transcends any geographic location, "Love divine all loves excelling." While Dryden celebrates the "Seat of Pleasures, and of Loves," Wesley realizes that something more enduring is required: "Joy of heaven to earth come down." While Dryden extols the goddess of spring and passion, "Venus here will chuse her Dwelling, / And forsake her Cyprian Groves," Wesley prays for something rooted in lasting reality: "fix in us thy humble dwelling, / all thy faithful mercies crown."

Dryden's patriotic poem romanticizes the state, picturing it in idyllic terms:

> *Cupid from his fav'rite nation*
> *Care and envy will remove;*
> *Jealousy, that poisons passion,*
> *And despair, that dies for love.*[40]

Although Dryden's poetry may sound dated, its intended effect lives on in our own age through rhetoric that idealizes our nation and claims it is divinely favored. Wesley, by way of contrast, is bluntly realistic about the entire human community. In the second stanza of his hymn, a stanza that is often eliminated or emended, he prays: "Take away our bent to sinning."[41] *For Wesley, perfection is not a politically attainable goal because of the broken character of humanity. Instead, he prays for the ongoing work of divine love:*

> Finish then thy new creation,
> pure and spotless let us be;
> let us see thy great salvation
> perfectly restored in thee;
> changed from glory into glory,
> till in heaven we see thy face,
> till we cast our crowns before thee,
> lost in wonder, love, and praise.[42]

This final stanza overflows with a stream of images and ideas from the apostle Paul and culminates in a vision from the book of Revelation: "If anyone is in Christ, there is a new creation" (2 Corinthians 5:17), "To present the church to himself in splendor, without a spot or wrinkle" (Ephesians 5:27), "And all of us . . . are being transformed . . . from one degree of glory to another" (2 Corinthians 3:18), "Then we will see face to face" (1 Corinthians 13:12), "They cast their crowns before the throne" (Revelation 4:10). The way the images pour out one after another gives an impetuosity to the hymn, as though the hymnist and those who sing his lines are being swept into the word of God and entering an altered state of being.

By transforming a patriotic song into a biblically informed contrafactum, Charles Wesley illumines both politics and religion. The hymn plays counterpoint to Dryden's paean to the nation. The poetic and theological contrast between the two would have sounded all the more clearly when the hymn was first sung because John Wesley "was apparently taken with his brother's parody of Dryden and its setting in Purcell's opera, and he set the hymn to Purcell's melody, altered as 'Westminster.'"[43] *People familiar with the Dryden/Purcell aria who later sang the hymn must have been struck by the boldly different direction Charles Wesley took. The contrast between the two texts makes a theological statement.*

After the violent upheavals of regicide and civil war that England had suffered in the 1600s, Dryden's description of the country enjoying pastoral bliss probably gave expression to a deep longing in the population. But Wesley's contrafactum provides a sobering perspective to Dryden's vision by reminding us that no nation is Eden, and it is God, not the state, who brings to humanity the sense of completion and wholeness that theology attempts to convey through the word "salvation."

Contrafactum in Charles Wesley's hands turns out to be far more than a literary device. Contrafactum is a theological method for developing an alternative consciousness. Contrafactum is a new way of seeing the world. Contrafactum is a reminder that we are a work in progress, a new creation that is yet to be finished and that finds its ultimate purpose in a meaning greater than the dimensions of mortal life and human accomplishment.

After the sermon, sing the hymn. It would be effective to print Dryden's poem in the service bulletin or to print the first stanza of the poem and the first stanza of the hymn, side by side or one above the other.

The contemporary American composer Alfred Fedak has set the words of Wesley's hymn to the original melody of Henry Purcell and adapted it as a choir anthem.[44] I can imagine having the choir sing the anthem following the sermon, and then using the church's more familiar hymn setting as the final hymn of the service. This would be a way of bringing the sermon home as people heard the text offered both to its original setting and to the one that has become established by tradition. The sound of contrafactum would be alive in the church.

EXPLORING CHRIST'S PASSION THROUGH HYMNS

Well-worn biblical passages and stories often challenge preachers to find a fresh perspective that can revitalize a congregation's engagement with the material. One way to do this is to trace the astounding variety of ways that hymn writers have treated the same story or theological theme through the centuries. Congregation members who think of a hymnal as an anthology of discrete pieces will discover that it is in fact a record of multiple and often conflicting interpretations of the basic claims and concepts of Christianity.

Consider, for example, the passion of Christ, his journey to suffering and death. Every Christian tradition I have worked with over the last forty years, whether or not they observe the entire liturgical year, focuses on the passion in some special way during the season of Lent and Holy Week. Exploring the passion through hymnody can fill the pastoral need of addressing the varied strategies that people use to respond to grief and suffering, to tragedy and brutality. Contrary to the fairly common assumption that there is a single way to interpret the passion of Christ that has remained constant over the centuries, the history of hymnody reveals a wide range of perspectives and interpretations, and they in turn can provide the preacher with multiple insights for sermons about the suffering and death of Christ.

When we sing passion hymns from different historical periods and cultures, we encounter strikingly different theological understandings of the passion of Christ. Putting some of the hymns side by side, we almost wonder if they are about the same event. Consider the dramatic contrasts among the following three texts that span 1,200 years of church history.

The first is a ninth-century passion hymn by Theodulph of Orleans (760–821). Theodulph was born in a noble family and became a high-level churchman in Charlemagne's court. He was often commissioned by the emperor to carry out important ecclesial and theological tasks. Near the end of his life, Theodulph was imprisoned. He found solace in the fact that the apostle Paul had also been imprisoned, and Theodulph's confident faith led him to write this hymn that was translated by John Mason Neale in 1854 and is used to this day by many churches on Palm Sunday:

> All glory, laud, and honor
> to thee, Redeemer, King,
> to whom the lips of children
> made sweet hosannas ring.
>
> In hastening to thy passion,
> they raised their hymns of praise;
> in reigning 'midst thy glory,
> our melody we raise.[45]

These lines exude an unqualified confidence that the passion leads to glory. The confidence is so great that Christ is pictured as "*hastening* to [his] passion."

Skip from the ninth century to the end of the twentieth century and consider how the poet Colin Gibson completely reenvisions the final procession to the cross in the first and third stanzas of his hymn "The Song of the Gallows Cart," a text that was inspired by a drawing of Hogarth that depicts a bloodthirsty mob jeering at a criminal:

See how the crowds are gathering
to watch the final kill;
they line the fearful roadway
that leads to Tyburn Hill.
And who will ride the gallows cart
beside the lonely one,
to share the jeers and bear the scorn
until the work is done?

And once I saw Christ Jesus
led on that way to die;
his face was pale with anguish,
I heard his lonely cry:
"O who will tear the gibbet down,
and who will stop this cart?
And when will love, not hatred, rule
in every human heart?"[46]

Instead of children singing sweet hosannas, there are crowds watching the final kill. Instead of a Christ "hastening" to his passion, he is "led" on the way to die in a gallows cart, his face "pale with anguish." Instead of "Glory, laud and honor," we hear Christ's "lonely voice" asking "when will love, not hatred, rule / in every human heart?"

Here is yet another approach to the passion by a hymn writer who presents an outright challenge to the interpretation that Theodulph of Orleans offered twelve centuries earlier:

How could a God whose name is love
seek blood to pay sin's price?
Are torture, shame, and senseless death
a holy sacrifice?
Each violent crime is tragic loss;
how could it be God's will?
How can we glorify the cross
when victims suffer still?[47]

In this case it is feminist theology that is "tearing up the turf" and " organizing rebellions and reconstructing disciplines." Instead, of singing "All glory, laud and honor," the poet questions how it is even possible to glorify the cross. Placing the hymn of Theodulph of Orleans side by side with the hymns by Colin Gibson and Ruth Duck demonstrates how radically different the theopoetic of the passion can be. I can imagine a sermon that would employ all three hymns and that would invite listeners to choose which hymn most nearly expresses their understanding of the passion of Christ.

I now turn to a broader cross section of passion hymns. Rather than arrange them in chronological order, I have organized them by how they draw upon the passion to strengthen faith or to cultivate certain forms of piety or to reshape our understanding of Christ's suffering. Like most taxonomies, my categories are somewhat porous, and it is best not to be too rigid about them. Hymn texts are a form of poetic literature, and they often exhibit multiple impulses. Nevertheless, it is homiletically suggestive to name some of the emphases that return again and again, although in very different forms through the centuries. The list is by no means exhaustive, but here are five recurring emphases found in passion hymns:

- The graphic description of Christ the crucified, his wounds and blood
- The passion as Christ's triumphant way to victory
- The devotion of the faithful to the crucified Christ as an expression of piety and often an occasion for introspection
- The theopoetic transformation of Christ's passion and cross to expand their imaginative idiom and symbolic meaning
- Personal, social, or ethical implications of the passion and death of Christ

Notice how the list of emphases is congruent with several of the overtones of beauty that we identified in chapter 1 and that we saw embodied in the Colossian hymn: that beauty is more than mere prettiness, that beauty has room for what is disturbing and difficult, and that beauty helps us to see honestly what is there. When we speak of the beauty of the church's song, we are in part referring to its treasury of hymns about the passion of Christ and the varied ways those hymns have illuminated people's understanding of suffering and death through the centuries.

The description of Christ crucified, his wounds and blood, appears in nearly every passion hymn. But the interpretation of his suffering varies, sometimes awaking sorrow, other times stirring celebration as the passion becomes a march to victory. We have already encountered this perspective in the ninth-century hymn "All Glory Laud and Honor":

> In hastening to thy passion,
> they raised their hymns of praise;
> in reigning 'midst thy glory,
> our melody we raise.

The triumph of Christ is an ancient and persistent theme in passion hymns. Many churches continue to sing triumphant passion texts such as "Sing, My Tongue, the Glorious Battle," written sometime in the sixth century by Venatius Honorius Fortunatus. We do not have the original setting, but it is often sung to plainsong.

> Sing, my tongue, the glorious battle,
> Sing the ending of the fray;
> Now above the cross, the trophy,
> Sound the loud triumphant lay:
> Tell how Christ the world's Redeemer,
> As a victim won the day.
>
> He, our Maker, deeply grieving
> That the first made Adam fell,
> When he ate the fruit forbidden
> Whose reward was death and hell,
> Marked e'en then this Tree the ruin
> Of the first tree to dispel.
>
> Tell how, when at length the fullness,
> Of th' appointed time was come,
> Christ, the Word, was born of woman,
> Left for us His heavenly home;
> Showed us human life made perfect,
> Shone as light amid the gloom.
>
> Lo! He lies an Infant weeping,
> Where the narrow manger stands,
> While the Mother-Maid His members
> Wraps in mean and lowly bands,
> And the swaddling clothes are winding
> Round His helpless feet and hands.

Thus, with thirty years accomplished,
Went He forth from Nazareth,
Destined, dedicated, willing,
Wrought His work, and met His death.
Like a lamb He humbly yielded
On the cross His dying breath.

There the nails and spears He suffers,
Vinegar, and gall, and reed;
From His sacred body pierced
Blood and water both proceed;
Precious flood, which all creation
From the stain of sin hath freed.

Faithful cross, thou sign of triumph,
Now for us the noblest tree,
None in foliage, none in blossom,
None in fruit thy peer may be;
Symbol of the world's redemption,
For the weight that hung on thee!

Bend thy boughs, O tree of glory!
Thy relaxing sinews bend;
For awhile the ancient rigor
That thy birth bestowed, suspend;
And the King of heavenly beauty
On thy bosom gently tend!

Thou alone wast counted worthy
This world's ransom to sustain,
That a shipwrecked race forever
Might a port of refuge gain,
With the sacred blood anointed
Of the Lamb of sinners slain.

To the Trinity be glory
Everlasting, as is meet:
Equal to the Father, equal
To the Son, and Paraclete:

God the Three in One, whose praises
All created things repeat.[48]

Part of the power of this text is the way it broadens and deepens the
homiletical possibilities for exploring the meaning of incarnation.
Preachers usually proclaim the incarnation during Advent, Christmas, and Epiphany, especially if they preach on the prologue to the
Gospel of John. But Fortunatus frames the birth narrative with the
passion and victory of Christ, thus suggesting that the full meaning
of incarnation is known only through all that Christ does and is. The
description of the infant Christ is unlike many of our favorite
Christmas carols. Instead of "little Lord Jesus no crying he makes,"
and instead of "Silent night, holy night / all is calm, all is bright," we
get a description of the child that foreshadows the sadness of his
passion:

> Lo! He lies an Infant weeping,
> Where the narrow manger stands,
> While the Mother-Maid His members
> Wraps in mean and lowly bands,
> And the swaddling clothes are winding
> Round His helpless feet and hands.

Those "helpless feet and hands" are a prefiguration of the stanzas that
follow and describe the crucifixion. The dramatic sequence of these
stanzas can deepen our Christmas as well as our Lenten preaching.

But for all of the hymn's attention to the suffering of Christ, the
opening stanza makes it clear that the passion ends ultimately in triumph,
and that is an enduring theme that returns again and again over the centuries. Consider, for example, stanzas 3 and 4 from Matthew Bridges's text
of 1851:

> Crown him the lord of love
> Behold his hands and side,
> rich wounds yet visible above
> in beauty glorified:
> No angel in the sky can fully bear that sight,
> but downward bends his burning eye
> at mysteries so bright.

> Crown him the Lord of peace,
> whose power a scepter sways
> from pole to pole, that wars may cease
> absorbed in prayer and praise:
> His reign shall know no end,
> and round his pierced feet
> fair flowers of paradise extend
> their fragrance ever sweet.

Here we contemplate the passion from the visionary perspective of the Revelation of John. Details of the crucifixion are still named, but the suffering is now over, so that instead of piling up the details of Christ's torture as Fortunatus does—"There the nails and spears He suffers, / Vinegar, and gall, and reed"—Bridges transforms the scene. He uses a more resplendent diction appropriate to the heavenly perspective of the angels. The wounds now become "rich" and transfigured by "beauty glorified," and the brutal story now leads to "mysteries so bright."

We find a similar transformation of the passion in a hymn by Henry Hart Milman:

> Ride on! Ride on in majesty
> Hark! all the tribes Hosanna cry;
> O Savior meek, pursue Thy road
> With palms and scattered garments strowed.
>
> Ride on, ride on, in majesty!
> In lowly pomp ride on to die!
> O Christ! Thy triumph now begin
> Over captive death and conquered sin.
>
> Ride on, ride on, in majesty!
> The winged squadrons of the sky
> Look down with sad and wondering eyes
> To see the approaching sacrifice.
>
> Ride on, ride on, in majesty!
> Thy last and fiercest strife is nigh;
> The Father, on His sapphire throne,
> Expects His own anointed Son.
> Ride on, ride on, in majesty!

> In lowly pomp ride on to die;
> Bow Thy meek head to mortal pain,
> Then take, O God, Thy power, and reign.[49]

The pulse of those first four single-syllable words gives a marching feel to the line that is repeated at the start of every stanza. Instead of hammered nails we get a drumbeat urging Christ on to his "triumph." The description of the passion never becomes more vivid than the command "Bow Thy meek head to mortal pain." Rather than provide graphic images of the wounds and blood, the poet gives us a more distant, abstract view of the passion, calling it the "approaching sacrifice" and the "last and fiercest strife."

Although the preceding hymns manifest varied ways of presenting the passion, each finds its impulse and structure in retelling the biblical story. This is different from the third category of passion hymns, which we might term meditative. They nurture devotion to the crucified as an expression of piety and as an occasion for introspection. Such devotion takes many hymnic forms.

Sometimes the passion is interpreted through a theological understanding of the Eucharist. For example, in 1263 the pope invited Thomas Aquinas to write a hymn for the then new office of Corpus Christi. The first stanza deals with the shedding of Christ's blood, while the rest of the text explores the mystery of the sacrament. The sacrament thus becomes a means of devotion to the sacrifice that Christ made through his passion.

> Now, my tongue, the mystery telling,
> Of the glorious body sing,
> And the blood, all price excelling,
> Which all mankind's Lord and King,
> In a virgin's womb once dwelling,
> Shed for this world's ransoming.
>
> Given for us and condescending
> To be born for us below,
> He, with men in converse blending,
> Dwelt the seed of truth to sow,
> Till He closed with wondrous ending
> His most patient life below.

That last night, at supper lying
'Mid the twelve, His chosen band,
Jesus, with the law complying,
Keeps the feast its rites demand;
Then, more precious food supplying,
Gives Himself with His own hand.

Word made flesh, true bread He maketh
By His word His flesh to be;
Wine His Blood: which whoso taketh
Must from carnal thoughts be free;
Faith alone, though sight forsaketh
Shows true hearts the mystery.

Therefore we, before Him bending,
This great sacrament revere;
Types and shadows have their ending,
For the newer rite is here;
Faith, our outward sense befriending,
Makes our inward vision clear.

Glory let us give, and blessing,
To the Father and the Son;
Honor, might and praise addressing
While eternal ages run,
Ever, too, His love confessing,
Who from Both with Both is One.[50]

In reading or singing these words, it is revealing to recall our earlier discussion about the sensorium. The full meaning of the text is not in the words alone but in the complete experience of the hymn as an act of worship in a particular sacred space. Imagine singing this hymn in a nave that features a crucified Christ, whose wounds are vividly present to the eye, while also before you is an altar with bread and wine. The passion as a story from the past—"That last night, at supper lying / 'Mid the twelve, His chosen band"—is present here and now: "Therefore we, before Him bending, / This great sacrament revere."

Just as the sacrament has served as a way of seeing and tasting the passion of Christ, so too has devotion to the Virgin Mary. The thirteenth-century Latin hymn "Stabat Mater" uses the image of Mary standing at the cross to awaken our participation in the sorrow of Christ's death:

> Who on Christ's dear Mother gazing,
> in her trouble so amazing,
> born of woman, would not weep?
> Who on Christ's dear Mother thinking,
> such a cup of sorrow drinking,
> would not share her sorrow deep?
>
> In the passion of my Maker
> be my sinful soul partaker,
> may I bear with her my part;
> of his passion bear the token,
> in a spirit bowed and broken
> bear his death within my heart.[51]

Protestant hymnody redefines meditation upon Christ's passion because of different understandings of the sacrament and a turning away from devotion to the virgin. But Christ's suffering still awakens the vivid language of a heartfelt piety. Here, for example, are lines from William Cowper (1731–1800), who found comfort in the Evangelical movement of late eighteenth-century England:

> There is a fountain filled with blood
> drawn from Emmanuel's veins;
> and sinners plunged beneath that flood
> lose all their guilty stains.
>
> Dear dying lamb, I saw the stream
> thy flowing wounds supply,
> redeeming love has been my theme,
> and shall be till I die.[52]

Given the iconoclastic character of Evangelical Protestantism and the resulting visual plainness of their houses for worship, the diction of the hymn is strikingly graphic: "a fountain filled with blood" and "the stream / thy flowing wounds supply." It is as if what the eye has suppressed springs forth in the language.

Sometimes, however, the pictorial representation of the passion is softened by substituting words of thought and feeling for the physical realities of crucifixion. While Fortunatus literally describes what happens—"From His sacred body pierced / *Blood and water* both proceed"—Isaac Watts, while mentioning the blood, transforms the scene through a theological interpretation of its meaning: "See from his head, his hands, his feet, / *sorrow and love* flow mingled down."

> When I Survey the Wondrous Cross
> where the young Prince of Glory died,
> my richest gain I count but loss,
> and pour contempt on all my pride.
>
> Forbid it, Lord, that I should boast
> save in the death of Christ my God;
> all the vain things that charm me most,
> I sacrifice them to his blood.
>
> See from his head, his hands, his feet,
> sorrow and love flow mingled down;
> did e'er such love and sorrow meet,
> or thorns compose so rich a crown?
>
> His dying crimson, like a robe,
> spreads o'er his body on the tree;
> then am I dead to all the globe,
> and all the globe is dead to me.
>
> Were the whole realm of nature mine,
> that were a present far too small;
> love so amazing, so divine,
> demands my soul, my life, my all.[53]

Although the Latin hymns and the Protestant hymns share a devotion to the passion, their expressive methods are different, especially if we take into account the distinctive sensorium of each tradition. The Aquinas text, "Now, My Tongue, the Mystery Telling," assumes a eucharistic setting that in most cases would feature a visual representation of the crucifixion. In a similar manner, the "Stabat Mater" was offered among images or statues of Mary. The singers of these hymns were not isolated individuals but participants surrounded by an environment of visual representation and sacramental action. The language of the Latin hymns is intertwined with an awareness of these realities as when Aquinas turns from describing the passion to describing the ritual action of bowing to honor Christ's presence in the sacrament:

> Therefore we, before him bending,
> this great Sacrament revere;
> types and shadows have their ending,
> for the newer rite is here;
> faith, our outward sense befriending,
> makes our inward vision clear.

Likewise, the Virgin Mary becomes in "Stabat Mater" a holy presence who helps the singers to look at the horrible suffering of Christ:

> O that blessed one, grief-laden,
> blessed Mother, blessed Maiden,
> Mother of th' all-holy One;
> O that silent, ceaseless mourning,
> O those dim eyes, never turning
> from that wondrous, suffering Son.[54]

By way of contrast, Cowper and Watts exercise a different kind of contemplation. It is the meditation of an individual whose sensorium lacks an elaborate ritual and visual context and depends instead upon the imaginings that are awakened by words alone. Thus the central image of Cowper's hymn, "a fountain of blood," has no external reference to a surrounding sacramental environment. The act of envisioning is exclusively an act of faith:

> E'er since, by faith, I saw the stream
> thy flowing wounds supply.
> redeeming love has been my theme
> and shall be, till I die.[55]

In the case of the Watts text, there is not a single reference either to an external visual environment or even to the church as the body of Christ. The contemplation of the passion does not lead to a deeper sense of interconnection to the rest of creation but rather to a complete disavowal of the world:

His dying crimson, like a robe,
spreads o'er his body on the tree;
then am I dead to all the globe,
and all the globe is dead to me.

Imagine singing this hymn in a New England meetinghouse: a white, clapboard, well-proportioned rectangular structure with clear windows. The sensorium reinforces the well-reasoned faith of the hymn as it builds to an irrefutable conclusion in the final stanza:

Were the whole realm of nature mine,
that were a present far too small;
love so amazing, so divine,
demands my soul, my life, my all.

Note the subjunctive mode, "*Were* the whole realm of nature mine." This is a classical rhetorical strategy. Watts effectively begins the stanza with an argument of "What if?" and then uses that hypothetical presupposition to reach a conclusion that is overwhelmingly persuasive. We respond to the passion not only with our feelings but also with our reason. Such an approach flows from the fact that "Watts was certainly a son of the Enlightenment" for whom "reason and revelation went together, with the result that his hymns 'were based on Holy Scripture, but they also represented the thoughts and feelings of a man who was engaged with the philosophical and religious ideas of his age.'"[56]

In comparing Latin and Protestant hymns, we gain insight into the profoundly different ways that faith through the ages has appropriated the passion of Christ. These differences include yet another emphasis that marks many passion hymns: the theopoetic transformation of Christ's passion and cross to expand their imaginative idiom and symbolic meaning. I believe the dynamic impulse for some of this poetic freedom can be traced back to the New Testament itself, and the fact that it uses both the word "cross" and the word "tree" to describe the instrument of torture on which Christ was executed. While the Gospels employ the word "cross," Acts 5:30 tells how the authorities killed Jesus "by hanging him on a tree." Whatever the exegetical issues may be in accounting for the difference, the fact that the scriptures use both "cross" and "tree" may help to account for later accretions and elaborations of the passion story. Thus the second stanza of Fortunatus's sixth-century hymn appears to arise from the legend that the tree on which Christ died was the planting of a shoot from the tree that bore the forbidden fruit in Eden. The stanza is usually eliminated from modern hymnals, but here are the words:

> God in pity saw men fallen,
> shamed and sunk in misery,
> when he fell on death by tasting
> fruit of the forbidden tree;
> then another tree was chosen
> which the world from death should free.[57]

There is something persistently attractive about this tree imagery, for many poets have written hymns that expand upon it. Here is a little-known text from the end of the nineteenth century that appeared as a hymn in *The Methodist Hymnal* (1905). Written by the American poet Sidney Lanier, it elaborates the tree imagery to the exclusion of any description of the wounds or bleeding. The word "forspent" is somewhat antiquated now, but it means "exhausted from hard work, fatigued":

> Into the woods my Master went,
> clean forspent, forspent;
> into the woods my Master came,
> forspent with love and shame;
> but the olives they were not blind to him,
> the little gray leaves were kind to him,
> the thorn tree had a mind to him,
> when into the woods he came.
>
> Out of the woods my Master went,
> and he was well content;
> out of the woods my Master came,
> content with death and shame.
> When death and shame would woo him last,
> from under the trees they drew him last:
> 'twas on a tree they slew him last,
> when out of the woods he came.[58]

I can understand why most hymnal committees have not kept this in the repertoire. It is not as immediately accessible as they want a hymn to be, but it remains a moving text. It gives witness to how deeply and forcefully the passion of Christ can work upon our visionary powers. It refreshes our understanding by reimagining the passion afresh. There is the picture of Jesus "forspent, forspent"—utterly fatigued by his work of love—yet finding amid creation the strength and contentment that will let him face his suffering:

> the olives they were not blind to him,
> the little gray leaves were kind to him,
> the thorn tree had a mind to him.

Unlike his sleeping disciples and unlike the violent solders, the natural order responds to Christ in a way that transforms him from being "forspent" to being "content." Some deep, dynamic transaction is going on here, as it does in dreams and reveries, and in prayer that is not overly controlled by our rationality. Lanier's lines mark an entirely different way of approaching the passion from Watt's tightly reasoned stanza, "Were the whole realm of nature mine." There is no need to choose one approach over the other, but preachers can deepen their sermons by drawing on both, thus expanding the imaginative idiom and symbolic meaning of Christ's suffering and death.

Another means of transforming the theopoetic of the passion and cross is for hymn writers to begin with their own historical situation and then use that as the context for remembering and reappropriating the passion in their own time and place. For example, after two world wars and many other violent conflicts that were accompanied by the hollow promises and brutal atrocities of dictators and tyrants, Martin Franzmann wrote a passion hymn in 1971 that opens by expressing the spiritual exhaustion of his era:

> Weary of all trumpeting,
> weary of all killing,
> weary of all songs that sing
> promise, non-fulfilling,
> we would raise, O Christ, one song;
> we would join in singing
> that great music pure and strong,
> wherewith heaven is ringing.

Captain Christ, O lowly Lord,
Servant King, your dying
bade us sheathe the foolish sword,
bade us cease denying.
Trumpet with your Spirit's breath
through each height and hollow;
into your self-giving death,
call us all to follow.

To the triumph of your cross
summon all the living;
summon us to love by loss,
gaining all by giving,
suffering all, that we may see
triumph in surrender;
leaving all, that we may be
partners in your splendor.

The world's loud, deceitful "trumpeting" in the first stanza contrasts with the supplication in the second stanza that Christ will "trumpet" a call to follow in the way of the cross. By the third stanza, empty trumpeting has given way to a vision of life that embodies the meaning of the cross. The hymn presents the passion as a counterforce to the propaganda and the horrors propagated by brutal power. It offers an alternative pattern of human existence in a world exhausted by unfilled promises. The progression of images from "Weary of all trumpeting" to the trumpet call that proceeds through the "Spirit's breath" to a life that finds its center by following Christ is a concise homily in poetry on how the passion can transform our lives here and now.

Hugo Distler had composed the melody that was to become the hymn's setting in 1938, thirty-three years before Martin Franzmann wrote the poetry. The Third Reich, having incorporated Austria into its boundaries, had charged Distler "to compose a suitable melody for the official text" celebrating the annexation. "Instead of being a triumphalist piece, Distler's melody has a sad strength about it."[59] The Nazis later characterized Distler's music as "degenerate," and the composer took his own life in 1942 rather than serve in the German army. That tragic story arises out of the "trumpeting" that the first stanza of the hymn decries. The text, the music, and the story behind them provide material for a homily that would reverberate with the overtone of beauty that helps us to see honestly the horrors of our human condition.

Our fifth and final framework for looking at passion hymns is a variation on the theopoetic transformation of the passion and cross. In this final category of passion hymns there is a strong statement about how we are to respond to Christ's suffering and death. The hymns name or explore the personal, social, or ethical implications of Christ's passion. Perhaps the most famous of these is the African American spiritual "Were You There?"

> Were you there when they crucified my Lord?
>   (were you there)
> Were you there when they crucified my Lord?
>   (were you there)
> Oh! Sometimes it causes me to tremble, tremble, tremble.
> Were you there when they crucified my Lord?
>   (were you there)
>
> Were you there when they nailed him to the tree?
>   (were you there)
> Were you there when they nailed him to the tree?
>   (were you there)
> Oh! Sometimes it causes me to tremble, tremble, tremble.
> Were you there when they nailed him to the tree?
>   (were you there)
>
> Were you there when they pierced him in the side?
>   (were you there)
> Were you there when they pierced him in the side?
>   (were you there)
> Oh! Sometimes it causes me to tremble, tremble, tremble.
> Were you there when they pierced him in the side?
>   (were you there)
>
> Were you there when the sun refused to shine?
>   (were you there)
> Were you there when the sun refused to shine?
>   (were you there)
> Oh! Sometimes it causes me to tremble, tremble, tremble.

Were you there when the sun refused to shine?
   (were you there)

Were you there when they laid him in the tomb?
   (were you there)
Were you there when they laid him in the tomb?
   (were you there)
Oh! Sometimes it causes me to tremble, tremble, tremble.
Were you there when they laid him in the tomb?
   (were you there)

The poetry is spare and direct. Reading or singing these lines, we cannot distance ourselves from the nailing and the piercing of the body. Every stanza shifts from the past to the present, from "Were you there," to "Sometimes it causes me to tremble, tremble, tremble." The use of the present tense draws the crucifixion out of history into the very moment of singing the spiritual. The use of the interjection "Oh!" to connect the two tenses heightens the impact. It is sung to a melisma, a series of slurred notes that gives the effect of the scene sliding through time into the heart of the singers and causing them to tremble, just as the earth trembled when Christ died (Matthew 27:51). Through our trembling we experience here and now what happened "when they crucified my Lord."

The use of "my Lord" in the first line had subversive connotations for the slaves who first sang this spiritual. Christ displaces the slave owner as "Lord." Instead of a master who is over them, Christ undergoes degradation and death, identifying with the slaves' own suffering. God is taking their side against the injustice and oppression that they suffer. They tremble not only for the suffering of their Lord but for the wonder of what God is doing and the liberation the divine action portends.

As I have noted in an earlier work,[60] the use of the word "refused" in the line "Were you there when the sun refused to shine?" is especially significant. It is based on Luke's account of Christ's death that reports "the sun was darkened" (Luke 23:45, KJV, the translation that the slaves would have known). Note the passive construction of the biblical verse. The darkening of the day for the biblical writer may well be an allusion to the darkening that Joel 2:31 predicts will accompany the day of the

Lord. But in the spiritual the sun is not passive. Instead of being "dark-ened," it becomes an active agent and refuses to shine. Slaves dared not refuse whatever their masters commanded them to do unless they were willing to risk a beating. In the spiritual, however, the death of Christ becomes an occasion for the sun to refuse to go along with the estab-lished order of things. Its refusal resonates with the hope of the slaves that the established tyranny of their world will be overturned by the Crucified Christ.

Although we do not know the name of the slave who first wrote and sang the spiritual, that profound soul is now part of "the whole company of heaven," whose witness is invoked in the liturgies of many traditions every time they celebrate the sacrament of communion. This is true not only of the creator of the spiritual but of all the hymn writers we have considered and all those whose voices still sound through the church at song and prayer. Surveying their work is a way for preachers to bring tradition alive, to help us sense anew the cloud of witnesses that surrounds us, to regain the wisdom that familiarity with their well-worn words may have hidden from us, and to be lifted up by the beauty of holiness that shines through their poetry and music.

THREE

Hear How the Whole Creation Longs

Preaching on Music

Ihave sometimes introduced a sermon based on music with the following exercise:

*I invite all of you to sit very still and listen to your breath. Become aware
of your lungs expanding and contracting, expanding and contracting. . . . Now
each time you exhale allow your voice to hum whatever fundamental pitch
comes out of you. . . . Increase the loudness. . . . Decrease the loudness and let it
fade away.*

*Next I would like you to find your pulse on your wrist and, sitting still,
simply feel it beating again and again. There is no need to figure out your pulse
rate. Just feel the constant beat. . . . Now every time your heart beats, say "beat,
beat, beat . . . ." Fade to silence.*

*Finally, let's have the left side of the congregation go back to humming as
they exhale, while the right side resumes speaking "beat, beat, beat" aloud. . . .
Fade to silence.*

You are a woodwind and a drum. Before you speak your first word
as an infant, you are a woodwind instrument that plays 12 million
breaths a year and a drum that beats 40 million times a year. And since
your vocal chords stretch over the path of your breath, you are also a
stringed instrument. From the moment of your birth you are an orchestra playing a perpetual concert through every moment of your life.

God has created us as musical creatures. But not only are we an orchestra, we are also automobile drivers, computer users, and house dwellers. Our steel boxes on wheels, our virtual reality, and our artificially cooled and warmed environments often make us forgetful. We forget our God-given identity as a woodwind, a drum, an orchestra.

Who will call us back to our primal identity as musical creatures?

It is essential that someone do it because when we human beings forget our creaturely identity as breathing, drumming orchestras whose music is the gift of God, we spawn illusions. Arrogant illusions. Dangerous illusions. The illusion that we are the masters of existence. The illusion that one group of human beings is superior to another group of human beings. The illusion that we can command and control the ecological web of life rather than live in harmony with it. The consequences are devastating to the environment, to the human family, and to all the other creatures who are also woodwinds, drums, and orchestras, fellow musical ensembles living with us on this sunlit, mossy stone we call earth.

Fortunately, we are not without hope. Music has the capacity to remind us of our primal identity as a drum, as a wind instrument, as an orchestra. Daniel Levitin observes: "Throughout most of the world and for most of human history, music making was as natural an activity as breathing and walking and everyone participated."[1] Levitin explores the complex neurological operations involved in listening to music: "The story of your brain on music is the story of an exquisite orchestration of brain regions, involving both the oldest and newest parts of the human brain, and regions as far apart as the cerebellum in the back of the head and the frontal lobes just behind your eyes. It involves a precision choreography of neurochemical release and uptake between logical prediction systems and emotional reward systems."[2] Note the words "orchestration" and "choreography." We are indeed a woodwind and a drum, a living orchestra. Levitin writes as a scientist. I write as a preacher and a poet. His science, my preaching and poetry point to the same conclusion: music restores us to our primal identity.

But music does not automatically do this, especially not in a culture that gives inadequate attention to developing the musical intelligence of its members, a culture where music is playing everywhere we turn. The result is a diminished capacity for attentive listening and its salutary

effects upon the human heart, the mind, and soul. Such diminishment
can happen as easily in church as elsewhere:

> My worry is that music, as an art form, is now so prevalent, we
> have forgotten how to listen actively. The music in the liturgy
> can all too easily become part of that ubiquitous tapestry of
> sound that our culture creates in the malls, in the elevator, the
> dentist office, the iPhone, the telephone, the gramophone.
> I suppose it's also part of the push in post Vatican II-life toward
> full, active, and conscious participation—which most often
> gets interpreted as of necessity moving one's mouth. In reality,
> do we categorically comprehend music better when our lips
> are moving as compared to when we are listening actively?[3]

I have sometimes heard people denigrate the singing of an anthem
or a solo in church because "it is just a performance." Missing in this
perspective is the active role of the attentive listener. When we listen to
an anthem or solo in church, the musicians are leading us in musical
prayer just as the priest or minister leads us in spoken prayer. Furthermore, the word "performance" means more than being passively enter-
tained. The word originally meant "to carry through to completion."[4]
The act of completing a piece of music belongs to the listeners as
they attend to the sound and receive the Spirit moving through the
music. The same is true of sermons that proclaim the Word of God: they
are completed only when they enter the hearts of the listeners who
then embody the Word in the world. Listening is performing. But
because the ubiquitous use of music has dulled the keenness of our
appreciation, we need to develop the art through practice. When the
church helps people to listen more attentively to music, it leads them
into deeper prayer, into a profounder awareness of the wonder and
glory of God.

Preaching on beautiful music and then having it performed as part
of the sermon is an act of spiritual restoration through which congregation members regain their God-given identity as musical creatures.
In the last chapter we provided spiritual nurture by explicating some
of the great hymn texts of the church. Our focus there was on the
language of the hymns and the historical and theological contexts from
which they arose. Now as we turn to major works from the traditions
of Western Christianity, we will continue to look at texts, but we will

become more attentive to the music, to the ways composers have worked with sound and rhythm, with instruments and voices to give glory to the One who has created us as woodwinds and drums, as living orchestras.

Music has often awakened caution and wariness among theologians. Thomas Aquinas, for instance, considered the spoken word "more valuable than a form of art, i.e. music, in instilling faith. It is almost ironic to note that Thomas undermines precisely the revelatory power of the art of music, which through the ages has made people concretely feel *and know* the existence and presence of the beauty of the divine."[5]

The propensity to set word against art, preaching against music is evident in Emil Brunner's statement that "the opinion often expressed at the present day that art—for instance, music—can become the means of expressing the Word of God as well as, and indeed better than, the human word, is based upon an error. Whoever asserts this does not mean by the Word of God the message of the God who is manifest in Jesus Christ."[6] Brunner's use of the term "message" is significant. The Word of God certainly includes "message," and Brunner is correct that language is a medium for sending messages. Nothing I write in the rest of this chapter devalues the "message" of preaching. But the Word of God is far more than "message." The Word is also the power to create all things that are (John 1:3) and the power by whom "all things hold together" (Colossians 1:17). The ranking of language and music, one over the other, results in a constricted understanding of the Word of God. A more faithful perspective is to view language and music as complementary elements whose mutually enriching presence in our worship brings us closer to the fullness of the Word. This way of framing the issue is congruent with the case Karl Rahner makes for a more holistic understanding of theology:

> If theology is not identified a priori with verbal theology, but is understood as man's total self-expression insofar as this is borne by God's self-communication, then religious phenomena in the arts are themselves a moment within theology taken in its totality.
>
> In practice, theology is rarely understood in this total way. But why should a person not think that when he hears a Bach

oratorio, he comes into contact in a very unique way with God's revelation about the human not only by the words it employs, but by the music itself? Why should he not think that what is going on there is theology? If theology is simply and arbitrarily defined as being identical with verbal theology, then of course we cannot say that. But then we would have to ask whether such a reduction of theology to verbal theology does justice to the value and uniqueness of these arts, and whether it does not unjustifiably limit the capacity of the arts to be used by God in his revelation.[7]

A theology that is overly reliant upon words often gives birth to worship that is prosaic and arid. Worship becomes so talky that the expansive mystery and wonder of God have little room to be manifest in the service. The impact is as detrimental to sacred speech as it is to the nonverbal dimensions of worship:

> Since the most vivid signs of God's presence among humans almost invariably involve the cooperation of acts and words, sacramental consciousness begins to fade when worship places a strong emphasis on words while at the same time neglecting actions (more "saying" than "doing"). In the process, words that once were charged with mysterious awe tend to lose their power and become commonplace.[8]

The apostle Paul offers an insight about prayer that reinforces why it is essential for theology to embrace the nonverbal dimensions of life as fully as it does language: "The Spirit helps us in our weakness; for we do not know how to pray as we ought, but that very Spirit intercedes with sighs too deep for words" (Romans 8:26). If our profoundest prayers are prayed for us by the Spirit in "sighs too deep for words," then any theology that is closed to the nonverbal is closed to the inarticulate intercessions of the Spirit of the living God, who is the reason for theology in the first place!

As convinced as I am about the need for a theology that embraces both the verbal and the nonverbal, I know that seasoned preachers inevitably ask of any theology: Will it preach? Is it possible to draw on the nonverbal dimensions of theology, such as the sound of pure music, to create a meaningful sermon for a congregation? The preachers' question deserves serious attention. For there are schools of thought that would argue pure music has no intrinsic meaning. Martin Jean observes that

> there has been in the history of musical criticism, a strong movement to dissuade us from thinking that music has any extra-musical meaning at all! Led by Eduard Hanslick in the 19th century as a kind of reaction against the Wagner movement, he claimed that music is just sound or sound structure. That its interest lies in the notes themselves, not in stories that they will represent or anything that they "mean." Peter Kivy calls music an art of "pure sonic design." There is, to be sure, explicit program music. And music sometimes combines with words or images to form a representational whole, as in song, opera, film and dance. But some will set aside these combinations as impure instances of music.[9]

Jean argues that human beings are creatures that make meaning, and drawing on the work of Kendall Walton, he points out "that music creates worlds, not unlike the pictorial or literary arts. Music, in similar ways to a play or a painting, induces our imaginings."[10] Jean then quotes a passage from Walton that summarizes many of the ways we describe the expressive qualities of music:

> We call passages of music exuberant, agitated, serene, timid, calm, determined, nervous. We speak of rising and falling melodies, of wistful melodies and hurried rhythms, of motion and rest, of leaps, skips, and stepwise progression, of statements and answering phrases, tension and release, resignation and resolve, struggle, uncertainty, and   arrival. Music can be impetuous, powerful, delicate, sprightly, witty, majestic, tender, arrogant, peevish, spirited, yearning, chilly. . . . [As we listen to it] we imagine agitation or nervousness, conflict and resolution.[11]

What strikes me, as someone who is both a homiletician and a musician, is how resonant this description of music is with what effective preaching stirs in a congregation, with the varied worlds of meaning that listeners create from what a preacher says.

Eugene L. Lowry has written extensively on how preaching works like music upon the listener because it too is a form of human expression that moves through time and, if effective, proceeds through conflict toward resolution: "One could speak of the basic *musicality* of any sermon. Music, after all, is also an event-in-time art form, with melody, harmony, and rhythm coming sequentially. No one *builds* a song; it is shaped and performed."[12]

In a similar fashion, Evans Crawford has developed the term "homiletical musicality" to describe

> the way in which the preacher uses timing, pauses, inflection, pace, and the other musical qualities of speech to engage all that the listener is in the act of proclamation. This musicality represents something much deeper than method. It is an expression of the holy God working through the preacher and the community, and it requires a rigorous and authentic spirituality on the part of both preacher and congregation.[13]

Preaching as an aural art converges with music, in the way it moves through time and in the emotions and intuitions it touches off in the heart.

Stephen Webb helps us see that homiletical musicality is part of a larger, more complex reality that he calls the "soundscape" of Christian theology:

> Surely it is the prayers of the faithful, both the vocal and the inarticulate longings of their hearts, that unite all Christians more than the jottings of the literate few: To God those prayers must sound like a constant humming emitted from the very properties of matter; a melody that accompanies the universe as it resonates with God's Word. By listening, God makes all of our sounds—from guttural moans of despair to tearful shouts of joy—matter.[14]

Preaching on music is one way to engage more effectively a congregation's soundscape. Of course, the preacher uses words to develop the message of the sermon, but the words emerge from the worlds of meaning that the music stirs in our hearts, from the imaginings that sound awakens. If the preacher does this artfully, the sermon will convey something of the generative energies of the music that gave birth to the language.

Although sermons later in this chapter will focus on compositions that dramatize sacred texts through tonal painting, I now present two sermons that can effectively be followed with an offering of purely instrumental music. The first, inspired in part by the stories of creation in Genesis 1 and of Pentecost in Acts 2, celebrates the ministry of music. The second expands on the relationship between music and the Spirit praying in us through "sighs too deep for words." I hope that each sermon demonstrates how a theology that embraces the nonverbal as well as the verbal will indeed preach.

Sermon: Genesis 1:1–2 and Acts 2:1–4

Perhaps it is because I grew up in the country on a mountain lake that I am enchanted by the sound of wind. Throughout the year I could hear it in the trees along the shore. In the summer when the windows were opened, I often awoke to the sound of wind-driven waves lapping against the rocks, and in the winter I heard the gusts roaring across the large central chimney that dominated our house. Maybe my sensitivity to the wind has been enhanced by the fact that I have played the flute since I was in fourth grade, and I have spent thousands of hours directing wind across an embouchure to set up vibrations in a silver pipe that poured into the air as melody.

When I blow on my flute, I am extending and elaborating the music that the wind is always making with trees and grass, with waves and water. Our ancient forebears must have been keenly attentive to that primal music, for "Musical instruments are among the oldest human-made artifacts we have found. The Slovenian bone flute, dated at fifty thousand years ago, which was made from the femur of a now extinct European bear, is a prime example. Music predates agriculture in the history of our species. We can say, conservatively, that there is no tangible evidence that language preceded music. In fact, the physical evidence suggests the contrary. . . . The archaeological record shows an uninterrupted record of music making everywhere we find humans, and in every era. And, of course, singing most probably predated flutes as well."[15]

I wish we knew the name of who it was that made the first flute. I would suggest the person ought to be canonized by musicians and listeners who love the sound of air moving through a pipe. That first flute maker is the ancestor to all of us who make music by moving air through a pipe or who take delight in listening. There is a ceaseless line of music making that moves from wind upon the water to wind in the trees to breath in a flute to air moving through the pipes of an organ. When we play or listen to the organ or any other instrument, when we blend our voices in song, we are joining in the music that God set humming by

blowing across the deep, the same God who inspired the psalmist to exclaim, "
Let everything that breathes praise the Lord!," the same God whose breath,
whose Spirit, came like a rush of wind at Pentecost.

Wind and breath and music remind us that God is not known simply as
an idea or as a theological definition or an abstraction. God is the vitalizing
energy that stirs our hearts and minds as air moves through pipes or across our
vocal cords and out through our mouths to sound forth music. Our music making
recapitulates the wonder of God's first act of breathing upon the deep. You might
call this a theology of wind or a theology of breath. It reminds us that words alone
are an inadequate witness to God. When we make or listen to music in the praise
of God, we are enacting the theology of wind and breath and Spirit. Our music
is a sonic witness to the one whose creative action did not start with words but
with wind upon the water. "In the beginning when God created the heavens and
the earth . . . . a wind from God swept over the face of the waters."

I recall hearing in a chapel one day a slightly nasal, reedy organ stop, the
kind of sound that intrigues the ear. The tonal quality was so rich and distinctive
that I felt if I reached out, I would touch the sound with my hands, as if it were
a substance suffusing the air. I saw others around me perk up their ears. This was
a far different experience from each of us listening to our tunes on an iPod.
Listening intensely as one body to the music, we became like those who gathered
at the first Pentecost, a congregation bound together in mutual understanding by
the power of the Spirit.

When I stepped outside after the service, the wind was blowing in the trees,
and I found myself carried by memory back to the shore of the lake where I grew
up, only the trees now sounded to me like the reedy stop on the organ. I left the
chapel with an overwhelming sense of the breath of the Creator moving across the
deep and the Spirit of Pentecost breathing upon the congregation. Our spiritual
energies for the work of ministry had been renewed as the word of God was
carried into our hearts by the sound of air moving through a pipe.

Sermon: Romans 8:26–27

Sometimes when friends lose a person very dear to them, we say, "I have no
words to tell you how sad I am for you." Sometimes when someone does some-
thing extraordinarily generous on our behalf, we say, "I can never express
adequately how grateful I am to you." Sometimes when we hear music that takes
us out of ourselves, we say to the singers and players, "Words cannot capture how
moved I was by your performance." And sometimes when we need to pray,

we discover that "the Spirit helps us in our weakness; for we do not know how to pray as we ought, but that very Spirit intercedes with sighs too deep for words." There is grief too overwhelming to speak, there is grace too extravagant to name, there is beauty too intense to articulate, and there is prayer too profound for our lips to shape into syllables.

To have the experience of being moved beyond language is essential to claiming our full humanity. Language carries with it the dangerous illusion that we can control reality through what we say and write, that if we can just find the perfect words, we will catch in our language the reality that we have encountered. As a preacher and a poet who has been teaching students how to preach and write poetry for decades, I acknowledge my great passion for artful, disciplined, eloquent language. Words can do astounding things, and for that I am grateful. But for all that language can accomplish, it is still a net filled with holes, and there are vast currents of existence that it will never catch. Rather than count this as a deficiency in the nature of things, Saint Paul helps us to see it as an opening to our dependence on the Spirit that prays through us in "sighs too deep for words."

The church has long had a "theology of the Word." But we need as well a "theology of sighing," a theology of the sound that is made by grief too overwhelming to speak, by grace too extravagant to name, by beauty too intense to articulate, and by prayer too profound for our lips to shape into speech. What do these "sighs too deep for words" sound like? How do we identify them?

Sometimes we identify them by the character of the voice that is speaking words. I think of those times when I have picked up the phone, and someone close to me is about to tell me something sad. They first speak their name when I answer the phone, and before they get out the bad news, I find myself saying: "Are you all right? Is something wrong?" Or if they are calling with some piece of glad news, I can hear it from the instant they say hello. The sound precedes the message. It is alive in the voice, and the voice is telling me already what is happening in the soul.

Sound is more primordial than language. It is what first reaches the heart. If you doubt this, think of people who say they forgive you, but their voice tells you they are still bitter. How do the vibration of the soul and the resonance of the Spirit become audible? We hear them in voices, we hear them in prayer, and we hear them when we awake from a dream that led us to waters so pure and sweet we knew we would never thirst again. But perhaps most regularly and reliably we hear those blessed sounds through music offered to the glory of God by singers and instrumentalists whose art becomes the vessel of the Spirit praying in sighs too deep for words.

The sermon concludes with an instrument playing something not too complex, but melodic and meditative, suggestive of the Spirit's "sighs too deep for words."

Many preachers realize there are dimensions to prayer and theology that extend far beyond language. But in my experience they still are reluctant to create sermons based on serious works of music for one of three practical reasons. They claim they are not musical, or they believe their people will not respond appreciatively, or their churches lack the resources to perform great music. Because I take these reservations seriously, I will answer each one in turn.

Although I studied flute seriously and have performed much of my life in various settings, I have never been formally trained in musicology, the discipline that examines music historically and scientifically. I have found, however, there is a wealth of musicological literature that is accessible to the nonspecialist. For example, many CDs come with essays explaining how a composer uses a particular instrument or how to listen for a recurring theme or some bit of historical information that makes a lively contribution to a sermon. It is also possible to go online and find extensive sites about composers and their major works. Furthermore, I have collaborated with scores of church musicians on developing sermons and services around a major work or anthem, and without exception they have welcomed my questions about the music that I was going to preach on and they were going to perform. In many cases they have sat at the piano or organ or had me come to rehearsal. They have helped me understand the interplay between the libretto and the music, showing how the composer explores, deepens, and heightens the meaning of the words. Good preachers are always learning about fields other than what they studied in school and using what they learn to proclaim God's word. There is no reason why preachers cannot broaden their knowledge about music, especially in light of people's God-given identity as musical creatures, as woodwinds and drums, as living orchestras.

As to whether or not a congregation will appreciate sermons on great music, I can attest that in scores of churches where I have preached on sacred music, people have responded with overwhelming gratitude. While writing this book, I received a letter from a layman who some years ago had visited a church where I was preaching on a Bach cantata.

Moved by the way the sermon and music flowed together, he developed a prayer service based on Bach's music, to the delight of his home congregation.

Sometimes there are individuals who doubt they will like the music on which the sermon is to be based. They fear it will be too arty. But often to their surprise, they find hearing the music in the context of worship opens their hearts to its power in a way that renews and strengthens faith.

Some churches lack the resources to do a major work, but that can often be solved by drawing together several church choirs. That has happened many times in my experience, and it has been a way of building ecumenical relationships. Or instead of doing a major work, your musicians can do smaller solos. In the sermons that follow, I offer examples of preaching not only on full-scale works but also on solo arias. If you explain to your musicians how you would like to build your sermon around an anthem or choral work or solo or series of solos, they will usually have many ideas that will generate sermons in you. Also, churches often have teenagers who play in school bands or orchestras and who have achieved a level of competence that will allow them to provide instrumental accompaniment.

Some pastors ask about using prerecorded music, but I have found it never to be as effective as live music. The common belief that the best music making is found on professional recordings is not true. It is a falsehood that has contributed to the diminishment of our musical intelligence. No recording can capture the sight and sound of live human beings breathing and moving to produce music. I have now seen and heard dozens of church music directors get excellent performances out of their amateur choirs. They have chosen music that was challenging but within the reach of the people they were directing. Often choir and congregation alike were astounded at the beauty of what they produced. Many times the performance was better than the recording that I listened to in preparing my sermon. There may have been mistakes, some faltering intonation, or a missed entrance, but the interpretation had a warmth, a directness, and conviction that were absent from the perfectly laundered disc. The Spirit moved through the performance into the hearts of the congregation.

Attending rehearsal, talking with the musicians, and reading background material, preachers will discover that for centuries there has been a dynamic relationship between music and theology. History, culture, and expanding knowledge are continually transforming both theology and music. A change in one often changes the other. By bringing in these historical perspectives, preachers can heighten the musical intelligence of the congregation and also can make them aware of the affective energies of the heart and the intellectual constructions of faith that find sonic manifestation in music.

Preaching on beautiful works of music is also a way of drawing more fully on tradition. Many denominations say that tradition is one of the important sources for a mature Christian faith, but preachers are often not as clear about how to draw upon tradition in their sermons as they are about how to use the Bible. Studying the historical and theological background of music can bring tradition alive and provide substantive sermonic material. It can reveal how the mutually transformative relationship between theology and music plays itself out in different cultures and historical periods, different genres and composers. This is more than fascinating information. It is a way of tracing how the Spirit of our Creator has inspired generation after generation of artists, and it thus can sharpen our attentiveness to where the Spirit is moving in our own day. We come to see that tradition, instead of being stale and static, is a continuously unfolding process that enlivens and deepens faith.

I call preaching on works of sacred music a form of theomusical homiletic. I have coined the word "theomusical" following the lead of Amos Wilder. As we noted in our earlier discussion of hymn texts, Wilder wrote about the role of the poetic imagination in vitalizing the language of faith, arguing that "a theopoetic means doing more justice to the role of the symbolic and the prerational in the way we deal with experience."[16] As a poet and a theologian, Wilder's primary concern is with language and the visionary imagination. I am indebted to Wilder's work for helping me understand my own efforts to revitalize the church's theopoetic imagination through new hymns and homiletics. However, in writing hymn and anthem texts for composers and in working with conductors and performers to create sermons based on major works of sacred music, I have become convinced that theology needs to grasp the importance of not only the theopoetic but also the theomusical. By "theomusical" I mean the way music can explore and extend the theology of texts and how the sound of music is a witness to the Spirit that prays in "sighs too deep for words."

Theopoetically speaking, the character of creation has been theo-musical from the beginning. As the biblical book of Job puts the matter, it was at creation that "the morning stars sang together and all the heavenly beings shouted for joy" (38:7). When we preach on works of sacred music, when our sermons explore the dynamic interrelationship of music and theology, we are helping our congregations to reclaim their theomusical identity as woodwinds, as drums, as living orchestras, as the musical creatures God created them to be.

A theomusical homiletic is more than musicology. I am indebted to musicologists for their research into the history of composers and their music and for their painstaking analysis of musical scores at a level I cannot master on my own. However, their work often stops short of making the explicit theological and biblical connections that a sermon requires. Thus I find it necessary to move beyond their musicological analysis to consider the theological implications and spiritual dimensions of what a composer has created.

A worshiping congregation is a different context from a secular concert. Just as changing the context in which we read the same words can lead us to see different meanings, so too hearing music as an act of prayer can bring out depths and possibilities that we miss when we listen to it purely as concert music. I have been told dozens of times by professional singers who have sung in worship services featuring great sacred music how they themselves had never been so moved by the music until they offered it in worship. Some of them were persons of faith and some were not, but all of them picked up the same thing: in hearing a sermon about the piece, and in offering their music amid prayers and hymns, they heard depths in the music that they had never realized before. Robin Leaver's perceptive reflection on the renewed interest in authentic performances of early music helps to explain this phenomenon: "Matters concerning the original pitch and tempo, original instrumentation and vocal resources are insufficient on their own for a true understanding of church music as church music. The quest for authenticity includes discussing the reason why such music was written."[17]

Before we turn to sermons that embody a theomusical homiletic, I offer this hymn text as a way of naming and celebrating the theological dimensions of music making. I have often used the hymn in conjunction with the exercise that opened this chapter. I have found that using the exercise and the hymn together is helpful in introducing and gaining support for the idea of sermons based on music.

> First find a steady beat.
> Your pulsing heart will do.
> Mark how the sounds repeat, repeat—
> a drum that drums in you.
> Then whistle, sing or hum
> melodic, flowing lines.
> You are a woodwind and a drum
> whose music intertwines.
>
> Next harmonize with birds,
> with ocean, wind and shore,
> whose hymns and anthems use no words
> but waves that beat and roar.
> Now cross beyond the sea
> where songs unlike your own
> reveal the world's diversity
> in rhythm, mode and tone.
>
> Through all the varied songs
> earth's many voices raise
> hear how the whole creation longs
> to sing the artist's praise
> who tunes the world for sound
> and sets our hearts to beat,
> and with a music more profound
> makes all our songs complete.[18]

Before reading the remaining sermons in this chapter, I suggest that preachers first find a recording of the music on which they are based.[19] Every work has been recorded countless times, and I have been able to find them easily in public and university libraries if I myself did not own a recording. All the discs I have consulted are accompanied by booklets with libretti, usually in the original language with English translations. When I preach, I always include a copy of the libretto in the service bulletin so that the congregation can easily follow along. Or one can go to a public library and see if it subscribes to Naxos, which is usually listed under databases. Naxos has online recordings of all the choral and solo works upon which the rest of the sermons in this chapter are based.

To get a feeling for how each of the following sermons and music fit together as one integrated whole, I suggest the following process:

First read the biblical texts, the libretto, and sermon in that order.

Then listen immediately to the work.

This will provide an idea of what happens in a worship service when sermon and music are offered as one integrated act of proclaiming the word of God. However, doing this in a study or a library or listening online is never as powerful as what happens when the proclamation is part of a well-planned service using congregational song, prayers, scripture readings, and sacramental action.

I have usually preached these sermons in the context of a church's standard order of worship. I do not try to re-create a service of an epoch long past that places the work in its original liturgical setting. I feel free to employ the full richness of a congregation's hymnody and song. Not every selection has to be in the same style or from the same era as the major work on which we are preaching. Our intention is not to make the church a musical museum. Instead, we are offering a sermon in word and music that is a contemporary witness to the living God here and now.

The first of these sermons is based on Cantata 180, "Adorn Yourself, O Dear Soul," by Johann Sebastian Bach.[20] The scripture lessons for the sermon are Isaiah 52:1–2, Revelation 19:6–8 and Matthew 22:1–14.

I am indebted for the translation of the libretto to Steve Finch, a gifted professional choral conductor, who among his many activities directs a volunteer church choir. He and I have frequently worked together. I preach, and he then conducts the cantata on which the sermon is based. While the choir members are all amateurs, he often hires professionals or music students for the more challenging vocal and instrumental parts. We always offer the cantata at the church's principle Sunday service. There are two advantages to this over performing the cantata at a concert. Because of people's busy schedules, they are more apt to come out to a regular service featuring special music than to return for a separate concert; more important, hearing the cantata in the context of worship with a sermon that is based upon it opens them to a deeper level of listening, an attentiveness that leads them into profound worship.

"The Libretto for Cantata 180
Schmücke dich, o liebe Seele
Deck Thyself, O Beloved Soul"

1. Coro
Schümke dich, o liebe Seele,
Laß die dunkle Sündenhöhle
Komm ans helle Licht gegangen,
Fange herrlich an zu prangen;
Denn der Herr voll Heil und Gnaden
Läßt dich itzt zu Gaste laden.
Der den Himmel kann verwalten,
Will selbst Herberg in dir halten.

Deck thyself, O beloved soul,
Let sin's dark hollow
Come to the bright light,
Now begin to shine with glory;
For the Lord with health and blessing
Hath thee as his guest invited.
He, of heaven now the master,
Seeks his lodging here within thee.

2. Aria (Tenor)
Ermuntre dich: dein Heiland klopft,
Ach öffne bald die Herzenspforte!
Ob du gleich in entzückter Lust
Nur halbgebrochne Freudenworte
Zu deinem Jesu sagen mußt.

Be lively now: thy savior knocks,
Ah, open soon thy spirit's portals!
Although thou in enchanted joy
Only partly broken words of gladness
To thy Jesus must utter now.

3. Recitativo e Choral (Soprano)
Wie teuer sind des heilgen Mahles Gaben!
Sie finden ihres gleichen nicht.
Was sonst die Welt vor kostbar hält,
Sind Tand und Eitelkeiten:

Ein Gotteskind wünscht diesen Schatz zu
haben und spricht:
Ach, wie hungert mein gemüte,
Menschenfreund nach deiner Güte!
Ach, wie pfleg ich oft mit Tränen
Mich nach dieser Kost zu sehnen!
Ach, wie pfleget mich zu dürsten
Nach dem Trank des Lebensfürsten!
Wünsche stets, daß mein Gebeine
Sich durch Gott mit Gott vereine.

How costly are the holy banquet's offerings!
No other like them can be found.
All else the world doth precious think
Is trash and idle nothing;
A child of God would seek to have
    this treasure and say:
Ah, how hungry is my spirit,
Friend of man, to have thy kindness!
Ah, how often I am weeping
For this treasure filled with yearning!
Ah, how often am I thirsting
For the drink from life's true sovereign!
Hoping ever that my body
Be through God with God made united.

4. Recitativo (Alto)
Mein Herz fühlt in sich Furcht und Freude;
Es wird die Furcht erregt,
Wenn es die Hoheit überlegt,
Wenn es sich nicht in das Geheimnis findet,
Noch durch Vernunft dies hohe Werk ergründet.
Nur Gottes Geist kann durch sien Wort uns lehren.
Wie sich allhier die Seelen nähren,
Die sich im Glauben zugeschickt.
Die Freude aber wird gestärket,
Wenn sie des Heilands Herz erblickt,
Und seiner Liebe Größe merket.

My heart feels fear and gladness;
It is with fear inspired
When it that majesty doth weigh,
When it no way in the secret findeth,
Nor with the mind this lofty work can fathom.
Only God's spirit can teach us through his word.
How here all spirits shall be nurtured,
Which have themselves in faith arrayed.
Our joy, though, is ever strengthened
When we the Savior's heart behold,
And of his love the greatness witness.

5. Aria (Soprano)
Lebens Sonne, Licht der Sinnen,
Herr, der du mein Alles bist!
Du wirst meine Treue sehen
Und den Glauben nicht verschmähen,
Der noch schwach und furchtsam ist.

Sun of life, light of feeling,
Lord, thou who art all to me!
Thou wilt see that I am true
And my faith wilt not disparage,
Which is weak and fearful yet.

6. Recitativo (Basso)
Herr, laß an mir dein treues Lieben,
So dich vom Himmel abgetrieben,
Ja nicht vergeblich sein!
Entzünde du in Liebe meinen Geist,
Daß er sich nur nach dem, was himmlisch heißt,
Im Glauben lenke
Und deiner Liebe stets gedenke.

Lord, let me in thy true love,
Which out of heaven hath driven,
Yes, not in vain have been!
Enkindle thou my spirit with thy love,

That it may only things
Of heavenly worth in faith be seeking
And of thy love be ever mindful.

7. Choral
Jesu, wahres Brot des Lebens,
Hilf, daß ich doch nicht vergebens
Oder mir vielleicht zum Schaden
Sei zu deinem Tisch geladen.
Laß mich durch dies Seelenessen
Deine Liebe recht ermessen,
Daß ich auch, wie jetzt auf Erden,
Mög ein Gast im Himmel werden.

Jesus, true bread of life,
Help that I may never vainly
Nor perhaps even in sorrow,
Be invited to thy table.
Grant that through this spiritual food,
I thy love may rightly measure,
That I too, as now here on earth,
May become a guest in heaven.[21]

Sermon: Isaiah 52:1–2, Revelation 19:6–8, and Matthew 22:1–14

Do you remember the favorite clothing you most liked to wear when you were a child? I recall when I was in kindergarten, it was my Gene Audrey outfit. When I was in second or third grade, it was my Davy Crockett hat. What was it for you? This may seem a naive and childish question. But in fact what we wear continues to be important to us most of our adult lives. What did you wear when you interviewed in an effort to get into the college of your choice? What did you wear to impress a prospective employer? What did you wear to win the heart of one you love?

What we choose to wear is often a statement of how we see ourselves and how we want others to see us. Indeed, the way we dress can influence our behavior. Picture yourself in a fine evening gown or a tuxedo. Then picture yourself in cutoff jeans and a T-shirt. You do not get down on your knees in the garden in an evening gown or a tuxedo. You do not go to a formal dinner in cutoffs and a T-shirt. The way you are dressed shapes your whole behavior.

For most of history the making of clothes was a labor-intensive activity. People did not shop in stores amid racks filled with ready-to-wear clothes. The biblical writers knew how demanding and time-consuming it was to make a garment. Therefore, when they wanted to convey the arduous work of living a life of integrity, they often turned to the metaphor of dressing. Isaiah says: "Awake, awake, put on your strength, O Zion! Put on your beautiful garments, O Jerusalem, the holy city." The author of Revelation envisions the church as the bride of Christ to whom "'it has been granted to be clothed with fine linen, bright and pure'—for the fine linen is the righteous deeds of the saints." And the parable from today's gospel stresses the seriousness of being rightly attired. The king who has invited people to a wedding banquet for his son asks: "'Friend, how did you get in here without a wedding robe?'"

Bach builds the opening chorale of today's cantata around the biblical metaphor of dressing ourselves in righteousness. As the choir sings "Adorn yourself, O dear soul," the accompanying instruments weave the finery with which the soul is to be attired.

To feel the wonder of the aria that follows, imagine yourself all decked out for your first formal date, and finally the doorbell rings. Of course, in the time of the Bible and in the time of Bach there were no electric doorbells. Instead there was a knock at the door. Bach gives the knock to the flute, and a very insistent knock it is, repeated again and again as if we do not answer instantly. There is even a section in the aria where we get the impression of our being unable to respond: there are eighth-note rests in the musical phrases that accompany the words "Only partly broken words of gladness," suggesting how we are speechless with joy at the arrival of our beloved. This speechlessness finally gives way to a great sustained note and flourish on the word "utter," suggesting we have finally found our voice. There is insight here into the state of the human soul getting ready to welcome God. We attire ourselves in all that is most beautiful and gracious, but when God arrives we are at first speechless. Then when we finally find our tongue, our utterance is boundless.

The combined recitative and chorale that follow take us into the depths of why we are slow to respond to God's knock at our hearts. The word "recitative" comes from the same root as the word "recite." A recitative is sung, but it has the quality of speech. The music starts in a straightforward declarative mode, then breaks into a chorale with a beautiful flowing cello line. The cello represents that ceaseless stream for which we yearn: the drink that will unite our soul with God. In many ways this recitative/chorale/aria is a sonic expression of the theology of Saint Augustine, namely, that God has made us to thirst for God, and God alone can quench that thirst.

The next recitative is sung by the alto. It features two high flutes that simultaneously seem to suggest the fear and gladness that are named in the text: "My heart feels fear and gladness." The high pitch suggests the fear while their sustained quality suggests an underlying certitude.

By contrast, the soprano aria that follows has a clear, bold theme announced in the very opening measures. The light of lights, the Lord who is all to me, takes over. It is as if all of our human tenuousness is dissipated by the shining brilliance of God that is expressed through an energetic sixteenth-note pattern. The music traces what happens to our spirits when we move from self-preoccupation to a sense of the presence of God: we are energized, renewed, abundantly alive.

The contrast between our human tentativeness and the shining brilliance of God leads to a prayer in the form of a recitative that God's love for us not be in vain. The very end of the recitative suggests that the prayer is answered because it moves from a recitative to a graceful melody, an arioso, suggesting that God's grace is beginning to dwell in the seeking soul. Bach's music here reveals insight about the nature of prayer. We often talk about whether or not prayer is "answered." Did we get what we asked for? By moving from a recitative to an arioso, Bach's music suggests that the prayer is answered in the very act of its being prayed. The answer to prayer is the relationship it establishes between us and God.

The soul that was exhorted at the beginning of the cantata to adorn itself for God is now attired by the grace of God. The final chorale suggests that the anxious soul wanting to prepare itself for God finally achieves peace at the table of God's hospitality. Bach's congregation was very familiar with the chorale. It was one of their beloved hymns, an invitation to dress their souls properly for a meal at the Lord's table so that, unlike the wrongly attired attendee in today's gospel, they will be warmly welcomed to the banquet.

The entire spiritual process that the cantata has led us through is not just about the individual soul but about the soul of the community, about the soul of the congregation as a whole. Through the cantata God calls us to become a holy community, attired with the integrity and faithfulness that can transform a broken world. Listening to this cantata is like standing before the mirror in which we check how we appear in some new clothes. The cantata reflects back to us the deepest anxieties and the greatest joys of the soul as we dress for royalty, as we prepare to welcome the holy one who stands at the door, the eternally hospitable host: Jesus, the bread of life.

In moving from J. S. Bach (1685–1750) to Gabriel Fauré (1845–1924), we leap from one musical universe into another, and yet there is this similarity: each composer in his unique way explores and expands the meaning of a sacred text, using voices and instruments, harmonies and rhythms that take us into a profounder encounter with the divine.

I have chosen the Fauré Requiem not only for its beauty but also because I have heard it performed in congregations using a range of musical instruments, from Fauré's original orchestration to keyboard accompaniment alone to keyboard plus a solo violin to bring out some of Fauré's intensely lyrical moments.

The sermon alternates word and music. The liturgical planners and conductor with whom I worked felt that it would be more effective as an act of worship if we interwove homily and music, alternating sections of the Requiem with theomusical reflections. I was struck by the large number of congregants who remarked afterward how effective this form of preaching is. I believe that speech and music complement each other in ways that awaken a greater attentiveness to what is heard. Speech prepares us to receive music; music prepares us to receive speech. The alternation keeps the soul alert and alive to the multiple dimensions of the divine Word as articulated by language and made sonically manifest through music.

Sermon, Part 1: Romans 8:31–39

The texts that are to be sung are printed in the bulletin. The musical performance of them is preceded by the preacher's theomusical sermon.

Introit et Kyrie

Requiem aeternam dona eis, Domine:	Grant eternal rest to them, Lord,
et lux perpetua luceat eis.	and let perpetual light shine on them.
Te decet hymnus, Deus in Sion,	A hymn befits you, God in Zion,
et tibi reddetur votum in Jerusalem:	and a vow to you shall be fulfilled in Jerusalem.
Exaudi orationem meam,	Hear my prayer,
ad te omnis caro veniet.	for unto you all flesh shall come.
Kyrie eleison.	Lord, have mercy upon us.
Christe eleison.	Christ, have mercy upon us.
Kryie eleison.	Lord, have mercy upon us.

Offertoire

O Domine Jesu Christe, Rex gloriae,	O Lord Jesus Christ, King of Glory,
libera animas defunctorum	free the souls of the dead
de poenis inferni, et profundo lacu,	from infernal punishment, and from the deep abyss,
libera eas de ore leonis.	free them from the mouth of the lion.
Ne absorbeat eas tartarus,	Do not let Hell swallow them up,
ne cadant in obscurum.	do not let them fall into the darkness.
Hostias et preces tibi, Domine, laudis offerimus.	Sacrifices and prayers of praise we offer to you, O Lord.
Tu suscipe pro animabus illis	Receive them for the souls of those
quarum hodie memoriam facimus.	whom we commemorate today.
Fac eas, Domine, de morte transpire ad vitam,	Lord, make them pass from death to life.
quam olim Abrahae promisisti	as you once promised to Abraham, and to
semini ejus.	his seed.

Sanctus

Sanctus, Sanctus, Sanctus	Holy, Holy, Holy
Domine Deus Sabaoth	Lord God of Hosts,
pleni sunt caeli et terra	the heavens and earth are filled
Gloria tua.	with your glory.
Osanna in excelsis!	Hosanna in the highest!

When the Requiem by Gabriel Fauré was first performed, there were many negative reactions. A lot of them came from religious people. The story of the Requiem and those negative reactions provide a case study in how difficult it is for people to accept the gracious character of God. The story confirms what the history of Christian theology reveals: it is very hard for many people to believe that God is above all a God of grace, not anger and judgment. God is more gracious than we want.

The text and the music of Fauré's Requiem are an exploration of the love of God. Many early critics did not like how Fauré himself made substantial changes to the official church text of the requiem mass. All of Fauré's changes to the text present God as less judgmental and more gracious and accepting of all human beings. For example, the official text of the offertory, the second movement, reads, "deliver the souls of all the departed faithful." But Fauré changed the text to read, "deliver the souls of the departed," or as other translations of Fauré's text render it: "free the souls of the dead." The composer's text makes the deliverance of souls utterly dependent upon God, not upon how much faith human beings have.

Some scholars speculate that Fauré may have rewritten the text because of his own uncertain belief. We do not know for sure if that is true, but Fauré himself acknowledged that in writing this requiem he was trying to do something different. Fauré was an experienced church organist, and he appeals to that experience in explaining his Requiem: "Perhaps instinctively I sought to break loose from convention. Look how long I've been accompanying funeral services on the organ. I've completely had enough of it. I wanted to do something different."[22]

When an interviewer pointed out that many critics considered the work pagan, Fauré retorted: "Pagan does not necessarily mean 'irreligious'!" The difficulty that critics had was that both the text and the music sounded too serenely confident. They wanted a more severe God. But that is not what Fauré gives us.

The Requiem opens with an Introit and a Kyrie. The Introit is a prayer for eternal rest. The Kyrie is a prayer for mercy. Both begin with the same musical motif, suggesting that the prayers are intertwined: to receive rest is to receive mercy, to receive mercy is to receive rest. Listen for an upward-moving pattern in the orchestra following the word eleison (have mercy), suggesting that grace is rising and lifting us up: our prayer for mercy is being answered even as we pray.

In the Offertory that follows, note how the music for the "king of glory" is not bombastic but gentle. The tenors and the altos sing without accompaniment the words "Christ thou all glorious king," and the score is marked double piano: very soft. The result is the glorious king is presented as an intimate, gentle ruler—one who knows our fear. This is a glory that welcomes and beckons rather than overwhelming us.

The petition to receive the departed is sung by the baritone. The amen, sung by the chorus, ascends as if the souls are now ascending to God.

In the Sanctus a solo violin spins sustained melodic lines while the other strings are plucked. The brass instruments then play in a bold, declarative style, *matching the way the chorus sings "Hosanna in the highest." But their musical exhortation gives way to a return of the solo violin over the pizzicato strings, as if in the presence of holiness even the sacred language of the angels melts into pure sound. To hear that pure sound in a service of worship is an act of prayer that draws our hearts deeper and deeper into the realization of Saint Paul's affirmation that nothing in all of creation "will be able to separate us from the love of God in Christ Jesus our Lord."*

We listen to the Introit and Kyrie, Offertory, Sanctus.[23]

Sermon, Part 2

Pie Jesus

Pie Jesus Domine,	Merciful Lord Jesus,
dona eis requiem,	grant them rest,
requiem sempiternam.	eternal rest.

Agnus Dei et Lux Aeterna

Agnus Dei, qui tollis peccata mundi	Lamb of God, who removes the sins of
dona eis requiem.	the world, grant them rest.
Agnus Dei, qui tollis peccata mundi	Lamb of God, who removes the sins of
dona eis requiem sempiternam.	the world, grant them eternal rest.
Lux aeterna luceat eis, Domine,	May eternal light shine on them, Lord,
cum sanctis tuis in aeternum quia pius es.	with your saints for eternity, for you are merciful.
Requiem aeternam dona eis, Domine,	Grant eternal rest to them, Lord,
et lux perpetua luceat eis.	and let perpetual light shine on them.

Libera Me

Libera me, Domine,	Free me, Lord,
de morte aeterna,	from eternal death,
in die illa tremenda	on that day of dread,

quando caeli movendi sunt et terra,	when the heavens and earth shall move,
dum veneris judicare saeculum per ignem.	when you shall come to judge the world by fire.
Tremens factus sum ego, et timeo,	I am made to tremble, and to fear,
dum discussion venerit, atque ventura ira.	when destruction shall come, and also your coming wrath.
Dies illa, dies irae calamitatis et miseriae, dies magna et amara valde.	O that day, that day of wrath, of calamity and misery, the great and exceedingly bitter day.
Requiem aeternam, dona eis Domine,	Grant eternal rest to them, Lord,
et lux perpetua luceat eis.	and let perpetual light shine on them.

Fauré, in writing about two other composers, César Franck and Charles Gounod, admires three qualities in their work—sensuality, purity, and tenderness— the very qualities that we hear in his Requiem, particularly in the Pie Jesu. Here, once again, Fauré has changed the official church text to present the character of God in a more gracious light. In the official text, this is the place where the "Dies irae" (Day of Wrath) appears. Although it was not uncommon in some churches to include the Pie Jesu in a requiem, what the critics could not abide was that at this point in the composition Fauré eliminates the Day of Wrath. Although he later presents it, here he replaces the fierce day of judgment with grace. The Pie Jesu is a lullaby for soprano, a gentle cradle-rocking song that reassures us our request for eternal rest will be granted.

The Agnus Dei starts serenely, then features more troubled music, on the phrase "that takest away the sins of the world," as brass and strings provide darker chords. But grace shines through as the light eternal starts with a long note on "Lux."

After the choir sings: "Grant eternal rest to them, Lord, and let perpetual light shine on them," the strings conclude with an ethereal melody, as if the request has been answered, and no more language is needed because the light has come.

Fauré follows the Agnus Dei with the Libera Me, "Deliver me, O Lord." These words were not associated with the official church requiem. They were instead words of absolution that came after the mass was finished. This is the one section where the day of wrath appears in the text, but the music does not match the fear of the words. While other composers have dwelt upon the terror and developed it to dramatic lengths, Fauré merely mentions it. What stays with us is the conclusion: the way it ends not in conflagration but in a prayer and decrescendo.

To hear the day of wrath transfigured by these gentle sounds in a service of worship draws our hearts deeper and deeper into the realization of Saint Paul's affirmation that nothing in all of creation "will be able to separate us from the love of God in Christ Jesus our Lord."

We listen to the Pie Jesu, Agnus Dei, and Libera Me.

Sermon, Part 3

In Paradisum

In Paradisum deducant te Angeli.	May angels lead you into Paradise.
In tuo adventu	At your coming
suscipiant te martyres	may martyrs receive you,
et perducant te	and may they lead you
in civitatem sanctam Jerusalem,	into the Holy City, Jerusalem.
Chorus Angelorum te suscipiat,	May the chorus of angels receive you,
et cum Lazaro quondam paupere	and with Lazarus, who once was a pauper,
aeternam habeas requiem.	may you have eternal rest.

The In Paradisum was never used in the standard versions of the requiem mass. It was instead sung outside the church as the casket was carried to the cemetery. But Fauré includes it in his Requiem, opening with high voices rising up as if the angels are taking the departed into paradise. The high voices are joined by the lower voices on the word "Jerusalem," as if the citizens of the heavenly Jerusalem are welcoming the departed.

The libretto ends with the same word on which it began: requiem (rest). It is a profound and holy rest that is communicated through chords on the harp and a long sustained note.

The Requiem starts with a strange-sounding sustained note. Even if we are not musically trained, its peculiar sound makes us wonder where it will lead. Will it blossom into a minor or major key? Will our prayers for the dead make us only sadder, or will our hearts brighten with confidence that the departed have been welcomed into God's eternal care? By the conclusion of the piece we have our answer. The Requiem ends in D major. It ends with the same kind of steady confidence that characterizes the apostle Paul's affirmation that nothing in all of creation "will be able to separate us from the love of God in Christ Jesus our Lord."

We listen to In Paradisum.

If a church choir is not able to perform a major sacred work such as a cantata or requiem, and if it is not feasible to join forces with other choirs, then an alternative is to do a sermon based on a smaller work or on a selection of arias. Rather than do one continuous sermon, I inter-weave word and music, preaching on the first aria and then having it performed, next preaching on the second aria and having it performed, and so forth. I usually use three or four arias that have contrasting musical qualities, such as fast followed by slow or loud followed by soft or percussive followed by melodic. The "sermon," the communication of the Word of God, equals the sum total of the homilies and the musical performances. Once again the response I have had from congregations indicates that this alternating of word and music makes for very listenable and comprehensible preaching.

Here is how I outlined such a "sermon" in the bulletin, using sub-headings to make it easy for the congregation to follow. All the arias are from various works by J. S. Bach.

One Human Heart: A World Too Vast to Chart
Psalm 139:1–6
Sermon, Part 1
Aria: From the Mass in B Minor

| Laudamus te, benedicamus te | We praise thee, we bless thee, |
| adoramus te, glorificamus te. | we adore thee, we glorify thee. |

The Heart in Turmoil and at Peace
Psalm 38:8–10
Sermon, Part 2
Aria: From Cantata 27

Gute Nacht, du Weltgetüm-mel!	Good night, you worldly tumult!
Jezt mach ich mit dir Beschluss;	Now I make an end with you.
Ich steh schon mit einem Fuss	I stand already with one foot
Bei dem lieben Gott im Himmel	With our dear God in heaven.[24]

The Infinite Dimensions of the Divine Heart
Psalm 139:7–12
Sermon, Part 3
Aria: From Cantata 198

Der Ewigkeit spahirnes Haus	Eternity's sapphire house
Zieht, Fürstin, deine heitern Blicke	Draws, Princess, your serene glances
Von unsrer Niedrigkeit zurücke	Away from our lowliness
Und tilgt der Erden Dreck-bild aus.	And effaces the mental image of the earth.
Ein starker Glanz von hun-dert Sonnen	A powerful radiance of a hundred suns,
Der unsern Tag zu Mitter-nacht	That turns our day into midnight
Und unsre Sonne finster macht,	And makes our sun dark
Hat dein verklärtes Haupt umsponnen	Has encompassed your transfigured head.[25]

The Heart Hastens to God
Psalm 27:7–9
Sermon, Part 4
Aria: From Cantata 78

Wir eilen mit schwachen, doch emsigen Schritten	We hasten with weak yet eager steps
O Jesu, o Meister zu helfen zu dir	O Jesus, O Master, for help to You.
Du suchest die Kranken und	You faithfully seek the sick and
Irrenden treulich.	straying
Ach höre, wie wir	Ah, hear how we
Die Stimme erheben, um Hülfe zu bitten!	Lift up our voices to pray for help!
Es sei uns dein gnädiges Antlitz erfreulich!	May Your gracious countenance be gratifying to us![26]

The preceding is what appeared in the worship bulletin. Here is the manuscript of the sermon I preached.

Sermon, Part 1: Psalm 139:1–6

One human heart holds a universe as complex and vast as the one in which our tiny little planet floats. To explore the universe beyond us, we send out space probes, and we train telescopes on distant galaxies. But how do we probe the human heart? How do we measure the distance between our faith and our fear? How do we account for the fact that the same heart that fills with love can rage with hatred? Who can measure the depths and heights of the human heart?

For the psalmist it is God who knows the human heart even better than we know it ourselves:

O Lord, you have searched me and known me . . . .
Even before a word is on my tongue,
O Lord, you know it completely . . .
Such knowledge is too wonderful for me.

This ancient belief that God knows us even better than we know ourselves found its way into one of the church's most beloved prayers, the collect with which our service opened: "Almighty God, unto whom all hearts are open, all desires known and from whom no secrets are hid . . ."

Although we can never know our hearts as perfectly and thoroughly as God, there are astronauts of the heart who dare to probe its farthest reaches. We call these astronauts "creative artists." One of the greatest astronauts of the human heart is Johann Sebastian Bach. Consider the first aria we will hear today, the Laudamus Te from his Mass in B Minor. Although the words "We praise thee" might suggest a joyful, declaratory theme, Bach opens with an extended solo for the violin that continues throughout the aria. The violin has long, arching phrases, suggesting the longing of the heart from which authentic praise and adoration arise. Listening to the yearning expressed by both the violin and the alto voice, we come to a more complex understanding of the praise of God. Our praise is not always joyful and ebullient. Praise means bringing all of who we are to God, the great yearning, aching desire of our hearts, as well as our gladness and thanksgiving.

We listen to the aria from the Mass in B Minor.

Sermon, Part 2: Psalm 4

One human heart can fluctuate wildly between peace and turmoil. It is a common experience to lie down in bed, eager for a good night's sleep, when the problems of the day come rushing back upon us. We toss and turn until we are more exhausted than when we turned out the light. Eventually we sleep, but only to have the turmoil wake us from our dreams.

Bach has written an aria that captures the experience. Before a single word is sung, the orchestra introduces two contrasting themes. The first is a slow phrase, but it leads immediately into much faster music. The bass enters singing "good night" on the slow theme but then follows it by singing the words "thou world in turmoil" to the much faster music. And so it continues, back and forth, back and forth, slow fast, slow fast. Sleep, turmoil, sleep, turmoil. The themes alternate and blend. We oscillate between a peaceful sleep and the world with all its worries. It is like tossing and turning in bed.

Then the music changes to a much more irenic quality as the soloist sings of already having one foot with God in heaven. The tossing and turning return briefly, but finally give way to a serene end. The orchestra plays the good-night theme and reharmonizes it. The new harmony suggests the harmony of a human heart that has come into the presence of God, a heart that at long last can say with the psalmist: "I will both lie down and sleep in peace; for you alone, O Lord, make me lie down in safety."

We listen to the aria from Cantata 27.

Sermon, Part 3: Psalm 139:7–12

One human heart can learn how the light of God transfigures even death and grief.

Queen Christiane Eberhardine was beloved by the people of Saxony. When she died in September 1727, a period of four months of mourning was ordered. Church organs were not even allowed to be played! Through the insistence of a musically knowledgeable nobleman, J. S. Bach was commissioned to write a cantata in Queen Eberhardine's honor. The text was not a sacred text but was commissioned for the occasion. There is nothing particularly biblical about the poetry with the possible exception of a vague allusion to the book of Revelation in the phrase "the sapphire house of eternity" and a light that makes our sun appear dark.

But Bach's music is another matter. The violins and continuo consistently keep a quarter note, quarter rest, quarter note pattern that suggests eternity. Above this recurring pattern, the flute plays a beatific melody that has a sense of stretching into infinity. The oboe has a sustained note suggesting eternity as the singer enters also with a sustained note. Several bars later, Ewigheit (Eternity) will be sung to an extraordinarily extended phrase of many notes. By sustaining "Eternity" on one note and then representing eternity through an architectonic phrase, Bach suggests both the simplicity and the complexity of that realm that remains beyond our comprehension.

Bach later in the aria uses the same kind of extremely sustained moving note phrase for the word umsponnen (transfigured), thus suggesting how the beloved queen now shares in the character of that which is eternal. The great fear of the human heart—that our lives are nothing but a brief moment of disturbance and confusion—is musically transformed into the assurance of an everlasting meaning that evades all our conceptual schemes. The human heart is embraced by the infinite dimensions of the divine heart.

We listen to the aria from Cantata 198.

Sermon, Part 4: Psalm 27:7–9

One human heart can utter an astonishing range of prayers. The Bible gives witness to a multitude of voices emerging from the depths of the human creature. Sometimes people rage at God: "How long, O Lord? Will you forget me forever?" Sometimes they give themselves to God in peace and serenity: "Into your hand I commit my spirit." Sometimes they ask for personal transformation: "Create in me a clean heart, O God, and put a new and right spirit within me." Sometimes they ask for the elemental necessities of life: "Give us this day our daily bread." Sometimes they face death with equanimity: "Even though I walk through the valley of the shadow of death, I fear no evil, for you are with me." Sometimes they cry out in panic and desperation: "Save me, O God, for the waters have come up to my neck." Sometimes they lose themselves in utter wonder and adoration: "Holy, holy, holy is the Lord of hosts; the whole earth is full of his glory."

J. S. Bach was attuned to the heart's vast repertoire of prayer. We have already heard him give voice to the yearning, the fluctuations, and the serenity of the heart. Now we hear him delightfully portray the way the heart hastens toward God. The lyrics and music together paint a picture of disciples who are running to Jesus for help: "We hasten with weak yet eager steps, O Jesus, O Master, for help to you." The soprano and alto sing in canon, one following the other with the same melody, suggesting in musical terms that they are following Christ. The buoyant music could be a film score for people running along a path to catch up with a friend who moves ahead more easily and swiftly than they do. The singers' sprightly canon stops for a moment, and they call out together to their Lord, "Ah, hear! Ah, hear! Ah, hear!" (Ach höre! in German.) The first two "Ah, hears" feature a musical rest between the interjection "Ah" and the verb "hear." It is as if Christ's followers have stopped running for a second and are so out of breath they can only pant one word at a time while they call to their Master. But on the third "Ah, hear" there is no musical pause. They are panting less now, and they take off again as the vigorous canon returns. Bach paints through music how joy, exertion, exhaustion, and renewed joy flow together in the human heart as it hastens toward the divine. We do not run continuously at a steady pace toward Christ. Sometimes our prayer is buoyant and robust, but then we slow down and call out, hoping to be heard by the One we are trying to follow. We are very much like the psalmist who exclaims: "'Come,' my heart says, 'seek his face!' Your face, Lord, do I seek. Do not hide your face from me. Do not turn your servant away in anger, you who have been my help."

As you listen to the aria, I invite you to imagine yourself one of the runners in the aria who is praying, "We hasten with weak yet eager steps." Next recall those times when, exhausted, you have called out: "Ah, hear! Ah, hear! Ah, hear!" Then finally let yourself pray for the confidence to say, as the psalmist does several verses later in the psalm, "I believe that I shall see the goodness of the Lord in the land of the living."

We listen to the aria from Cantata 78.

As a way of drawing the entire service to a coherent close, I supplied the following hymn text, based on the theme of the sermon and sung to "Terra Beata."

> One human heart can hold
> a world too vast to chart.
> For time and space cannot enfold
> the reaches of the heart
> that span our hope and tears,
> the breadth and depth and height
> that separate our faith and fears,
> the shadows and the light.
>
> O God, your heart alone
> can plumb and measure ours.
> The whole expanse is grasped and known
> by your discerning powers.
> You touch the wounds and scars
> where violence leaves its mark.
> You see our hopes as bright as stars
> that shine against the dark.
>
> Although we cannot know
> as we are known by you,
> the visions of our hearts can grow
> to see all hearts anew.
> We dream how each appears
> in your unbounded sight:
> a universe of joys and tears,
> of sorrow and delight.

> And through our dream we see
> the life that you intend:
> to honor the complexity
> of stranger, foe and friend,
> to welcome every heart
> and help each heart recall
> through worship, music, service, art
> your heart embraces all.[27]

So far we have considered how preachers can create sermons that proclaim the Word of God as it is manifest both in pure music and in music with words. In all the preceding sermons the musical composition served as the primary "text" for the preacher in the same way that a biblical passage is usually the text for developing the preacher's message. I am not suggesting that preaching on music is something preachers ought to do all the time or even frequently. Instead, I am offering this as a way of expanding a preacher's repertoire of homiletical forms, and as a way of being attentive to the prayers that the Spirit makes through "sighs too deep for words." Most of the time we can attend to those sighs simply by singing a congregational song or listening to an anthem or an instrumental piece. There is no need to comment all the time on what is played and sung. But if preachers never preach on music, then the culture's use of it as entertainment or as background noise is apt to pervade the congregation's consciousness. The members of the congregation may no longer understand that music in church is a form of prayer. Periodic sermons on musical compositions can deepen a church's receptivity to how the Spirit is moving through the music they sing and hear.

There is yet another way to use music homiletically. In this sermonic form music does not provide the text from which the preacher works. The sermon, however, concludes with a piece that complements and summarizes the substance of what the preacher has said. The music can take any number of forms. The only restriction is that the spirit and tone of the piece should flow seamlessly out of the Word that has been proclaimed. The music might be a grand choral anthem for a sermon celebrating the risen Christ or a mournful solo for a sermon lamenting the world's brutality or a congregational hymn for a sermon honoring the biblical injunction "Let everything that breathes praise the Lord!"

I am indebted to many African American preachers who have made powerful use of this form throughout my thirty years of teaching homiletics. I have encountered the form now and then in other traditions, but it is in African American preaching that I have heard it used most frequently. Often the preacher will break into song and sing a solo. Other times the choir or congregation will join in the music. The sermon has not ended. Rather, the sermon has been transformed from speech into music that carries us into the presence of God.

There is no reason that this sermon form need be limited to one tradition. It can be used effectively in any tradition that has a rich treasury of music for worship. To demonstrate the method's versatility, I conclude with two sermons that employ very different repertoires. The first draws once more on a Bach aria, but unlike the earlier set of sermons on arias, there are only a few brief words about the piece, and they all come right at the end. The second uses a spiritual that was sung unaccompanied by a soloist.

Sermon: John 2:13–22

My wife and I used to live in a house that had an unusual arrangement of rooms. A door led directly from the guest room into our master bedroom. It was awkward whenever visitors were staying with us. But most of the time the guest room was not occupied, and because the door was close at hand the room became a convenient, oversized storage place. We kept our bedroom neat by piling the guestroom with newspapers, half-read articles in journals and magazines, books, sewing projects, and clothes that needed to be put away for the season. But there would always come a day when we looked at each other in panic because overnight guests would soon be staying with us. We scrambled through the clutter, discovering that much of it was now dated and needed to be thrown out. We put the room right, and looking around the trim and tidy space, we vowed that never again would we clutter that room with junk. But a few days after the guests had left there was a half-read article that I had every intention of finishing in the future. I put it in the guest room. That was soon followed by a book and then some small project and then . . . and then . . .

That room filled up with clutter in the same way that the house of religion keeps filling up with clutter. The Gospel of John pictures the temple filled with "cattle, sheep, and doves and the money changers," all of whom Jesus drives out, pouring out the coins and overturning the tables. John places this scene near the beginning of Christ's ministry whereas Matthew, Mark, and Luke all place it near the end. I will leave it to scholars to disentangle whose account may be the more accurate. Instead of fretting about the precise history behind the story, I want to consider what it might mean that the four Gospels, when read as a whole, picture Jesus cleaning out the temple at the beginning of his ministry and at the end of his ministry. Since temples are buildings that point beyond themselves to the ineffable realities of religious faith, we might consider a symbolic reading of Christ's cleaning out the temple at the beginning and end of his ministry: the two cleansings remind us that the house of religion keeps getting cluttered with what is not essential, and again and again it needs a thorough cleaning out.

It is clear why our guestroom became a storage place for all kinds of junk: the door from our bedroom gave us easy access. But why does the temple, the house of religion, keep getting filled with what it does not need? In Matthew 12, Jesus tells a brief parable that helps us understand the root of the problem: "'When the unclean spirit has gone out of a person, it wanders through waterless regions looking for a resting place, but it finds none. Then it says, "I will return to my house from which I came." When it comes, it finds it empty, and brings along seven other spirits more evil than itself, and they enter and live there; and the last state of that person is worse than the first. So will it be also with this evil generation.'" It is not adequate simply to clean house. If the rubbish that has accumulated in the house of religion is tossed out but nothing excellent is put in its place, it will quickly refill with junk, and its latter state may be worse than before!

In John's account of Christ's cleansing the temple, the disciples attribute his action to "zeal" for the house of God. Christ does not settle for simply cleaning house. He replaces what he throws out with a "zeal" for what God intends. The word "zeal" frightens many people, and for good reason. It is often associated with extremism, including the zealotry that feeds religious bigotry and violence. Fortunately, the other three Gospels provide a fuller description of the nature of Christ's zeal. In Mark's account, for example, Jesus follows the cleansing of the temple with his "teaching and saying, 'Is it not written, "My house shall be called a house of prayer for all the nations?"'" Christ's zeal is a passion for spiritual hospitality, for welcoming into the temple all peoples of the earth. There is no word qualifying "all." All means all: everyone, every nation, every culture, every kind of person, no one left out. All! Christ's zeal is an intense longing to bring the whole human community together into the presence of the living Spirit.

When this kind of zeal is missing from the house of religion or from the soul, then the evil spirits take up residence. Fear, prejudice, hostility, ignorance, superstition, and stacks of other rubbish routinely pile up in the house of religion. One has only to think of the sad and tragic history of the church justifying slavery, starting religious wars, fighting the early development of science, treating women as inferior to men, nurturing the anti-Semitism that led to the Holocaust, and supplying theological rationales for racism and homophobia. Although that is only a brief list, it is long enough to understand why many people eschew all forms of religious faith and appeal to the salutary effects of living by reason and the scientific method. The problem with this solution is that it ignores the thirst of the human spirit for the Spirit of the living God, for the source and core of being, for the One who creates and sustains us. Forever in the heart there springs a hunger that our science and reason, wonderful gifts that they are, can never fill. If we put the soul in well-reasoned order while leaving it empty in the center, bad spirits will make it their home.

The antidote to rotten theology and all the pathologies it spawns is not the demolition of theology but the robust zeal of Christ for the godly well-being of the whole human community. The way to bring that healthy passion into our lives is for us to welcome Christ into our hearts. We need to reenact the temple cleansing by clearing out the rubbish of fear and prejudice that accumulates in our hearts and then inviting Christ to enter.

J. S. Bach captures the spirit of the process in his aria "Open My Whole Heart." The soprano repeatedly sings her prayer as a beautiful melodic line. But in the middle of the aria, the music slows down as she takes stock of her creaturely status, "I am but dust and earth." The contrast between the flowing melody and the honest acknowledgment of her true state gives witness to the spiritual health that we seek. Listen. Let the aria be a prayer for the house of religious faith, a prayer that we who dwell in that temple may throw out everything not essential in order to make room for what we cannot live without: the Christ who bears to all people and to the whole creation the eternal love of God.

Öffne dich, mein ganzes Herze,	Open, my whole heart:
Jesus kömmt und ziehet ein.	Jesus comes and moves in.
Bin ich gleich nur Staub und Erde,	Though I am but dust and earth,
Will er mich doch nicht verschmähn,	Yet He would not disdain

Seine Lust an mir zu sehn,	To find his pleasure in me,
Dass ich seine Wohnung werde.	So that I might become his dwelling.
O wie selig werd ich sein!	Oh, how blessed I shall be![28]

A Sermon: 2 Kings 2:1–12, Psalm 121

"The Lord will keep your going out and your coming in from this time on and forevermore."

Going out and coming in, going out and coming in. It is part of the deep rhythm of life. What keen memory of a particular going out do you have? Perhaps it was when you left home for college. Perhaps it was much earlier in life, when you were a small child and your family moved across the country, and you had to leave the only neighborhood you had ever known. Perhaps it was later in life when you left the hospice after someone you loved had died, and you felt you were setting off into a land you had never walked before. Perhaps it was some great intellectual venture that would take you into realms of knowledge that opened new worlds to you.

"The Lord will keep your going out and your coming in from this time on and forevermore."

Going out and coming in, going out and coming in. What keen memory of a particular coming in do you have? Perhaps it was coming in to a circle of friends where you felt more at home than in any other group you had ever been a part of. Perhaps it was coming in to your own as you realized you were no longer a novice but really an expert at what you did for a living. Perhaps it was coming in to a dangerous situation that took you by surprise and left you feeling threatened and vulnerable. Perhaps it was coming in to a stage of life where you had finally made peace with the hard things of your past.

"The Lord will keep your going out and your coming in from this time on and forevermore."

The story of Elijah and Elisha parting at the river Jordan is a story about going out and coming in. Elijah is ready for going out of this world and coming into his eternal home. The old prophet knows it is his last day on earth, and he is set to go. But his apprentice, Elisha, is not at all ready for Elijah's going out and coming in. When Elijah tries to leave him behind in Gilgal and head for Bethel, Elisha insists, "'As the Lord lives, and as you yourself live, I will not leave you.'" When they arrive in Bethel and a company of prophets asks Elisha if he knows that this is Elijah's last day, he retorts, "'Yes, I know; keep silent.'"

Although it is Elijah's last day on earth, it is astounding how physically active he is. First he walks with Elisha from Gilgal to Bethel. Gilgal was a town seven miles north of Bethel. Seven miles! That is a good long walk for any day of someone's life, but especially impressive on the last day of life.

Once again Elijah tries to shake his clinging apprentice, asking him to stay behind while he proceeds alone to Jericho, but Elisha, as stubborn as ever, persists at his mentor's side while they walk together eleven miles to Jericho, where another company of prophets asks if Elisha realizes what is to happen, and he once more answers: "'Yes, I know; be silent.'" By now they have walked eighteen miles! But the journey is still not over.

The old prophet senses that God is now sending him from Jericho to the river Jordan. One more time, Elijah and Elisha replay the same scene. Elijah asks his apprentice to stay behind, and Elisha says, "'As the Lord lives, and as you yourself live, I will not leave you.'" And so together they proceed to the river Jordan, another five miles away. Add up the mileage. On his last day on earth Elijah walks seven miles from Gilgal to Bethel, eleven miles from Bethel to Jericho, five miles from Jericho to Jordan. Seven plus eleven plus five equals twenty- three. Twenty three miles in one day! Have you ever walked twenty-three miles in one day? I did just once in my life, when my wife and I were hiking the coast-to-coast path in England. Twenty-three miles in a day is exhausting. One would think that by now Elisha would feel so tired that he would be ready to let Elijah go. But instead the apprentice prophet asks: "'Please let me inherit a double share of your spirit.'"

While Elisha's final request hangs in the air, I repeat to myself the places to which the two prophets have walked this day: Bethel, Jericho, Jordan. Those are more than geophysical locations. They are fabled places in the landscape of the heart of faith. The words start to repeat in my mind like a chant: Bethel, Jericho, Jordan. Bethel, Jericho, Jordan. Bethel, Jericho, Jordan. Suddenly it dawns upon me: Elijah and Elisha have walked much farther than twenty-three miles. They have walked across the centuries of God's keeping watch over the going out and the coming in of the community of faith.

Jacob was going out, running away from his family, when he lay down at Bethel with a stone for a pillow. That night he had a vision of a ladder with angels ascending to heaven and descending to earth. He woke up and realized, "'Surely the Lord is in this place—and I did not know it!'" To go to Bethel is to return to the place of visionary powers, to recall anew the ladder of connections between earth and heaven, between the mortal and the eternal, between human inadequacy and divine fulfillment.

To travel to Jericho is to remember when Israel was coming in to the promised land and to recall how

> *Joshua fought the battle of Jericho, Jericho, Jericho.*
> *Joshua fought the battle of Jericho,*
> *And the walls came a tumbling down!*

To go to Jericho is to be reminded that God has the power to take down the walls of human division.

To travel to the river Jordan is to remember that God opened a path through deep waters when the Hebrew slaves were going out of Egypt and when they were coming in to the promised land. To go to the river Jordan is to renew our confidence that God can make a way to freedom when it seems no way is possible.

When Elisha makes his request for a double share of his teacher's spirit, Elijah's response is provisional: it depends on whether or not Elisha sees him as he is taken away. Yet Elijah has already blessed his apprentice. For he has walked Elisha across the centuries of the community of faith to receive an extravagant blessing. It is the blessing of the Lord watching over the going out and the coming in of generation after generation, the same Lord who is there when at last the chariot of fire and horses of fire separate the two prophets, the same Lord who is there when this prayer arises as the final song of our mortal life.

A soloist sings:

> *Swing low, sweet chariot,*
> *coming for to carry me home!*
> *Swing low, sweet chariot,*
> *coming for to carry me home!*
>
> *I looked over Jordan, and what did I see,*
> *coming for to carry me home?*
> *A band of angels coming after me,*
> *coming for to carry me home.*
>
> *If you get there before I do,*
> *tell all my friends I'm coming too.*
>
> *The brightest day that ever I saw,*
> *when Jesus washed my sins away.*

> *I'm sometimes up and sometimes down,*
> *but still my soul feels heavenly bound.*[29]

After the singing of the spiritual, the preacher gives the following blessing as the conclusion to the sermon.

The Lord of Bethel, the source of visionary powers and dreams, will keep your going out and your coming in from this time on and forevermore.

The Lord of Jericho, the power who brings down the walls of human division, will keep your going out and your coming in from this time on and forevermore.

The Lord of the Jordan, the liberator who makes a way through waters that threaten to drown you, will keep your going out and your coming in from this time on and forevermore.

The Lord will keep your going out and your coming in from this time on and forevermore.

Quick-Eyed Love Draws Near

Preaching on Poetry

It is a common illusion to consider poetry a rarefied aesthetic domain that interests only the literati. The great twentieth-century American poet Wallace Stevens challenged the inadequacy of such a narrow view and asserted that the word "poet" ought to mean "any man of imagination,"[1] any woman of imagination. Poetry, understood as our capacity to be imaginative, gives vivid expression to the intimations of mystery that draw us more closely to the deep dear core of things. Poetry is the idiom of our visionary powers. It articulates the intangible realities that we sense through the yearning soul and the heart alive to wonder. It opens us to the ineffable substance of the Spirit: "Poetry tries to get at something elemental by coming out of a silence and returning us—restoring us—to that silence. It longs to contact the mysteries; hence its kinship to prayer."[2] As one who prays and also reads and writes poetry, I have become intimately acquainted with the "kinship" of the two. Praying often moves me to write poetry. It has fed all the hymns I have created. Likewise, reading or writing poetry often awakens prayer because of the way poetry works upon the heart and mind: "The poem surprises us in words by formally delivering a sense of overpowering spiritual immensity. It instills us with a feeling of what cannot be possessed, and it lets the soul have its way with us. The poem is a soul in action through words."[3]

Despite the kinship between poetry and prayer, there is a persistent suspicion of the artful eloquence that characterizes a great deal of poetry. It often rears up when people are afraid that attention to the beauty of language will displace plain biblical truth. As Fred Craddock has observed:

> There still lives among us the ancient notion that there is an essential enmity between form and content. Let someone give valuable and needed attention to form and style, and soon comes the charge that substance and content are to the writer inconsequential. Let a book on any subject reveal literary artistry on the part of the author, and immediately its scholarship is questioned. Such thinking persists in spite of the fact that Luke put the lie to this dichotomous reaction long ago by producing a Gospel in which the Christian message is happily joined to conscious literary art.[4]

As long as we "lack a 'poetic theology,'"[5] preachers, even if now and then they quote from poems in the pulpit, will not consider using a poem as the primary text for a sermon. Here, then, are some observations and principles that provide a theological rationale for preaching on poems as a way to proclaim the word of God.

Andrew M. Greeley, a sociologist, builds a strong case for understanding religion as poetry. He uses the word "poetry" in its broadest sense to refer to the "symbols, stories, community culture and rituals (all of which could be lumped under the rubric 'religious language' or 'religious poetry')."[6] Although I am using the word "poetry" in the more confined sense of artfully crafted verse, Greeley's definition places what I am doing in a larger framework that reveals why preaching on poetry can be highly effective. Greeley claims that far from being merely incidental or ornamental, the poetic is essential to understanding any religion. He challenges approaches to religion that stress the institutional while ignoring the poetic: "If I therefore pay little attention to the voluminous literature on religious institutions, the reason is not that I think that institutions are unimportant but that I am interested in that which is more primordial and more fundamental to religion—its poetry."[7]

The recognition of the "primordial" nature of the poetic does not abnegate the need for reasoned reflection, which Greeley knows to be "often necessary and always useful."[8] However, for Greeley it is the poetry of religion that encodes experiences of the renewal of hope, experiences that "are prior to and richer than propositional and ethical religion and provide the raw power for the latter."[9] Thus to turn to poetry is to revisit the source that can renew our moral concern. One way poetry does this is by expanding our feeling for others: "In the end, the true poet is a microcosm of all life, and that is what makes sympathy possible: we cannot sympathize with what we cannot truly imagine, and we cannot truly imagine what we do not inwardly know."[10] Poetry helps us to "inwardly know," to glimpse how the world appears to another, to stand in someone else's shoes, to see things through a different set of eyes. The result is a deeper empathy and a broader capacity to be compassionate to others. One way the church can cultivate that empathic consciousness is to use poetry as a resource for its preaching and worship.

The poetic impulse lies deep in the nature of our humanity as created by God and as manifest in the early development of oral communication. Long before there was writing, human sound evolved into speech. Our ancient forebears preserved the primacy of speech in the way they pictured God creating the world. Genesis 1 does not read "God *wrote,* 'Let there be light,' and there was light," but rather "God *said,* 'Let there be light,' and there was light." God did not fill out a work order to bring things into existence. God spoke them into being. The ancients preserved the aural, musical qualities of human speech through poetry because

> all poetry was originally oral. It was sung or chanted; poetic scheme and musical pattern coincided, or were sometimes identical. Poetic form as we know it is an abstraction from, or residue of, musical form, from which it came to be divorced when writing replaced memory as a way of preserving poetic utterance in narrative, prayer, spell, and the like. The ghost of oral poetry never vanishes, even though the conventions and patterns of writing reach out across time and silence all actual voices.[11]

Not only do the musical origins of poetry survive as a "residue" in our various forms of verse, but the pleasures of oral communication also persist in a multitude of manifestations: our incessant conversation on cell phones, our love of talk shows, our delight in the lyrics of popular songs and beloved hymns, our susceptibility to jingles that entice us to buy things, and the news broadcast that comes to us in sound bites. All of these, some for good and some for ill, appeal to the human imagination by engaging the ear with the music of speech. They employ the same oral qualities that gave birth to poetry and that are preserved in our various forms of written verse.

Since we have the capacity to enrich or diminish life by stirring the imagination through the music of speech, preaching on great poems can be a way of redirecting the heart toward those things that matter most: doing justice, loving-kindness, and walking humbly with our God (Micah 6:8). "Wanting to live well, we need guidance in both private matters relating to personal relationships and in public questions of social and political relationships. Poetry preeminently supplies this guidance. Neither abstracted to philosophical precept nor confined to the literalness of history, poetry can speak with special vividness and comprehensiveness."[12]

As we have already seen in examining hymn texts (chapter 2), the church has long recognized how poetry speaks with "special vividness and comprehensiveness." Donald Davie observes about the church's use of hymns: "Among the pleas, never long stilled, that poetry be brought 'to the people,' we habitually overlook this poetry [hymnody] that *has* been brought to the people, and still abides with them."[13] It is wrong to assume that congregation members have no interest in poetry when one of the major ways they participate in worship is by singing poems to God, a way of praying that connects them to their ancient forebears.

But no matter how much hymns feed our worship, it is a diminishment of the church's imagination to confine its use of poetry to the texts of congregational song. Edward Hirsch, a contemporary poet and literary critic, draws upon Paul Celan's metaphor that a poem "'can be a message in a bottle, sent out in the—not always greatly hopeful—belief that somewhere and sometime it could wash up on land, on heartland perhaps.'"[14] Heartland is of course the land that preachers also aim to reach, and poetry can help their sermons get to the heartland of their listeners because, as Hirsch says in his own words: "The spiritual life wants articulation—it wants embodiment in language. The physical life wants the spirit. I know this because I hear it in the words, because when I liberate the message in the bottle a physical—a spiritual—urgency pulses through the arranged text."[15]

Preachers can convey that urgent pulse through a sermon that is an exposition of the "arranged text" of a poem in the same way that they regularly provide expositions of biblical passages. Preachers are not strangers to interpreting poetry. I think of all the sermons I have heard and all that I have preached on great poetic texts in the Bible such as the Twenty-third Psalm, the suffering servant songs of Isaiah, the Lamentations of Jeremiah, and the Magnificat of Mary. Preachers can create a sermon by paying the same close attention to a poem that is not from the Bible. They can tend to its metaphors and images, to the music of its language, to its allusions, to the connotations and associations set off by particular words, to the era when it was created, and to its unfolding process of thought and experience. For poems, though different from tightly reasoned arguments, are not without their own logic. As the Jesuit poet Tommaso Ceva (1648–1737) puts the matter, poetry is "'a dream dreamed in the presence of reason.'"[16] By blending dream and reason, poetry can give expression to the interfusion of transrational and rational elements that characterizes the state of our hearts and minds when we are in deep prayer. This helps to account for the phenomenon that Enda McDonagh has observed: "Poetry which trembles on the edge of prayer may be found in all languages and religious traditions."[17]

In a similar fashion, poetry can also tremble on the edge of prophecy. The words of the biblical prophets "are poetry, are image and symbol as well as meaning, are sound and rhythm, maybe above all are passion, they set echoes going the way a choir in a great cathedral does, only it is we who become the cathedral and in us that the words echo."[18]

One way for preachers to achieve some of the poetic power of the prophets is to create sermons that move back and forth between a poetic text and its explication, between feeling and logic, between metaphor and concept. The sermon recapitulates the dialogical process between poetic and conceptual thought that marks the scriptures and that has characterized much of Western intellectual history, including the development of theology. Andrew Greeley offers his own succinct summation of this essential dialectic: "Humans need both experience and reflection, both poetry and prose, both fiction and nonfiction."[19] Preaching on great poetic texts is, then, more than an appealing communications method. It is a way of participating in the dialogical process of God's transforming human life with the wonder of divine glory.

When we are swept into that process through sermons that use great poetry as their primary texts, we discover that "it is not only the love and personal relations which characterize God that one human being can mediate to another: this is also true of divine creativity. . . . The beauty of the poetry . . . can thus equally act sacramentally, pointing beyond itself to the beauty of the divine. God's love, intelligibility and grandeur are thus disclosed in and through the writer's art."[20]

There are, then, strong theological reasons for preaching sermons on poems:

- Religion is itself a kind of poetry.
- Poetry nurtures compassion by developing our empathic imaginations.
- Poetry lies deep in our humanity as oral creatures.
- Poetry helps preachers to reach the heartland of their listeners.
- Poetry gives articulation to the spiritual life.
- Poetry is one of the major literary genres of the Bible.
- Poetry often "trembles on the edge of prayer."
- Poetry helps to empower the prophetic word.
- Poetry is a necessary part of theology's dialogic process.
- Poetry can function sacramentally to disclose God's love.

I find that preaching on poems is somewhat different from preaching on well-known hymns whose words people often know by heart. Preaching on hymns, I usually supply more historical background in order to revitalize the depth and meaning of a familiar text. But when I preach on lyric poems that are not part of a congregation's repertoire, I find it necessary to do several things to highlight the text. I print the poem in the bulletin or on an insert. I read it aloud before preaching, and I often repeat lines from the poem in the body of the sermon. Finally, the plot or outline of the sermon unfolds from the flow of the poem. The sermon is an exposition of the poem in the same way that many sermons are expositions of a biblical text. In the case of most of the poems I choose to preach on, I do not have to worry about neglecting the Bible, because the poems are often filled with allusions to the images, language, and theology of the scriptures.

Sometimes the poem has been set to music and is offered by the choir as an anthem following the sermon. Although I may make brief observations about how the music draws out the meaning of the text, I do not develop my musical commentary as completely as when I am preaching on a full-scale choral work (chapter 3). Instead, the bulk of the sermon attends to the poem and its literary, theological, and practical implications for the life and faith of the congregation.

There is a vast treasury of poems from which preachers may draw to create and deliver sermons. The process I went through in choosing poems to use for this book reveals the abundance of available riches. I own a substantial number of poetry anthologies and single-author collections. When I started pulling them off the shelves and thumbing through them, I soon had so many stacks of books about me that I realized I could have dedicated this entire book to nothing except creating sermons based on poems! However, since my primary intention is to build a case for the place of beauty in preaching and worship by using classic works, I narrowed my criteria to two poets from two different eras of history whose work is easily available and in the public domain. This allowed me to tend closely to voices from the cloud of witnesses and to demonstrate how vibrant the tradition is with wisdom for our own age. I needed poems brief enough to fit easily in a worship bulletin yet profound enough to give birth to a sermon and to be worth people's taking a copy home for personal prayer and reflection. I wanted poetry that is accessible but that bears up well so that repeated readings keep disclosing new perspectives and insights that were initially missed. I wanted one poet to be a man and one to be a woman. I also thought that by limiting myself to two poets I could use more than a single poem by each, thus allowing for a fuller appreciation of their distinctive poetic voices.

There is no need for preachers to be bound to the restrictions I set for myself for the purposes of this chapter. Depending on the occasion, preachers might decide to search for a poem based on a season of the liturgical year or a pastoral need they want to address or a theological idea they seek to present with imaginative energy or an anthem the choir is singing, especially if it is a setting of a poem that calls out for commentary and exposition. The only one of my guidelines that I believe preachers will want to follow is that the poem be brief enough to fit easily in a worship bulletin yet profound enough to give birth to a sermon and to be worth people's taking a copy home for personal prayer and reflection.

The two poets I ended up choosing are George Herbert (1593–1633) and Alice Meynell (1847–1922). I begin with Herbert and end with Meynell.[21]

I chose Herbert for a number of reasons. Not only is he one of the great English poets,[22] he is also easily accessible, writing memorable lines that only now and then require a gloss in order to understand the meaning of an antiquated word or phrase. By offering sermons on three of his poems, I seek to convey something of the breadth of his work and theological insight in much the same way that preaching through a whole book of the Bible more accurately presents the richness and scope of the author's thought. Herbert is a great enough poet that he can easily feed a sermon series.

In addition to the beauty and accessibility of his work, Herbert has long enjoyed an ecumenical audience. Even though he was an Anglican priest, other traditions that separated from the established church of England found his poetry inspiring. With candor and wit Herbert captures the joy of faith as well as the struggles of the human heart to accept the grace of God. The poet's language gives witness to the complexities of the human soul in a manner that resonates with a wide range of believers and seekers.

Furthermore, Herbert has a sophisticated and holistic understanding of the Bible, taking delight in the scriptures yet maintaining an admirable humility that saves him from the dogmatic illusion that he fully understands them:

> O that I knew how all thy lights combine,
> And the configurations of their glory!
> Seeing not only how each verse doth shine,
> But all the constellations of the story.[23]

What John Hollander, a poet and literary critic, writes about the sonnet form rings true about Herbert's verse: it "channels strong feelings into deep designs."[24] Channeling strong feelings into deep designs is one of the characteristics of powerful preaching; therefore, Herbert can help us as preachers learn how to fuse the affective vitality of faith with the form and structure that make for homiletical clarity and insight.

The Call

Come, my Way, my Truth, my Life:
Such a Way, as gives us breath:
Such a Truth, as ends all strife:
And such a Life, as killeth death.

Come, my Light, my Feast, my Strength:
Such a Light, as shows a feast:
Such a Feast, as mends in length:
Such a Strength, as makes his guest.

Come, my Joy, my Love, my Heart:
Such a Joy, as none can move:
Such a Love, as none can part:
Such a Heart, as joys in love.[25]

Sermon: John 14:6

Artists have sometimes painted themselves into their pictures of biblical scenes. They become part of the story. George Herbert does the same in his poetry: he paints himself into the story of grace and redemption. He gives witness to what faith means to him personally, the joys and struggles of belief and doubt. You can see this in his poem "The Call," familiar to many congregations as the hymn "Come, My Way, My Truth, My Life."

The poem draws upon John 14:6, in which Christ says: "'I am the way, and the truth, and the life. No one comes to the father except through me.'" Notice how Herbert transforms the biblical verse. The poet personalizes it. In the Gospel of John, Jesus describes himself as the way, the truth, the life. But Herbert invokes Christ as my way, my truth, my life. The poem gives witness to an essential insight about religious belief: the power of faith is never fully manifest until it becomes personally true in our own lives. It is when something becomes true for us in the core of our heart that it changes us, that it mobilizes our energies to act and speak and live in a distinctive way. Personal truth is much more gripping than truth in the abstract. It is one thing to have general ideas about child rearing. It is entirely another thing to be a parent. It is one thing to have general ideas about how to deal with pain and suffering. It is entirely another thing to see someone you love die a slow, agonizing death. It is one thing to have general ideas about how to change society. It is entirely another thing to pass a piece of legislation. It is one thing to have general ideas about Jesus Christ, to read in an ancient gospel that he is the way, the truth, the life. It is entirely another thing to call upon him as my way, my truth, my life. Religion is no longer a chess game in the mind. It is how I live and act and speak day by day. How I treat my neighbor. How I seek reconciliation with my enemy. How I work for justice. How I pray with urgent, heartfelt intensity:

> *Come, my Way, my Truth, my life:*
> *Come, my Light, my Feast, my Strength:*
> *Come, my Joy, my Love, my Heart.*

When Herbert prays, he is not seeking some vague spiritual experience. He wants to feel the impact of Christ upon our life:

> *Come, my Way, my Truth, my Life:*
> *Such a Way, as gives us breath:*
> *Such a Truth, as ends all strife:*
> *And such a Life, as killeth death.*

"Such a Way, as gives us breath." *Perhaps the line means: come into our life by giving us the Spirit. For breath is often equated with the Spirit. In the Gospel of John, Christ breathes the Spirit upon the disciples. But the line* "Such a Way, as gives us breath" *might also mean quite literally: come as the very source of breath, the inhaling and exhaling of my lungs. For Christ is the Word through whom all things were made. And when that Word becomes personal for us, when Christ becomes my way, when Christ becomes your way, then there is a heightened sense of how our breath and pulse are a gift that we have done nothing to earn.*

Have you ever thought of this: How second by second you are receiving the gift of pulse and breath? You and I did not do a single thing to start our lungs breathing. You and I did not do a single thing to start our hearts beating. "Such a Way, as gives us breath" *is a way that makes us aware that our breath is a gift, that our heartbeat is a gift. Instead of griping about all that we lack, we start giving thanks. We realize that to exist is to receive gift upon gift every second that we live.*

> *Come, my Way, my Truth, my Life:*
> *Such a Way, as gives us breath:*
> *Such a Truth, as ends all strife:*

What kind of truth ends all strife? Is it the truth of some sacred text or creed? Judging from the way religious people have tortured and killed and accused each other of heresy over different interpretations of sacred texts, I can only conclude, no, the truth that ends all strife is not a sacred text.

Is it some scientific truth, a law of nature empirically tested and verified? Judging from our capacity to use our scientific knowledge for destructive and violent ends, I can only conclude, no, the truth that ends all strife is not a scientific truth.

Not a sacred text. Not a scientific law. The truth that ends all strife is Christ, the living embodiment of God's peace, God's wholeness, God's shalom.

If we look at this broken world, if we consider all the grief and alienation that have marked our own lives, then many of us would say we have known precious little of such a truth as ends all strife. And yet I have had glimpses of such a truth, momentary and fleeting though they have been. I think of a colleague. Bitter disagreement had separated us. My colleague took the initiative to come to me. He spoke. Then I spoke. Sentence by sentence we exchanged verbal snapshots of each other's world. We gave up trying to change each other. We settled for understanding each other. Alienation gave way to respect. And when my colleague left, we shook hands and said to each other, "Grace and peace." For a moment, a brief moment that had the quality of eternity about it, we knew "Such a Truth, as ends all strife."

> Come, my Way, my Truth, my Life:
> Such a Way, as gives us breath:
> Such a Truth, as ends all strife:
> And such a Life, as killeth death.

What kind of life has the power to kill death? It is usually death that is killing life. A life that is not haunted by the fear of death is "such a Life, as killeth death." For the worst of death is not death itself but our fear of it.

Several years ago there was a priest in Zaire who during the reign of the ruthless dictator Idi Amin faced death at the hands of his henchmen. The assassins showed up one day in the vestry of the priest's church. They told him they were going to shoot him right there on the spot. They asked the priest if he had anything to say before he died. He told the assassins that he was alive in Christ and that they were already dead in their sin. Then he promised them that after they had shot him and he came into the full presence of Christ, he would pray for them. The priest shut his eyes and waited for the rain of bullets. Nothing happened. He opened his eyes. They put down their guns, and they asked if the priest would pray for them now, here on earth. Yes, of course he would. They shut their eyes. The priest kept his eyes open and prayed for the men who had come to kill him. Not only did they not shoot the priest, many of them became part of the resistance, helping people to escape assassination. "Such a Life, as killeth death."

> Come, my Way, my Truth, my Life:
> Such a Way, as gives us breath:
> Such a Truth, as ends all strife:
> And such a Life, as killeth death.

Imagine what it would mean if the poet's prayer became our prayer. Imagine how much change that might bring in us, in the world. If the poet's prayer became our prayer we would know every breath is a gift from God. I wonder what that would do to the greed that feeds our plunder of the environment.

If the poet's prayer became our prayer, we would see the world through the eyes of our enemies. I wonder what that would do to the bitterness that feeds our conflict and violence.

If the poet's prayer became our prayer, we would live no longer haunted by the fear of death. I wonder what that would do to our cowardice in the face of injustice.

If the poet's prayer became our prayer, we would be changed. We would be empowered to change the world. Change that profound does not happen in an instant. Change that profound has to be nurtured over time. Change that profound requires that we pray for Christ to feed us, to mend us, for Christ to be our joy and our love and our heart. And so today we join with George Herbert and offer the poet's prayer as our own prayer:

> Come, my Light, my Feast, my Strength:
> Such a Light, as shows a feast:
> Such a Feast, as mends in length:
> Such a Strength, as makes his guest.

> Come, my Joy, my Love, my Heart:
> Such a Joy, as none can move:
> Such a Love, as none can part:
> Such a Heart, as joys in love.

> Antiphon (I)
> Let all the world in ev'ry corner sing,
>   My God and King.

The heav'ns are not too high,
His praise may thither fly:
The earth is not too low,
His praises there may grow.

Let all the world in ev'ry corner sing,
My God and King.

The church with psalms must shout,
No door can keep them out:
But above all, the heart
Must bear the longest part.

Let all the world in ev'ry corner sing,
My God and King.[26]

Sermon: Acts 16:16–34

It was a strange place for a musical performance. It was a strange time for a musical performance. And strangest of all: the appearance of the musicians, two prisoners in shackles. "About midnight Paul and Silas were praying and singing hymns to God, and the prisoners were listening to them" (Acts 16:25).

Think of all the music you have heard and sung in church, week after week, season after season, year after year at an appointed time in a sacred space dedicated to word and sacrament, music and prayer. But Paul and Silas are singing at midnight, in a dungeon, in some forsaken corner of the mighty Roman Empire. Why don't Paul and Silas respond like the psalmist in Babylon who laments: "How shall we sing the Lord's song in a strange land?" (Psalm 137:4 KJV). Why don't they cry out: "How shall we sing at midnight, our bodies bruised and hurting from having been beaten with rods, our feet and hands in chains?"

Midnight: the hour when the memory of evening light has vanished, and it seems that dawn will never arrive. Midnight: the hour when patients are restless with fear and pain. Midnight: the hour when the young child wakes from a scary dream. Midnight is more than a moment in time. It is a state of soul, a waiting in the depths of darkness. And yet we read: "About midnight Paul and Silas were praying and singing hymns to God." What is the secret of their song? What gives them strength to sing hymns at midnight in a prison?

Although George Herbert would not write his poem "Let All the World in Ev'ry Corner Sing" until 1,600 years after the time of Paul and Silas,

I believe he knows the secret of their song. Even if the story of Paul and Silas were not in the poet's mind while he was writing, still the poem is in touch with the spirit of singing hymns at midnight.

> Let all the world in ev'ry corner sing,
>   My God and King.

Not just in church. Not just in concert halls. But in ev'ry corner sing. In shackles in a prison at midnight.

To sing "My God and King" is to recognize the sovereignty of God. To sing "My God and King" is to confess that no matter how cruel and oppressive the empires of this world may be, their power is neither ultimate nor eternal nor impervious to the power of faith.

> Let all the world in ev'ry corner sing,
>   My God and King.

African American slaves whether, or not they knew Herbert's words, lived the truth of them. Torn from their homeland, their families frequently sold away to other masters, whipped and chained, the slaves sang in ev'ry corner:

> Nobody knows the trouble I've seen
> Glory Hallelujah.

And through their song they received strength to survive, to press on, to keep alive the dream of freedom.

> Let all the world in ev'ry corner sing,
>   My God and King.

The civil rights advocates of the 1960s singing in the streets lived the truth of Herbert's words. The people of South Africa working against apartheid and singing their freedom songs lived the truth of Herbert's words.

> The heav'ns are not too high,
> His praise may thither fly:
> The earth is not too low,
> His praises there may grow.

And that is exactly what happens when Paul and Silas sing at midnight in prison: God's praises grow. The other prisoners listen to their song. There is an earthquake. The prison doors open. The prisoners' chains are broken. The jailer and his household are baptized. God's praises grow.

Music and especially music in the praise of God has power to transform the world in ways that set off earthquakes. Any comprehensive account of social change needs to trace how often music has been a motivating and sustaining source of movements for reform and justice. For example, during the reformations of the 1500s, one of Martin Luther's opponents observed that Luther had won more converts with his hymns than with his sermons and treatises. You can refute a sermon or a book or an argument. You can jail or even kill an opponent. But there is something irrepressible about the praise of God in song. It cannot be stopped or suppressed or buried. After the authorities threw Paul and Silas into jail, they probably let out a sigh of relief: "There, that ought to silence those troublemakers." What the authorities had not counted on was the songful resilience of faith. You cannot stop faith from singing. As Herbert observes at the start of the second stanza:

> The church with psalms must shout,
> No door can keep them out.

The praise of God is irrepressible. It bubbles up in the babble of a baby. It hums in the hum of whales. It sings in the song of birds. It roars in the roar of lions. It drums in the drum of the thunder. It whistles in the windswept trees. It beats in the beat of the waves. It sounds in the hymns and prayers of the oppressed. When Herbert writes

> Let all the world in ev'ry corner sing,
> My God and King,

he is telling the world to let loose what is built into its very nature. To sing God's praise is to fulfill what God created us to be and to do: to love God and enjoy God forever.

I recall one day I was walking home through the park. It was a beautiful sunny day. Flowers were out. Birds were chirping. A woman was walking a hundred yards in front of me. She was swinging her arms and dancing as she walked. As I drew closer, I could hear her singing. I do not remember what the song was, except that it was an ebullient, infectious tune. The woman had a lovely voice, liquid and pure. I was lost in the delight of her music. Suddenly the woman heard my footsteps and turned around. She stopped singing, obviously embarrassed, and muttered: "I'm sorry. For my song, I mean."

"Oh, don't be sorry. I loved your song. I was so glad to hear it." As I walked on, the woman remained silent. But when I had gotten some distance

away her song drifted to me on the breeze. Not even her embarrassment could stifle the music in her soul.

> Let all the world in ev'ry corner sing,
>   My God and King.
>
> The church with psalms must shout,
> No door can keep them out:
> But above all, the heart
> Must bear the longest part.

We have been created for the praise of God, but that does not mean our song takes no effort on our part. In the last two lines Herbert's knowledge of music is apparent:

> But above all, the heart
> Must bear the longest part.

Anyone who has played in an orchestra or a band or a chamber music group, anyone who has sung in a choir, knows about the strain of bearing the longest part. As a flutist, I can think of various obbligatos I have played where my part went on and on without a break in the melodic line. I was bearing the longest part. I wondered: When will I ever get a chance to breathe?

Herbert uses the longest part as a metaphor to make clear how demanding the praise of God is.

> But above all, the heart
> Must bear the longest part.

When Paul and Silas were singing at midnight, it was the heart that had to bear the longest part. It was the heart that had to keep faith while they were imprisoned in the darkness of the dungeon. When the slaves sang,

> Nobody knows the trouble I've seen:
> Glory Hallelujah!

it was the heart that had to bear the longest part. It was the heart that had to keep alive the vision of hope through abuse and degradation. When the freedom movement in South Africa stood up to apartheid, it was the heart that had to bear the longest part. It was the heart that had to keep believing liberation is possible. When you sit by the bed of one who is dying, it is the heart that has to bear the longest part. It is the heart that must keep singing with faith when the voice is too choked with grief to sound a note.

The individual heart grows weary. Like my lungs at the end of a long phrase on the flute, the heart gasps for life and wonders how it will continue. The very title and form of Herbert's poem suggest how the heart will bear the longest part. The poem is titled "Antiphon (I)." *An antiphon is a devotional composition sung responsively during worship. The form of Herbert's poem follows the form of the psalms as they were sung or recited in the daily services that George Herbert led as a priest. Thus the form and title of the poem remind us that we do not sing alone. We sing together, we sing responsively, we sing as the body of Christ. When our individual hearts can no longer bear the longest part, then there are others who can bear that part for us.*

I can think of times in my own life, tragic times, when grief made it impossible for me to sing the hymns and responses. I would stand or sit in the pew, my heart unable to bear the longest part. And I would tell God, "Let the others sing for me. They will help my heart bear the longest part."

Ralph Vaughan Williams's setting of Herbert's text captures perfectly our need for one another's voice. As the anthem proceeds, the words of the chorus

> *Let all the world in ev'ry corner sing,*
> *My God and King*

are echoed back and forth, between the different parts, the melody sometimes carried by the singers, sometimes by the accompaniment. No one musician carries the longest part all the time. And what is true of the ministry of music is true of all the other ministries of the church. None of us possesses a heart that can bear the longest part all the time. No single heart can bear the longest part in the struggle to feed or to heal or to press for justice. No single heart can bear the longest part in giving witness to the life and ministry of Jesus Christ. We need each other's actions. We need each other's words. We need each other's prayers. We need each other's presence. So together as one body we declare with George Herbert:

> *Let all the world in ev'ry corner sing,*
> *My God and King.*

> *The church with psalms must shout,*
> *No door can keep them out:*
> *But above all, the heart*
> *Must bear the longest part.*

> *Let all the world in ev'ry corner sing,*
> *My God and King.*

Love (3)

Love bade me welcome: yet my soul drew back,
    Guilty of dust and sin.
But quick-eyed Love, observing me grow slack
    From my first entrance in,
Drew nearer to me, sweetly questioning,
    If I lacked anything.

A guest, I answered, worthy to be here:
    Love said, You shall be he.
I the unkind, ungrateful: Ah my dear,
    I cannot look on thee.
Love took my hand, and smiling did reply,
    Who made the eyes but I?

Truth Lord, but I have marred them: let my shame
    Go where it doth deserve.
And know you not, says Love, who bore the blame?
    My dear, then I will serve.
You must sit down, says Love, and taste my meat:
    So I did sit and eat.[27]

Sermon: Isaiah 55:1–2 and John 6:48–51

I recall a story that a father told me more than thirty years ago when I was a young pastor. One evening the man was at home reading. He looked up and saw his teenage daughter across the room working on some project. He studied the intensity of her face and realized how much she meant to him, and spontaneously, without any calculation at all, words came to his lips. He said to her, "I love you."

She looked up. Startled. Then puzzled. "Why, Dad? Because I did the dishes tonight?"

He shook his head no.

"Because I had a good report card?"

No, he shook his head again.

"Because I helped you outside today?"

"No, no, it has nothing to do with anything you have done."

"Well, then why, Dad?"

"Because. Because you are who you are. I just love you. That's all I meant."

"Oh," she said, and returned to her project, still obviously baffled by her father's statement of affection.

I will never forget the sadness in the man's voice when he told me this story. It sounded like the sadness that I imagine in the heart of God at our inability to accept that God simply loves us.

> Love bade me welcome: yet my soul drew back
> Guilty of dust and sin.

The poem uses an extended metaphor of being invited to a banquet, one of Jesus' favorite images for the reign of God, a table with all kinds of people coming from everywhere and gathering around for a feast.

To get in the spirit of Jesus' invitation, and the spirit of Herbert's poem, imagine yourself invited to a great party in a grand hall. You are reluctant to come from the moment you receive the engraved invitation that is addressed to you in elegant calligraphy. You have nothing suitable to wear. You fear you will not know anybody else there. They are not your kind of people. You have not the foggiest idea why you were invited. You check the name and the address and the zip code on the envelope. Sure enough, it is addressed to you.

By the grace of God you finally get up enough courage to go. But you approach the front door trembling and embarrassed, hoping you can sneak in to be seen for a little while, then sneak away. You knock timidly at the door, and the minute it opens, there is the host speaking to you, giving you a warm and gracious welcome. But at the very sound of that welcoming voice you feel inadequate:

> Love bade me welcome: yet my soul drew back,
> Guilty of dust and sin.
> But quick-eyed Love, observing me grow slack
> From my first entrance in,
> Drew nearer to me, sweetly questioning,
> If I lacked anything.

Now begins a tug-of-war between the hospitable host and you, the reluctant guest. You are filled with excuses, all of them familiar to everyone of us who has ever struggled to accept that we are accepted by God.

But this host is quick-eyed love, not blind love, not mercurial love, not fickle love, but quick-eyed love, observant love, attentive love, who for every excuse has the perfect answer:

> But quick-eyed Love, observing me grow slack
> From my first entrance in,

> *Drew nearer to me, sweetly questioning,*
>> *If I lacked anything.*
> *A guest, I answered, worthy to be here:*
>> *Love said, You shall be he.*
> *I the unkind, ungrateful: Ah my dear,*
>> *I cannot look on thee.*
> *Love took my hand, and smiling did reply,*
>> *Who made the eyes but I?*

These simple lines convey a profound theological insight: in rejecting the love that invites us to feast in the reign of God, we are rejecting the very one who made us and whose image we bear. This insight and the pattern of Herbert's language reflects Exodus 4:10–11 as translated in the King James Version. When Moses is called by God, Moses protests: "O my Lord, I am not eloquent . . . but I am slow of speech, and of a slow tongue." To which God replies, "Who hath made man's mouth? . . . Have not I the Lord?"

By the end of the poem, we are not told that the guest has finally overcome all reservation and shame. Herbert is too humble, and too much the realist to think that his art can argue us into a state of grace. Instead, he depends at the end not upon his art but upon what will happen if we eat what Christ offers us.

> *Love took my hand, and smiling did reply,*
>> *Who made the eyes but I?*
>
> *Truth Lord, but I have marred them: let my shame*
>> *Go where it doth deserve.*
> *And know you not, says Love, who bore the blame?*
>> *My dear, then I will serve.*
> *You must sit down, says Love, and taste my meat:*
>> *So I did sit and eat.*

In the musical setting of this poem by Ralph Vaughan Williams, the choir during the final stanza sings a lovely sustained melody, as if the protesting guest has finally given up making excuses and at long last enjoys the meal that the host has been wanting to serve from the beginning of the poem.

Herbert's poem brings to mind a former missionary who reminisced about the first communion service he had led years ago on a far Pacific island. The vast majority of attendees were not Christian. They had come to the service out of curiosity about this strange new religion. When the missionary issued the invitation to come forward for the bread and wine, they completely ignored the directions that "all baptized Christians were welcome at the table." Every single person came forward, the vast majority of them not baptized. They all came to the table ready to eat. They might not have doctrine straight in their heads, but they knew a meal was about to begin, and they wanted to join in. The missionary heard in his heart the voice of Christ saying: "I am not going to turn these people away. Everyone, baptized or not, is welcome at my table." And so the missionary, even though it was against what he had been taught and what he believed, welcomed them all and fed every last one of them in the name of Christ.

I wonder what would happen if the church were, in every time and place, as welcoming to all persons as that missionary was. Would that not give witness to the hospitality of Christ, who ate with every kind and class of person? Perhaps if the church were that open and receptive, people would sense love taking them by the hand. Instead of arguing them into belief, our behavior would declare: "Love bids you welcome." And to every excuse we would respond by repeating what we ourselves have heard from quick-eyed Love: "You must sit down, says Love, and taste my meat."

Alice Meynell was in her own day so respected as a poet that she was considered for the poet laureateship of England. Over the decades since her death in 1922, her reputation as a poet has diminished, although there has been renewed attention to her essays and her work on childhood issues. Nevertheless, a few of her highly compressed and polished lyric poems have continued to appear in anthologies, and all of her verse is now available online and in the public domain.[28]

Sometimes her language may sound dated to postmodern ears because her diction is soulful and, as Edward Hirsch observes, "We have almost lost the word *soul* as a figure of deep spiritual essence outside the terms of organized religion. When we lose a word we also lose its meaning. The depletion in our vocabulary leads to a dire loss of soulfulness."[29] I agree with Hirsch, except that in my experience, "soul" has also become a neglected term in most of the preaching and theological discourse I hear and read. Alice Meynell's beautiful and enduring poems help us recover from our "dire loss of soulfulness" through an art that is suffused with reflection on the mysteries of faith. She conveys theological insight through a deceptive simplicity. A preacher who lives with these poems will find they have the depth and directness of a sound homiletical idea. G. K. Chesterton, a literary critic and contemporary of

Meynell's, said of her work: "'She never wrote a line that does not stand like the rib of a strong intellectual structure; a thing with the bones of thought in it.'"[30]

In addition to Meynell's clarity of thought, there is a refined music to the language that brings pleasure to the ear when the poems are read aloud. Part of that pleasure is in the poet's keenly developed use of rhyme and meter. Because serious poetry since Meynell's era has usually been in free verse and because free-versers have been "opposed not only to conventional meter, but also to end rhyme,"[31] there may be some readers who would disparage her lyrics by categorizing them as "verse" rather than poetry. However, Timothy Steele has written a trenchant apologia for poetic form, demonstrating that the distinction between verse and poetry is a modern phenomenon. He makes a strong case for poetic form and "the memorability and delight its symmetries and surprises give to readers."[32]

Memorability, delight, and surprises are indeed present in Meynell's carefully crafted poems. But Meynell's use of meter and rhyme carry for her profounder implications. In "The Laws of Verse" she reveals that the challenge of form is what makes it possible for her to feel her pulsing heart and gives to her the "weight of life" so that she is not just a lightweight "feather" that "merely floats" but rather a bird capable of flight, a poet whose verse can soar:

> Dear laws, come to my breast!
> Take all my frame, and make your close arms meet
> Around me; and so ruled, so warmed, so pressed,
> I breathe, aware; I feel my wild heart beat.
>
> Dear laws, be wings to me!
> The feather merely floats. O be it heard
> Through weight of life—the skylark's gravity–
> That I am not a feather, but a bird.

I believe that Wendell Berry, one of our most distinguished living poets and critics, is close in spirit to Meynell's lines: "When understood seriously enough, a form is a way of accepting and of living within the limits of creaturely life."[33] Meynell believes that the limits of creaturely life, "the skylark's gravity," are essential if her poetic voice is to be effective. Skylarks ascend into the sky by swooping up, then slightly descending, then swooping up yet higher, then slightly descending, then swooping up yet higher. It is the force of gravity as well as the substance of air that makes it possible for the creature to fly. Just as the bird's flight depends on the laws of gravity, force and matter, so too Meynell will take flight by entrusting her lines to the laws of verse. Because of the theological dimension of many of her poems, including all the poems on which I will offer sermons, this commitment to working within "the laws of verse" is also an acknowledgment of the discipline required to live faithfully within the bounds of the world God has created: "She saw, when she was scarcely grown up, the shape that she wished her spiritual life to take, and she perceived that without the bonds of a moral law she could never attain it, never be wholly free of the domination of heart and passions."[34]

Although the best of Meynell's work stands on its own artistic and theopoetic merits, there is an additional reason for listening to her. "An ardent feminist [who] called herself a Christian Socialist,"[35] she was committed from an early age to the equality of the sexes. When she was eighteen she wrote: "'Of all the crying evils in this depraved earth, the greatest, judged by all the laws of God and of Humanity is the miserable selfishness of men that keep women from work.'"[36] Meynell defines "work" as "study or business or laborious pleasures," the strenuous endeavors that in her day were open only to men.[37]

Her theological insights expressed through beautiful and rigorously disciplined poetry give us a glimpse into the lively intellect and imagination of a Roman Catholic, feminist, socialist laywoman living through the Victorian era. Her art adds to that chorus of women's voices from the past that the church too often forgets and ignores.

The first poem I have chosen is based on the same biblical text as George Herbert's "Come, my Way, my Truth, my Life": John 14:6. By comparing the two poems, preachers may find themselves seeing the text from angles that never before occurred to them, perspectives that suggest fresh homiletical ideas.

I am the Way

Thou art the Way.
Hadst Thou been nothing but the goal,
I cannot say
If Thou hadst ever met my soul.

I cannot see—
I, child of process—if there lies
An end for me,
Full of repose, full of replies.

I'll not reproach
The road that winds, my feet that err.
Access, Approach
Art Thou, Time, Way, and Wayfarer.

Sermon: John 14:6

There are many goals we never reach. Maybe we wanted to enter a particular profession as our life's work, but when we went off to school we took an elective course and discovered a whole new world that led us far away from our initial goal. Maybe we dreamed that when we grew up we would settle in a particular place that we had read about and seen pictures of so that it existed in our imagination as the ideal place to live. But as things turned out we never even visited there. Or maybe we had set our heart on attaining a particular level of accomplishment and recognition in our field, but the economy went bad or our health deteriorated or some other unforeseen circumstance intervened and we had to settle for far less than we had hoped. Or maybe we dreamed of attaining a faith in God so clear and certain that it would never waver, never dissipate into times of feeling abandoned and hopeless.

Or maybe it was something much smaller than these major life goals. Maybe it was like the day I went climbing up a mountain whose elevation was more than 14,000 feet. I was eager to catch the magnificent view from the peak far above the tree line. But the thin air had slowed my pace to a crawl, and before the summit was even in view I abandoned my goal, turned back, and started down lest I not return to the trailhead before nightfall.

Whether it is a career or a place or a level of accomplishment or a faith or a mountain summit, if it becomes clear we will never reach our goal, we turn in other directions. That is why the poet is so grateful that Christ is not only the goal of faith but also the way of faith:

Thou art the Way.
Hadst Thou been nothing but the goal,
I cannot say
If Thou hadst ever met my soul.

What a revelation there is in the distinction between "way" and "goal"! If Christ were "nothing but the goal," then the poet might never have encountered Christ. She might have heard of Christ. She might have dreamed that it would be a good thing to live as Christ lived. She might have learned about Christ and his teaching. She might have listened to others give witness about what Christ meant to them. But in all these things Christ would have remained "nothing but the goal," as far off as the distant mountain peak I never reached. She would not even be able to say, "If thou hadst ever met my soul." Christ as "nothing but the goal" is too grand, too vast, too splendid, too far beyond her reach.

But Christ is not only the goal. The poet opens by declaring what makes it possible for Christ to meet her soul: "Thou art the Way." A "way" is what she needs, because, as she acknowledges:

> *I cannot see—*
> *I, child of process—if there lies*
> *An end for me,*
> *Full of repose, full of replies.*

We often use the phrase "child of" to account for someone's talents or character: "He grew up as a child of the depression." "You can tell she's the child of gifted musicians." "He is a child of the X generation." What we are "children of" helps to explain why we think and act the way we do. By identifying herself as a "child of process," the poet explains why it is inadequate for Christ to be "nothing but the goal." The phrase "child of process" suggests she is always in a state of becoming, always traveling, always moving on. Christ as the goal lies beyond her range of vision: "I cannot see . . . if there lies / An end for me, / Full of repose, full of replies." However, Christ "the way" can meet her soul wherever she is traveling, long before the journey reaches its goal.

Because Christ is the way, the poet is freed from the heavy burden of perfectionist religion. She does not have to despair because she does not have all the answers, because she does not have a faith that points to a specific terminus that is "Full of repose, full of replies." Instead of bemoaning her incomplete state, she has the freedom to be grateful for the journey:

> *I'll not reproach*
> *The road that winds, my feet that err.*
> *Access, Approach*
> *Art Thou, Time, Way, and Wayfarer.*

What wisdom there is in her vow that she will "not reproach" those times when her feet err, when she gets off course and is lost. We often waste energy blaming ourselves for our inconstancy, for the way our faith wavers and stumbles. But Meynell was aware that life itself, and in particular the life of faith is inevitably marked by what she termed "periodicity." In an essay entitled "The Rhythm of Life," she writes that even saints "endured, during spaces of vacant time, the interior loss of all for which they had sacrificed the world."[38] *If that happens to saints, then surely it will happen to us, and when it does it would be prudent not to curse "The road that winds, my feet that err."*

In the final two lines of her poem Meynell gives a list of synonyms for the word "Way," capitalizing them as if they were other names for Christ.

> *Access, Approach*
> *Art Thou, Time, Way, and Wayfarer.*

The string of words is precisely arranged. An access to something is usually the immediate entrance, whereas the approach is just a little farther off. The approach leads to the access. Access and approach are the two last stages of a journey before travelers reach their goal. But "Time, Way, and Wayfarer" are long-term elements of a journey. A wayfarer sets out to travel upon the way through time. The last line of the poem reminds us of the long journey that lies ahead, and it thereby reinforces the insight with which the poem began: if Christ had been "nothing but the goal," the poet and Christ might never have met.

Christ is "Time" because he is "'the Alpha and the Omega'" (Revelation 1:8), the beginning and the end of all things, the one who is present in time and who encompasses the totality of time. Time is also the reality through which a "child of process" travels. To call Christ Time is to realize that the process of our lives takes place in Christ, through Christ, and with Christ, so that he is our travel companion, our fellow "Wayfarer." Christ can relate to a "child of process" because Christ himself is a child of process, a Wayfarer, one who walks with us. The image resonates with Christ's observation about his own travels upon this earth: "'Foxes have holes, and birds of the air have nests; but the Son of Man has nowhere to lay his head'" (Matthew 8:20). Christ is indeed a Wayfarer as well as the Way.

Take this poem home. Put it on your refrigerator or wherever you post important photos and cards and recipes. And when you are feeling as though you are far, far, far off from God, read Meynell's poem, and then try opening a prayer with these words: "O Christ, O You who are Access, Approach, Time, Way, and Wayfarer, walk with me. Walk with me."

Advent Meditation

Rorate coeli desuper, et nubes pluant Justum
Aperiatur terra, et germinet Salvatorem.[39]

No sudden thing of glory and fear
Was the Lord's coming; but the dear
Slow Nature's days followed each other
To form the Saviour from His Mother
—One of the children of the year.

The earth, the rain, received the trust,
—The sun and dews, to frame the Just.
He drew His daily life from these,
According to His own decrees
Who makes man from the fertile dust.

Sweet summer and the winter wild,
These brought him forth, the Undefiled.
The happy Springs renewed again
His daily bread, the growing grain,
The food and raiment of the Child.

Sermon: Luke 1:26–56

I am always impressed when I see an angel, and I see a lot of them this time of year. They are prominent on many of the Christmas cards I receive. Quite frequently the cards feature an Italian Renaissance painting of the Annunciation, the visit of the angel Gabriel to Mary. The painter has placed the encounter in a courtyard or regal chamber. In the background there is a pastoral scene of distant hills with a shepherd playing a flute and sheep grazing around him. Near the center foreground of the painting is Mary, bowing demurely to the angel. She is usually clothed in a blue velvet or silk robe of extraordinary richness. The artist has painted the folds of the robe with great skill. They look so real that it appears you would feel the texture of the fabric if you reached out to touch it. Gabriel, with splendid arching wings, stands to the side of the virgin.

Whenever I see such a picture, I study it for a moment, and I imagine how I would respond if an angel that substantial and with wings that impressive appeared to me. I probably would exclaim: "Wow! An angel! Just tell me what you want, or I mean, what God wants. I'll do it." But nothing like this actually happens in the biblical text. Instead of being wowed, Mary is "much perplexed," and she engages the angel in a conversation about the message he brings: "'How can this be, since I am a virgin?'" It is noteworthy that Mary does not accede to Gabriel immediately after he explains, "'The holy Spirit will come upon you and the power of the Most High will overshadow you.'" One might expect that Mary would interject some kind of response to the angel's weighty theological pronouncement. But she keeps still and does not assent until the angel has informed her that her kinswoman Elizabeth is now pregnant. Then, and only then, does Mary say: "'Let it be with me according to your word.'"

When the angel departs, Mary goes "with haste" to see Elizabeth. It is not until Elizabeth greets her and confirms the message of the angel that Mary breaks into her magnificent song of praise: "'My soul magnifies the Lord, and my spirit rejoices in God my Savior.'" Why does Mary wait to sing until this moment in the presence of Elizabeth? Why did she not sing earlier to Gabriel? Perhaps it is because the most convincing angels are not those with splendid wings but rather the people we love and trust. The word "angel" means "messenger," and the people we love and trust are the most convincing messengers we know. We believe them when they tell us: you are lovable, you matter immensely, you have the capacity to bring to birth what is holy and good.

Luke tells us that Gabriel suddenly appears, delivers his message, and then just as suddenly departs. But Elizabeth opens her heart and home to Mary for three months! The most convincing angels are the most enduring angels, the ones who are in it for the long haul with us and who realize as Alice Meynell puts it in her poem:

> *No sudden thing of glory and fear*
> *Was the Lord's coming; but the dear*
> *Slow Nature's days followed each other*
> *To form the Saviour from His Mother*
> *—One of the children of the year.*

Alice Meynell was the mother of eight children. She knew about the physical demands of pregnancy and the waiting and the wondering as a child's being is gradually knitted together. She uses this intimate understanding to make clear that when "the word was made flesh," it involved the same period of gestation as for all other human beings. Instead of a "sudden thing of glory and fear," it involves "the dear / Slow Nature's days." The Saviour did not instantly exist from the moment Mary was pregnant, but rather it was necessary "To form the Saviour from His Mother." We can read the word "Mother" in the poem at two levels. "Mother" means Mary, Christ's earthly parent. Christ, like any child, is formed from cells and nutrients the mother's body provides. But Meynell has capitalized the word so we can also read it as the divine Mother.

Whatever way we interpret "Mother," the "slow" days lead in time to the birth of "One of the children of the year." By describing Christ as nothing more than "One of the children of the year," Meynell reminds us that the savior comes in the ordinary processes of life, and because of its ordinariness we might easily miss the profound significance of the infant's arrival. Perhaps this is why she includes as her superscription to the poem the words from Isaiah 45:8 that are frequently used in the mass during the season of Advent: "Drop down dew, ye heavens, from above, and let the clouds rain the just. Let the earth be opened and send forth a Saviour." Quoting them in Latin as they appear in the Vulgate frames the poem with ecclesial solemnity and sets up a dialectic between liturgical tradition and Meynell's reflections on the forming of the savior. The tradition alerts us not to treat the ordinary too casually or we may miss the theological significance of Christ's birth. But in turn Meynell's poetry alerts the tradition not to forget the earthy reality of pregnancy lest we miss how the miracle of Advent happens through life's deep cycles of gestation, birth, and nurture.

The quotation from Isaiah provides the poet with images for the second stanza:

> The earth, the rain, received the trust,
> —The sun and dews, to frame the Just.
> He drew His daily life from these,
> According to His own decrees
> Who makes man from the fertile dust.

The language echoes Jesus' teaching that God "maketh his sun to rise on the evil and on the good, and sendeth rain on the just and on the unjust" (Matthew 5:45, KJV). Jesus is born into the created order of things that his teaching describes. His existence is not privileged to special treatment. He must live "According to His own decrees." By naming them "His own decrees," the poet captures the mystery of what is happening in the incarnation: the very Word, the Logos, by whom all things were made (John 1:3), is now subject to the world he created. Jesus' teaching about the rain landing on the just and unjust alike is as true for him as it is for us. Christ enters completely into the materiality of being a creature on whom the sun shines and the rain rains without any discrimination.

Sweet summer and the winter wild,
These brought him forth, the Undefiled.
The happy Springs renewed again
His daily bread, the growing grain,
The food and raiment of the Child.

Once more Meynell's diction echoes Christ's teaching. The phrase "daily bread"
comes from the prayer Christ teaches his disciples, and the word "raiment" recalls
a famous passage from the Sermon on the Mount: "'And why take ye thought
for raiment? Consider the lilies of the field, how they grow, they toil not, neither
do they spin: And yet I say unto you, That even Solomon in all his glory was
not arrayed like one of these" (Matthew 6:28–29 KJV). The poet is making an
acute theological observation. Christ is brought forth by the very processes that he
takes to be signs of God's unceasing attentiveness to the natural world and to us.
Christ's teaching grows out of the way he arrived in the world, which is identical
with the way all of us arrived in the world: "No sudden thing of glory and fear,"
but coming through "dear / Slow Nature's days."

Meynell calls her poem "Advent Meditation." The poem is not simply to
be read once and then put away. It is an invitation to continue in reflection on
the coming of Christ. Instead of leaving us to drift in some vague spiritual ether,
the poet points us to gestation and creation. Those elemental, material processes
are the way that God makes us "from the fertile dust," and the way that God's
redemptive love becomes pulse and breath and flesh on earth. A wonder this or-
dinary and yet this splendid is enough to make us join Mary as she sings: "'My
soul magnifies the Lord, and my spirit rejoices in God my Savior.'"

The Unknown God

One of the crowd went up,
And knelt before the Paten and the Cup,
Received the Lord, returned in peace, and prayed
Close to my side. Then in my heart I said:

"O Christ, in this man's life–
This stranger who is Thine—in all his strife,
All his felicity, his good and ill,
In the assaulted stronghold of his will,

"I do confess Thee here,
Alive within this life; I know Thee near

Within this lonely conscience, closed away
Within this brother's solitary day.

"Christ in his unknown heart,
His intellect unknown—this love, this art,
This battle and this peace, this destiny
That I shall never know, look upon me!

"Christ in his numbered breath,
Christ in his beating heart and in his death,
Christ in his mystery! From that secret place
And from that separate dwelling, give me grace!"

Sermon: 1 Corinthians 10:16–17

Years ago I had a colleague and friend who had many wise sayings that he would share at just the appropriate moment when someone could use the insight or comfort that the saying provided. He never spoke with arrogance but always with a gentleness and an awareness of how burdened life often is. One of his sayings became a favorite of mine, something I have repeated again and again when I have been baffled by human behavior or utterly puzzled about how to reach out to someone in distress. My friend credited this adage to an anonymous medieval mystic, and though I have often looked for a more precise source, I have never found one. The saying is: "Another human being's soul is a far country to travel to." How often I have found that to be the case. I have experienced the reality of the soul's far country in trying to bring comfort or help to people who were depressed or grieving or bitter or afflicted by any other adversity. And I have experienced the truth of the saying when other people were attempting to bring help and comfort to me but never reached the far country of my soul. Sometimes we do break through to each other, but often we fail because it is in fact the case that "another human being's soul is a far country to travel to."

The saying offers wisdom to all of us who want to help others. We should not assume that we understand what others are going through, that we know exactly what they feel. Very often we do not. If, instead, we honor their souls as a far country to travel to, then the help we do extend will be more effective because our action will not carry with it the unattractive burden of presumptuousness.

Alice Meynell has written a poem, entitled "The Unknown God," that hallows the far country of the soul by seeing how the deep, dear core of another human being participates in the larger reality of Christ. The poem begins:

> One of the crowd went up,
> And knelt before the Paten and the Cup,
> Received the Lord, returned in peace, and prayed
> Close to my side. Then in my heart I said:
>
> "O Christ, in this man's life—
> This stranger who is Thine—in all his strife,
> All his felicity, his good and ill,
> In the assaulted stronghold of his will."

The word "crowd" in the opening line conjures up scene after scene in the Gospels, all the crowds that follow Jesus, all the crowds that Jesus preaches to, all the crowds he feeds and heals. The second line reveals that this "crowd" is a congregation receiving the sacrament of holy communion. A communicant returns from the altar and prays close to the side of the poet. There are only two assumptions the poet makes about the praying man. The first is that Christ dwells within him. In some ways this is not an assumption, since the man has just received the body and blood of Christ in the sacrament. The second assumption is that the man contends with the conflict and the happiness, the good and the ill that are the common lot of humanity.

> "I do confess Thee here,
> Alive within this life; I know Thee near
> Within this lonely conscience, closed away
> Within this brother's solitary day.
>
> "Christ in his unknown heart,
> His intellect unknown—this love, this art,
> This battle and this peace, this destiny
> That I shall never know, look upon me!"

Although there is so much that she "shall never know" about the man, although his soul remains a far country to travel to, still the poet is profoundly connected to him through Christ who dwells in him. Because they both participate in the sacrament and in the mystery of Christ, she can confess that Christ is "Alive within this life . . . Within this brother's solitary day." Note the word "brother." In Christ they are brother and sister, even though she does not have access to the secrets of his soul. Profound relationship does not always depend on interpersonal intimacy. Sometimes it does, but not always.

Although his "heart" and "intellect" will forever remain "unknown" to her, the poet believes that through this man she can be blessed by Christ.

> *"Christ in his numbered breath,*
> *Christ in his beating heart and in his death,*
> *Christ in his mystery! From that secret place*
> *And from that separate dwelling, give me grace!"*

The man's "numbered breath" and "his beating heart" and "his death" tell us that no matter how hidden the far country of his soul, the poet realizes this simple but profound truth: he belongs to the same species of mortal creatures as she. And from that awareness arises her final petition: "give me grace!" Grace is the unmerited favor of God toward human beings, the quality that makes it possible for us to move beyond our self-interests in acts of generosity and compassion toward others. The poet's respect for the far country of the man's soul leads not to withdrawal and lack of concern for her fellow creature but to a prayer for the very gift that can empower her to be a neighbor to the one who is a stranger.

In our present age, when people are continually texting and communicating with one another, Meynell's poem calls us to a deeper communion, the communion that the apostle Paul describes to the church in Corinth: "The cup of blessing which we bless, is it not the communion of the blood of Christ? The bread which we break, is it not the communion of the body of Christ? For we being many are one body: for we are all partakers of that one bread" (1 Corinthians 10:16–17, KJV).

Meynell calls her poem "The Unknown God." With a title like that we might expect a more philosophical or abstract poem. Instead, Meynell writes a poem about a human being whose body is right next to hers, "Close to my side," she says. The poet reflects at length on this stranger by praying to Christ, "'O Christ in this man's life—this stranger who is thine.'" Her prayer suggests that "The Unknown God," the Christ whose blessing she seeks and for whom we, too, hunger and yearn, is right next to us, as near as the stranger who has just returned from receiving the bread and the wine, and is now kneeling close to our side.

FIVE

Wonder Reborn through Beauty

In chapter 1 we discovered that defining beauty is like trying to cage a butterfly. Instead of a definition we considered the metaphor of overtones. Just as a musical instrument sounds a series of overtones that we identify as its distinctive voice, so too we identify beauty through a number of its "overtones," through certain intuitions and principles of judgment, that we may or may not have articulated to ourselves. These include the following:

- Beauty is more than prettiness.
- Beauty has a gift like, gracious quality.
- Beauty can be a vessel of God's creativity.
- Beauty is culturally durable.
- Beauty has ample room for what is disturbing and difficult.
- Beauty helps us to see honestly what is there.
- Beauty is judged to fill certain standards of value.
- Beauty is best understood by a dialogue between our concepts and experience.

The overtones do not give us a precise, once-and-for-all definition of beauty. We do not cage the butterfly. But we do have a clearer sense of the standards, the hopes, the values that are feeding people's understanding of what beauty is and how it functions in them.

Not every overtone of beauty sounds in every work featured in this book, and sometimes certain overtones are more dominant than others. However, nearly all the works are characterized by the overtone "Beauty is culturally durable." Congregations have sung for generations and are still singing "There Is a Balm in Gilead," "Christ the Lord Is Risen Today," "Love Divine, All Loves Excelling," and most of the hymns on Christ's passion that we explored. People are still performing and listening to Bach and Fauré. New editions of George Herbert's poems have kept appearing since his death nearly four centuries ago, and Alice Meynell's poems still appear in anthologies. However, of all the artists in this book, Meynell is the least well known. In the course of writing this book and sharing her poetry with colleagues, only one of them immediately recognized her name, although all of them were impressed by the poems I cited. Given the excellence of her work, she is a reminder to us that cultural durability may be a harder standard to apply than we initially think. It involves something more than merely surviving in the popular consciousness. It is not unknown for a work of enduring value to disappear for several generations, only to be rediscovered at a later date and finally appreciated for its extraordinary quality. For example, Johann Sebastian Bach did not take his prominent place in the canon of great European music until his work was championed by Felix Mendelssohn. Even in the case of Herbert, his reputation waned after thriving for several decades only to be restored by Coleridge's high evaluation of him in the 1799 edition of *Biographia Literaria*.[1] But over the long haul the hymns, compositions, and poems under our consideration have endured because, although culture is perpetually changing, they resonate with the perennial character of the human quest for healing and reassurance, for beauty and wonder.

I find the rest of the overtones to be divided up among the various works. "There Is a Balm in Gilead" features the overtones "Beauty is more than prettiness" and "Beauty has ample room for what is disturbing and difficult." These overtones arise not only from the spiritual itself but also from the context that brought the spiritual to birth and the way it nurtured hope and healing in a people who were enslaved and oppressed. Those disturbing and difficult conditions, as well as the haunting refrain and the sliding notes on the word "whole," blend to make the spiritual too potent, too deep to call it merely "pretty."

As a contrafactum to John Dryden's paean to England, "Fairest Isle, All Isles Excelling," Charles Wesley's hymn "Love Divine, All Loves Excelling" sounds with the overtone "Beauty helps us to see what is actually there." The contrast between idealizing the state and placing the love of God at the center of human existence helps us to see more sharply the over-extended claims and promises of the political order.

The overtone "Beauty has a giftlike, gracious quality" sounds with special strength in "Christ the Lord Is Risen Today" and in all the poems of George Herbert and Alice Meynell. This is the result of the master-fully crafted poetic structures that mark both the hymn and the poems. In the Easter hymn every seven-syllable line flows inevitably to "Alle-luia!" The combination of metric impetuosity and the musical ebullience of the setting taps into our deepest wells of gratitude and gladness. We feel the resurrection lifting our lives here and now.

The gracious quality of the Herbert and Meynell poems arises from language that is intensely compressed but overflowing with wis-dom. Not one word is wasted. Yet despite the economy of the language, the poetry is filled with spiritual and theological insight. Herbert helps us trace the dramatic twists and turns of the life of faith: how the gos-pel story becomes our own story, how the heart needs the support of others so it can "bear the longest part," and how the human soul resists divine hospitality. Meynell expands our understanding of Christ as the way, as a child who arrives through the natural processes of creation, and as a stranger close to our side. Through the grace-filled beauty of their verse, Herbert and Meynell give vivid expression to substantial theology.

Tracing hymns about the passion of Christ, we heard again and again the overtones "Beauty has ample room for what is disturbing and difficult," and "Beauty helps us to see honestly what is there." Those hymns depict the cruel world of torture and oppression. But they also celebrate the compassion of God who enters that world and takes the side of the unjustly accused, the brutalized, the suffering, and the dying.

The musical works by Bach also repeatedly sound the overtone "Beauty helps us to see honestly what is there." Instead of idealizing human faith as a simple monochromatic response to God, the composer provides a candid exposition of what goes on inside us: everything from joy and trust in the Lord to the restless, anxious seeking of the human soul. Through rhythm, melody, and orchestration, Bach captures the cogitations of the human soul and offers it all to the glory of God.

In the case of the Fauré Requiem, I hear the overtone "Beauty can be a vessel of God's creativity." Although we have no conclusive proof that Fauré lost his faith as he grew older, there is evidence that faith and religion mattered much less to him than before. Nevertheless, he composed his irenic, ethereal Requiem, changing the official church text to emphasize the all-inclusive and gracious character of God, and generating a musical idiom that speaks profoundly to people of faith. Whatever the state of his own personal belief, Fauré's music is a work of beauty, a vessel of God's creativity.

We considered above how Herbert's and Meynell's poems sound the overtone "Beauty has a giftlike, gracious quality," but now I want to consider how they also feature the overtone "Beauty is judged to fill certain standards of value." The overtone sounds in two ways: through the music of their language and through the ecumenical attractiveness of their theology. Their language rings with a cadence and clarity that appeal to both our ears and our hearts. Read aloud any of Herbert's opening lines: "Come, my Way, my Truth, my Life," "Let all the world in ev'ry corner sing, My God and King," "Love bade me welcome: yet my soul drew back." The lines feature mostly single-syllable words, and they draw us instantly into the substance of the poem. Herbert's verse fills the poetic standards of euphony and concision. But it also manifests the values of a nonsectarian theology that draws on the riches of a vital relationship to God. It is a theological beauty that brought pleasure and insight to both Anglicans and Puritans, despite their fierce differences and conflicts.

Meynell has her own music that rings with delight on the ear. Her work again and again sounds the overtone "Beauty is judged to fill certain standards of value." As we saw earlier, one of the key standards for Meynell is what she called "The Laws of Verse," those forms and conventions of rhyme and meter that challenge the poet's mastery of her craft. Meynell practiced the truth of what Wendell Berry has written: "The mind that is not baffled is not employed. The impeded stream is the one that sings."[2]

The final overtone—"Beauty is best understood by a dialogue between our concepts and experience"—is found in the response of the congregation members who participate in services of worship using these works to the glory of God. The recurrent pattern of all the sermons and services is a dialogue between our concepts (my sermonic interpretations of the poetry and music) and our experience (actually singing or listening to the music and poetry). The final overtone of beauty arises from the experience of the sermon and the art being offered together as an integrated act of worship that awakens new insights and fills the heart with a sense of the wonder and beauty of God. The overtone of beauty is in a congregation member saying, "'Balm in Gilead' has kept me going so many times, and now I know why." The overtone of beauty is in a congregation member exclaiming, "I wanted to sing all ten stanzas of 'Christ the Lord Is Risen Today.'" The overtone of beauty is in the tears of a singer who performs in one of the Bach services and later reflects, "I've sung this music for years, but today for the first time I sang it as prayer." The overtone of beauty is in a string player after the Fauré Requiem service who says, "This is what I dream church could be." The overtone of beauty is in someone who realizes, "Love has bade me welcome, and I have withdrawn, but I don't want to any longer." The overtone of beauty is in the coffee hour conversation that turns from superficial chatter to people sharing deep matters of the Spirit that have been stirred by the poetry or music.

I believe these overtones sound with particular strength because the music and the poetry are offered in the context of prayer and worship. How we receive these works often changes with the venue in which we hear or perform them. Not for a minute would I give up reading great poetry in private, either to myself or to my wife. But hearing a poem read aloud in church and listening to a sermon spun from its visionary world brings an enrichment of its meaning, insight into its spiritual depths, and awareness of how the disciplined and generous use of the imagination can vitalize our faith and strengthen our own creative powers.

I do not want artists to give up performing sacred musical works in concert halls and other nonreligious settings. But hearing such compositions in a sacred space as worship offered to God after listening to a sermon that explores the theological significance of the music can bring a congregation to a place of attentive prayer and overflowing gratitude for the source of every good and perfect gift. Of course, these things can also happen in the concert hall. I think of the story I recounted at the beginning of chapter 1: my wife's wanting to sing the doxology after a concert performance of Anton Bruckner's Fifth Symphony. Instead, we simply kept applauding the musicians, even though the praise of God was bursting inside us for outward expression. But if we had been in church, we would have sung our hearts out, we would have prayed our hearts out, which is exactly why I want preachers and liturgists to let the beauty of what poets and musicians create burn brightly in the worship of God.

In some ways it is strange to have to argue for the place of beauty in preaching and worship because in earlier eras it was assumed that artistic beauty, especially the beauty of sacred art, belonged in church. All the music we have considered in this book was written for worship, for the church gathered in prayer. The creators of the spirituals were not thinking of the concert hall when they first sang those great expressions of their souls yearning and aching for liberation and for God. And Bach was not writing his cantatas to be played on CDs or performed in a program of major choral works. He wrote them because Sunday was coming, and he needed music that would help convey the meaning of the gospel to a church congregation. My colleague Martin Jean tells how his "atheist Renaissance music teacher from grad school would laugh at choral majors who would schedule" the kind of music we have been exploring "in their recitals. 'That piece has no business being on a concert stage,' he would say. 'It belongs in a liturgy!'"[3] As I have already made forcefully clear, I am delighted to hear this music on the concert stage. I only quote Jean to show how strange it is that the church too often neglects its own inheritance of beauty, work that was created for worship in the first place!

As you have listened to the music and read the poems and sermons you may have come to different conclusions than I have. But if that is the case, I hope the metaphor of overtones will help you articulate the basis of your judgment. What overtones led you to your conclusions? If you can identify these, then you and I can have a mutually illuminating conversation about our varied responses. Such conversation among congregation members may provide an opening for profounder exchanges about the life of the Spirit and how God is known. When beauty takes its rightful place in preaching and worship, a congregation's sense of wonder is reborn, and that wonder renews their energies for being a community, doing justice, and showing compassion. Wonder requires the nourishment of beauty because moving from childhood to adulthood inevitably brings with it a diminishment of wonder. Wordsworth captures the poignancy of the process when he reflects:

> There was a time when meadow, grove, and stream,
> The earth, and every common sight,
> To me did seem
> Apparelled in celestial light,
> The glory and the freshness of a dream.
> It is not now as it hath been of yore;—
> Turn wheresoe'er I may,
> By night or day,
> The things which I have seen I now can see no more.[4]

Later the poet presents this loss of wonder in the starkest possible terms:

> Heaven lies about us in our infancy!
> Shades of the prison-house begin to close
> Upon the growing boy.[5]

Although we cannot shrink ourselves down and reverse the process of biological maturation, it is possible for us adults to regain a sense of wonder. The importance of wonder is implied by Jesus' teaching that unless we become "like children," we will "never enter the kingdom of heaven" (Matthew 18:3). The beauty of great art does not infantilize us, but it can awaken a godly wonder, a delight, a joy so deep that it penetrates even grief and fear, transforming us and giving us the grace to be agents of transformation. I think of the light shining through the eyes of people in the pews as they stand to sing "There Is a Balm in Gilead," "Christ the Lord Is Risen Today," and "Love Divine, All Loves Excelling." I remember the rhapsodic expression of worshipers as they listened to the intertwining lines of Bach's choruses and arias. I see again in my mind's eye God's peace descending on the faces of a congregation as they heard Fauré's Requiem escorting the souls of the departed into the eternal care of God. I recall someone who wrote me after hearing a sermon on George Herbert's verse, telling me how the poet had opened a door to God that he had never before tried. I think of a woman who responded in utter delight to Alice Meynell's poetry. These are holy happenings, acts of worship through which the Spirit stirs the heart and mind to a renewed sense of wonder and replenishes the energies of faith. These things can happen again and again when preachers preach on art that has the capacity to engage the depths of the human soul with the glory of God.

It is essential to remember that I am not advocating such preaching and worship as the regular, week-to-week practice of preachers and congregations. There is a certain rhythm to the life of every worshiping community just as there is a certain rhythm to our most cherished relationships. We arise in the morning and go through our standard rituals: plugging in the coffee, taking out the dog, getting the newspaper, pouring the cereal, saying, "Good morning. How did you sleep?" Day after day we do these things. But then amid the ordinary march of days, we happen to have a profound conversation with one another, so deep and true and mutually helpful that our hearts brim over with thankfulness for each other and what we share. It is a moment of utter beauty, and then we go to bed, and the next morning we find ourselves again plugging in the coffee, taking out the dog, getting the newspaper, pouring the cereal, saying, "Good morning. How did you sleep?" We do not return to last night's splendid conversation, but now our common rituals seem to have a freshness about them, like the freshness of the earth after a welcome rain. We could never live at the intensity of beauty we knew in our conversation the night before, especially when sleep is still draining from our bodies, but that conversation deepens how we see and cherish our ordinary life.

That is the same dynamic that I have experienced in periodically preaching on works of great artistic beauty that are offered to the glory of God in a worship service. The congregation does not need a steady diet of such preaching, but periodically preaching in this way refreshes and revitalizes the normative weekly ritual life of the church. When I was a young pastor, a lifetime regular churchgoer told me that sermons were like the meals his mother had cooked for him growing up: he did not remember each particular meal, but he was thankful that she had prepared them all and he had eaten them. As a young preacher, I found it a wise and helpful analogy. But now I wonder if the man did not remember some of the special meals: What was served at Thanksgiving, at Christmas, at his graduation? My hunch is that he would have remembered some of those meals: who was there, what was served, a story that was told, how many helpings of a favorite dish he had taken. The next day he would have returned to his usual diet, but the memory of that great meal probably returned again and again, and sometimes when he was eating just a common meal, he would enjoy it all the more because of the memory of the great meal.

In the same way, sermons on works of great artistic beauty often take residence in the long-term memory of a congregation. I think, for example, of congregation members who were present when I preached on "Love Divine, All Loves Excelling" as a contrafactum. They said to me over the years afterward, "We never sing that hymn but that I remember your sermon on contra something. I can't recall the word, but it was contra something." "Contrafactum." "That's it! I cannot keep the word in my head, but I still remember the sermon." Sometimes the memory is not this pointed. It is instead a feeling or it is music that still echoes in the heart or an intimation of wonder that returns more regularly during times of prayer and song.

In awakening intimations of wonder, we are doing more than simply enriching each individual's awareness of the depths of creation and life. We are also engaging the cultures in which our people live and that fashion their values and behavior for good and for ill: "Worldviews are not neatly written propositional paragraphs that can be explicated and critiqued in rational and discursive fashion. Rather they are, in their origins and their raw, primal power, tenacious and durable narrative symbols that take possession of the imagination early in the socialization process and provide patterns of meaning and response that shape the rest of life."[6] All the hymns, choral works, and poems on which the sermons in this book are based are related to that deep core of "tenacious and durable narrative symbols" that lie at the heart of a broadly ecumenical Christianity. To preach on them is to tap into their "raw, primal power," to engage the congregation's "patterns of meaning and response that shape the rest of life." One of my favorite metaphors for this process is the spiderweb: if you tap the web at any point, the whole thing moves. When we preach on a beloved hymn or a choral work rooted in scripture or a poem that explores our relationship to God, then we touch the "web of faith" at a junction point that is interconnected to the whole vast network of meanings and values that constitute our theological understanding of life. The whole web picks up the vitality that the work of art imparts.

But works of art do not simply confirm and reinforce the completed web of faith. They also take faith in new directions. Andrew Greeley sees this not as something completely novel but as a continuation of the dynamic process that we encounter in the scriptures:

So too the apostles' experience with Jesus, who was dead and now alive again, was an experience of men steeped in the religious language, the religious poetry, of Second Temple Judaism and interpreted in the very experience itself in the poetry of that heritage, a poetry that was forever transformed by that experience. Their attempts to explain it afterward made use of all the rich imaginative resources of their own heritage (Adam, Moses, David, Suffering Servant, Son of Man, Anointed One) but put a new "spin" on the meaning of these resources. They used the same metaphors but with meanings drawn from the metaphors . . . that had not been drawn from them before and that *created new trajectories for the future use of the metaphors.*[7]

We have seen those "new trajectories" in nearly every piece of art we have considered. The African American slaves saw "new trajectories" of healing in the spiritual, "There Is a Balm in Gilead." "Jesus Christ Is Risen Today" takes the resurrection and extends it forever into the present moment. "Love Divine, All Love's Excelling" celebrates a trajectory that leads away from the idealization of the nation. Bach's arias, both the vocal and instrumental parts, provide a sonic idiom that illuminates the complex interactions of faith and doubt, yearning and hope. Fauré revises the text and musical expression of the Requiem so as to expand our sense of the graciousness of God. Herbert helps us face up to our resistance to God as well as our delight in God's intimate company. Meynell celebrates the natural processes through which the Word of God is made flesh and gives us a glimpse into the sacred mystery of a stranger's soul. All these artists continue the dynamism of the biblical witness, reminding us that we are most faithful to the scriptures not when we simply repeat their ancient formulae, but when we allow the biblical witness to create "new trajectories for the future use of the metaphors."

Among those trajectories is a broader vision of God, including a move away from an exclusively masculine understanding of deity. Sometimes the move is implicit in the poetry. Although the gender is not specified, the host in "Love Bade Me Welcome" appears to be a woman. It is possible that "There Is a Balm in Gilead" was written by a slave woman seeking to soothe her discouraged family and community, and Alice Meynell describes the incarnation in ways that draw us to see the holiness of the feminine: "the dear / Slow Nature's days followed each other / To form the Saviour from His Mother." But even when the poet or musician is not a woman, the very nature of the art moves us beyond rigid dichotomies of sexual stereotyping. For example, Bach's music is as demanding for the sopranos and altos as it is for the tenors and the basses. Or I think of the way Fauré completely changes the character of the angry, judging God, traditionally associated with God the Father, through his modifications of the text of his Requiem and to the placement and musical idiom of the "Dies Irae" (Day of Wrath). Preaching on such works of artistic beauty is a potent way to loosen the rigid imagination of the church not by rationally arguing people into a more inclusive vision of God and the church, a strategy that is seldom effective, but by leading them into the liberating experience of such a vision.

John Ruskin (1819–1900), the famous English art critic, sees this visionary approach to homiletics as an alternative to a pattern of preaching that is overburdened with a fierce and demanding God:

> The reason that preaching is so commonly ineffectual is that it calls on men oftener to work for God, than to behold God working for them. If, for every rebuke that we utter of men's vices, we put forth a claim upon their hearts; if for every assertion of God's demands from them, we could substitute a display of his kindness to them; if side by side with every warning of death, we could exhibit proofs and promises of immortality; if, in fine, instead of assuming the being of an awful Deity, which men, though they cannot and dare not deny, are always unwilling, sometimes unable to conceive, we were to show them a near, visible, inevitable, but all beneficent Deity, whose presence makes the earth itself a heaven, I think there would be fewer deaf children sitting in the market-place.[8]

The beauty of the gospel lies in the beauty of the God it reveals: "A spendthrift lover is the Lord / who never counts the cost / or asks if heaven can afford / to woo a world that's lost."[9] I preach on works of artistic beauty as a way of removing the burdens of heavy religion and helping listeners to feel instead how God is "near" and "beneficent" and working for them. In aiming toward that theological goal, I have used the work of past artists for at least three reasons. First, as I explained in the opening chapter, I am concerned that the church not lose touch with the treasures of imaginative art that are part of its sacred legacy. Second, when we attend closely to these treasures, we appreciate anew the daring, imaginative, visionary quality of the Christian tradition. The artists in this book reveal that the trajectory of the tradition, as manifest in their creations, is more inclusive than the official dogmas and pronouncements of the church. My hope is that the willingness of artists from the past to risk "new trajectories for the future use of the metaphors" of faith will give us courage to be as bold in our own time as they were in theirs. I have written this book as a prelude to a homiletic that will employ the work of contemporary artists. It is a necessary prelude because in my experience preachers will not risk new things unless they believe deeply that the tradition not only validates but inspires and commands such work. By drawing on core works of hymnody, choral music, and poetry, I have hoped to demonstrate that this is exactly what the tradition does.

Third, I draw upon works from the past because, although they are culturally related to us, they are qualitatively different from the works of our electronic, technological age. They give us some desperately needed perspective on the distortions of our time, and they challenge us with a different set of values: "A technical culture is voracious, devouring; it consumes all the other nontechnical aspects of culture by turning everything into a skill, a knowledge of how to do it, a *means*."[10] Certainly the works of artistic beauty that we have explored demonstrate extraordinary skill, sophisticated knowledge, and rigorous discipline, but their beauty is not a "means" to achieve wealth or status. To experience their beauty takes us into another realm of value, another dimension of reality:

> In the right encounter with the beautiful, we transcend the realm of profit or utility. We also leave behind a morality that speaks with an unattractive "must." Those who know beauty will never choose a morals [sic] of "must," detached from value. Rather, in wonderment, gratitude and joy, they sense the beautiful in all its delicacy and refinement, and soon discover that the beauty in nature and art opens new vistas to the stream of beauty that waters the earth through the moral sensibilities of its people.[11]

When the church neglects beauty, it risks diminishing the sense of the numinous and holy so that it becomes less and less a community that celebrates the Spirit of God moving in, around, and through its gathered members. It loses its ability to offer an alternative way of being and living to the utilitarianism that prevails in our culture: "What may be most missing in this highly technological world of ours is beauty. We value efficiency instead. We want functionalism over art. . . . A loss of commitment to beauty may be the clearest sign we have that we have lost our way to God. Without beauty we miss the glory of the face of God in the here and now."[12]

In summary, I have used works of artistic beauty from the past because I am eager that the church not abandon its legacy, because these works demonstrate how daring and imaginative the tradition is, and because they offer an alternative set of values to our current culture. I am not interested in using the past in order to make the church a museum. All the services and sermons in which I have employed these works of artistic beauty were fashioned to empower the congregation members to live their faith in God more fully here and now. I believe that a vital appropriation of such works gives people courage to continue the dynamic tradition of creating new trajectories for faith that are relevant to ministering to a wounded and fragmented world.

Of course, preaching on works of artistic beauty will not bring about the immediate transformation of a world in crisis. But if instant effectiveness is the standard by which we judge preaching, then no preaching measures up. God's word, Isaiah reminds us, does not work that way. Instead, it is much more like the processes of nature that fulfill their purpose over time and whose results we must await with the patience of farmers who trust the seeds they have planted will eventually bear fruit:

> For as the rain and the snow come down from heaven,
>   and do not return there until they have watered the earth,
>   making it bring forth and sprout,
>   giving seed to the sower and bread to the eater,
>   so shall my word be that goes out from my mouth;
>   it shall not return to me empty,
>   but it shall accomplish that which I purpose,
>   and succeed in the thing for which I sent it. (Isaiah
> 55:10–11, NRSV)

Isaiah's wisdom applies to preaching the Word of God through works of artistic beauty as much as it does to all other forms of preaching and possibly even more, since "art has no power to change the world, for great art exerts a different kind of power—not the power of violence and revolution, but the potent vulnerability of imagination and memory, of mourning and of hope. Art is powerless in itself, and yet it stands as an obstacle in the path of every destructive and oppressive force. That is why every tyrant and ideologue has sought to silence or to control the artistic imagination."[13] And it is why the church must not play into the hands of tyrants and ideologues by neglecting art. The "potent vulnerability of imagination and memory, of mourning and of hope" is the power that the church needs to build community, renew faith, and energize people for the work of ministering to the world. Beauty is a resource for tending to the anguish of human life and providing pastoral care: "Beauty sustains the human heart in the midst of pain and despair. Whatever the dullness of a world stupefied by the mediocre, in the end beauty is able, by penetrating our own souls, to penetrate the ugliness of a world awash in the cheap, the tawdry, the imitative, the excessive and the cruel. To have seen a bit of the Beauty out of which beauty comes is a deeply spiritual experience. It shouts to us always, 'More. There is yet more.'"[14]

In light of what beauty has the potential to do, it is sad to acknowledge that creating a place for beauty in preaching and worship can be challenging because religious people often resist the artistic imagination:

> Christian authorities have always had an ambivalent attitude towards the power of the arts to communicate the truth of the Christian story, from the iconoclastic controversies of the early Church through the Reformation and beyond. The artistic imagination has eluded the control of theology and doctrine with their rationalizing and authoritarian tendencies, and it still lays before us a more visceral and compelling account of the story of Christ than those theological tomes gathering dust in libraries which cater to a bygone era.[15]

I believe there are two reasons for resistance to the use of art in the church and in its preaching. The first is the fear that art will corrupt faith with what an older style of prayer called "the vain imaginings of the heart." The second reason, perhaps more germane to our age, is the fear that attention to beauty will divert energies from the pressing needs of the world. Tina Beattie speaks to this fear with candor and wisdom: "Of course, art alone will not feed the hungry nor visit those in prison nor clothe the naked, but it may answer to a much deeper need than our basic physical needs. It may be of the very essence of our humanity that we hunger for beauty as much as we hunger for food, and those who seek to do good in the world must be providers of beauty as well as of food to those in need."[16]

Beattie's words are very close in spirit to Jesus' response to the first temptation in the desert. When the devil asks Jesus to command stones to be turned into bread, he responds by quoting from Deuteronomy 8:3: "'One does not live by bread alone, but by every word that comes from the mouth of God.'" Sometimes our theology gets into a single track, and we effectively settle not for "every word that comes from the mouth of God," but for our personally favorite words that come from the mouth of God. But every word that comes from the mouth of God embraces the whole of reality: from the need for bread to the need for beauty. If we eliminate either one of them, we constrict the fullness of being that characterizes God, we put limits on the divine vocabulary and no longer seek to live by *every* word that proceeds from the mouth of God. In the economy of holy grace, bread and beauty work in concert with each other. If we polarize them as opposites, we will probably also polarize reason and imagination, science and religion, pragmatism and art. Preaching on works of artistic beauty can help us realize that

> artistic and scientific knowledge, religion and rationality are not competitors for the same space in the spectrum of human wisdom. Science cannot provide the answers to every human question, for scientific knowledge does not encompass all the ways of knowing that human consciousness is capable of. Art and beauty, creativity and imagination, provide a connecting narrative between the endeavours of science and the endeavours of religion. They invite us into conversations without violence, dialogue without closure.[17]

My experience with preaching on works of art has been that they do indeed "invite us into conversations without violence, dialogue without closure." I think in particular of a number of Jewish listeners who attended a series of services in which I preached on Bach cantatas, immediately followed by their performance as part of the church's regular liturgy (chapter 3). Seeing an advertisement for the services in the newspaper had drawn the Jews to attend because they loved the music of Bach. Afterward they told me how moved they were even though the prayers and hymns as well as the cantatas were explicitly Christian. They said the beauty of the music, especially because the sermons had helped them listen more knowledgeably, carried them beyond the words to a state of prayer and worship that was congruent with their own faith. In a world where religious conflict is a major issue, these services allowed us, Jews and Christians together, to maintain the integrity of our different faiths while affirming through art and beauty our common humanity and the holy gifts of delight and wonder. What a purely rational theological conversation cannot achieve was realized in a shared experience of beauty in the context of worship.

David Daiches offers a way of understanding this ability of art to transcend theological difference. He identifies himself "as someone brought up in an orthodox Jewish family yet who from childhood has had a passionate love affair with English poetry, so much of it deeply rooted in Christian faith."[18] Daiches understands such art to be "a *communication,* which illuminates an area of experience for the reader in ways quite undefinable outside that particular work of art. The communication authenticates itself by its achievement of an increasingly reverberating meaning, not by the literal truth of any assumption taken for granted by the author while he is writing."[19]

Preaching on art and beauty is a way of releasing that "increasingly reverberating meaning" into the prayer and worship of the church. It is a meaning deep and broad enough to have resonance with those who have faith in Christ, those who are doubters and seekers, and those who hold an entirely different faith perspective. As that meaning reverberates through the church's worship, we come to see that "the creative imagination is the true home of faith. It occupies that furthest extreme where words creep to the very fringes of silence, and life tiptoes along the edges of death. In the darkest recess of the imagination's cave, the human spirit shapes its questions about otherness, death and love in the delicate traceries of art, the haunted longings of music, the poetic shaping of silence."[20]

Artists, because of their visionary powers and the mastery of their craft, can help train our homiletical imaginations to give beauty its rightful place in preaching and worship, in the proclamation of the gospel and the praise of God: "Most of us give lip service to the fact that preaching is an art as well as a science, but then we become afraid that someone will think we speak of preaching as an art as an excuse for ambiguity, sloppy thinking, and poor reasoning."[21] What our close study of these works of artistic beauty has shown us is that art may often convey ambiguity, but if it is effective art, it also manifests a disciplined imagination. Imagining is not "sloppy thinking and poor reasoning," but precise thinking and profounder reasoning. Imagining is the hard work of bringing what is inchoate to fuller and clear articulation. Imagining moves us beyond homiletics as technique to homiletics as a means of embodying the intuitive, the visionary, the rhapsodic elements of human experience through which we taste anew the Spirit of God—the very qualities we encountered through these works of artistic beauty. The more we work with our imaginations, the more we realize what all these artists must have realized as well: "There are, it seems, two Muses: the Muse of Inspiration, who gives us inarticulate visions and desires, and the Muse of Realization, who returns again and again to say, 'It is yet more difficult than you thought.' This is the muse of form."[22]

Alice Meynell wrote a poem that shows why meeting the demands of the "Muse of Inspiration" is worth the hard labor. The poem provides a metaphor, drawn from the Bible and liturgical tradition, for understanding how the imaginative process that creates beauty is a religious pilgrimage. The poem is written in such a way that the act of creativity can be understood as belonging to both the poet and the reader.

The Courts
A Figure of the Epiphany

The poet's imageries are noble ways,
Approaches to a plot, an open shrine.
Their splendours, colours, avenues, arrays,
Their courts that run with wine:

Beautiful similes, "fair and flagrant things,"
Enriched, enamouring,—raptures, metaphors
Enhancing life, are paths for pilgrim kings
Made free of golden doors.

And yet the open heavenward plot, with dew,
Ultimate poetry, enclosed, enskied,
(Albeit such ceremonies lead thereto)
Stands on the yonder side.

Plain, behind oracles, it is; and past
All Symbols, simple; perfect, heavenly-wild,
The song some loaded poets reach at last—
The kings that found a Child.

The superscription, "A Figure of the Epiphany," is significant for interpreting the poem. The Epiphany is the manifestation of Christ to the Gentiles, the story of the Magi's visitation to the newborn infant in Matthew 2:1–12. Epiphany is also the name given to the day when that Gospel story is remembered and celebrated, January 6, and it is the name given to the liturgical season that follows. To call the poem "A Figure of the Epiphany" is to frame our reading of it even before we get to the first line. Because we know the story of the Epiphany is the story of a long journey that culminates with finding Christ, we are prepared to go on a journey. As soon as we begin the poem, we discover that the journey will take us not across ancient Palestine but through the visionary heart and mind: "The poet's imageries are noble ways, / Approaches to a plot, an open shrine." A shrine is usually a building constructed to honor the holy, but here it is described as "a plot, an open shrine," as though it were some field in the landscape of the heart. It is a sacred space without walls, but it is no less a shrine for the poet. The image suggests that the act of imagining is the way the poet draws near to the Holy. Her "imageries" are "Approaches," not the destination itself. The epiphany journey will be undertaken by using the imagination and the visions that flow from it: "splendours, colours, avenues, arrays, / Their courts that run with wine."

The poet makes her visions available to us through the literary devices of her craft: "Beautiful similes" and "raptures, metaphors." They provide an alternative kind of wealth to the world's understanding of what it means to be rich. The "pilgrim kings," the Magi, are no longer shut up in their royal chambers but are "Made free of golden doors" as they take the "paths" provided by the poet. The imagination sets us free by "Enhancing life" through the beauty and wonder provided by the creative artist.

But the poem does not end here. The poet does not conclude that what she or any artist creates is the ultimate destination of the journey. In the third stanza, the poet returns to the vision of the shrine, describing it this time as "the open heavenward plot, with dew, / Ultimate poetry, enclosed, enskied." The shrine is still open, but now the openness is given a direction: "heavenward." The shrine is open to heaven, but because it "Stands on the yonder side," it is from our earthly perspective "enclosed, enskied." Our works of artistic beauty are not altogether without value. "(Albeit such ceremonies lead thereto)"—the "ceremonies" are the poet's "imageries" that have helped lead us toward the open shrine. She terms them "ceremonies," suggesting their sacral function. At the same time she puts them in parentheses, indicating that no matter how "Enriched, enamouring" they are, they pale before the "Ultimate poetry."

When in the final stanza she names the qualities of "Ultimate poetry," it is striking how she leaves behind the rich diction of the opening stanzas and uses much simpler words. The "Ultimate poetry" is "Plain," "simple," "perfect, heavenly-wild." These qualities are utterly different from the character of Meynell's own poetry. Instead of plain and simple, we have had up to this point a parade of "splendours." And instead of being "heavenly-wild," Meynell's work is tightly crafted. The contrast between her poetry and "Ultimate poetry" is a figure for the relationship between works of artistic beauty created by humans and the beauty created by God. She does not disparage human "imageries." Indeed, she is grateful for how they "lead" to "Ultimate poetry," to the divine. But she sees that their final purpose extends beyond themselves to something that is "past / All symbols," past "Beautiful similes" and "raptures, metaphors." It is the "The song some loaded poets reach at last—The kings that found a Child." The poets are "loaded" with the riches of their imagination, "Their splendours, colours, avenues, arrays," just as the Magi were loaded with the gifts of gold, frankincense, and myrrh. But like the Magi bearing gifts, the "song" they ultimately reach is "a Child." They arrive at Christ.

Through her poetics Meynell takes us on a journey of the imagination as the beauty of art leads us toward the "Ultimate poetry," the numinous, the Holy, the Christ. As "A Figure of Epiphany," the poem moves us from the court of the Magi to the court of the Holy One, hence the title, "The Courts," plural not singular. Her act of creating the

poem is an epiphany, and our act of entering the poem and understanding it is an epiphany: a manifestation of the divine to mortal
humanity

The poem compresses into sixteen lines the complex process of
interfusing art and prayer in the worship of God that I have been tracing
throughout this book. In Meynell's piece, the sacred story and the
beauty of the art are continually interrelated, each illuminating the
other, and together drawing us into the presence of God. Her poem
embodies the theological and artistic complementarity that is achieved
when beauty takes its rightful place in preaching and worship and there
is an epiphany in the congregation.

George Herbert, the preacher-poet-priest whose work we considered earlier, provides us with yet another "figure" for understanding how
we encounter God through the beauty of artistic creation. Herbert employs
the figure of a stained glass window. It may initially seem a much more
static image than Meynell's pilgrimage of the Magi, but a close reading of
Herbert's text reveals a dynamic process that has many resonances with
Meynell's understanding of the journey to Christ through art.

The Windows

Lord, how can man preach thy eternal word?
He is a brittle crazy glass:
Yet in thy temple thou dost him afford
This glorious and transcendent place,
To be a window, through thy grace.

But when thou dost anneal in glass thy story,
Making thy life to shine within
The holy Preacher's; then the light and glory
More rev'rend grows, and more doth win:
Which else shows wat'rish, bleak, and thin.

Doctrine and life, colours and light, in one
When they combine and mingle, bring
A strong regard and awe: but speech alone
Doth vanish like a flaring thing,
And in the ear, not conscience ring.[23]

Unlike Meynell's "Courts," Herbert's poem starts off not in splendor but by contrasting God's "eternal word" with a candid assessment of the human creature: "He is a brittle crazy glass." The word "crazy" meant in Herbert's day: "Full of cracks or flaws; damaged, impaired, unsound; liable to break or fall to pieces; frail, 'shaky'"[24]—not exactly the qualifications we would expect God to look for in one who is called to preach! It initially seems as if the way of art and the way of preaching proceed in very different paths. The poet begins with "noble ways," with "splendours, colours, avenues, arrays," and the preacher starts with his (her) pitiable condition: "brittle crazy glass."

But no sooner has Herbert delivered his somber verdict on the human condition than he makes the astonishing affirmation:

> Yet in thy temple thou dost him afford
> This glorious and transcendent place,
> To be a window, through thy grace.

Herbert's sacred space, unlike Meynell's "open shrine," is a temple, an enclosed structure. But that structure provides a "glorious and transcendent place." "Temple" means for Herbert more than a physical edifice for the worship of God. It also refers to his major collection of poems entitled *The Temple,* from which "The Windows" is taken. According to Herbert, *The Temple* provides "a picture of the many spiritual conflicts that have passed betwixt God and my Soul, before I could subject mine to the will of Jesus my Master."[25] The individual poems of *The Temple* are titled after acts of worship, the architecture and furnishings of a church, the particular seasons of the liturgical year, the sacraments, or the struggles of the soul. To read *The Temple* is to enter the imaginative world of Herbert as shaped by the symbols and traditions of the church and to find ourselves in the sacred space of a cavernous soul, one that is resonant with the echoes of our own hopes and agonies. The first and longest poem is entitled "The Church-Porch," suggesting that we are at the point of entry. We are on the verge of sacred space. We are about to move into the depths and heights of encountering the holy, the wonder and mystery that flow from the deep dear core of things.

The Temple is, to use Meynell's word, a "figure" for the imaginative space in which God affords Herbert, the poet/preacher, the sacred role of being "a window, through thy grace." Herbert describes this place as "glorious" and "transcendent," adjectives denoting that God's presence is known through the poet/preacher's creative imagination. However, the poet/preacher insists that when he does become a window, it is utterly "through thy grace." To reinforce that it all depends on God, the poet/preacher in the next stanza pictures God as an artisan who fashions the poet/preacher as a stained glass window:

> But when thou dost anneal in glass thy story,
> Making thy life to shine within
> The holy Preacher's; then the light and glory
> More rev'rend grows, and more doth win:
> Which else shows wat'rish, bleak, and thin.

The word "anneal" means "to burn in colours upon glass."[26] It is the fiery process by which the pieces of glass that make up a stained glass window receive their brilliant reds, oranges, and golds, their deep blues, purples, and greens. The "glass" here recalls the description of the human creature in the first stanza: "a brittle crazy glass." God is taking the raw material of the human condition and refashioning it as an artisan who creates a stained glass window. In the imaginative space of the poet/preacher, *The Temple* , we encounter God as an imaginative artist! The creative work of God and the work of the human artist who is creating the poem converge. The element that God infuses into the glass of the preacher is God's "story," the story of creation, fall, exodus, prophets, exile, incarnation, crucifixion, resurrection, and Pentecost, the story of salvation that makes God's "life to shine within / The holy Preacher's" life. God's art has brought about a splendid transformation. In the first two lines of the poem, it sounds as though the human creature would never be adequate for the task of preaching, but now that same broken creature has been fashioned by the art of God into a "holy" preacher. The preacher is "holy" because he has been shaped by the holy God, and the result is "the light and glory / More rev'rend grow, and more doth win." The effectiveness of the preacher, the ability to "win," to persuade more people of the eternal word of God, is not a function of homiletical method but a function of God's own art. Without God the color, the vivacity of the window drains away as the light pales, becoming "wat'rish, bleak, and thin."

The final stanza replays the contrast between preaching that is sustained by the divine artist and preaching that is not:

> Doctrine and life, colours and light, in one
> When they combine and mingle, bring
> A strong regard and awe: but speech alone
> Doth vanish like a flaring thing,
> And in the ear, not conscience ring.

There is homiletical wisdom in these lines. Preaching that awakens "regard and awe" is neither purely doctrine nor purely life nor purely art ("colours") nor purely light. "Regard and awe" result when all the elements "combine and mingle" into one coherent whole, the very thing that Herbert has done in this poem and throughout *The Temple* . The poet's art combines and mingles the doctrine of "grace," the preacher's life, "colours" as found in the annealed glass, and the light of God. The poem enacts what it preaches. Herbert's integrative imagination brings together the varied elements into a work of artistic beauty. Beauty and art are not in themselves enough to make the preaching "win more." But neither are they merely ornamental. They are as essential as the other elements, and it is not any one of them alone but the interfusion of them all that brings the community to a state of "regard and awe."

The alternative is an ineffectual witness to the gospel that relies merely on the preacher's talking:

> but speech alone
> Doth vanish like a flaring thing,
> And in the ear, not conscience ring.

A "flaring thing," something that flames up and dies swiftly away, is the opposite of "the light and glory [that] More rev'rend *grows*" when God's story has been annealed in the preacher. The word "conscience" in the final line carries an earlier meaning that was common in Herbert's day: "Inward knowledge or consciousness; internal conviction," and "Inmost thought; mind, 'heart.'"[27] It is not possible to reach the place of inmost thought by "speech alone" because language without all the other elements, without the "Doctrine and life, colours and light," leaves us back where we started. We are only "a brittle crazy glass" instead of a window annealed by God with the story of God so that the life of God shines through us.

In describing how "speech alone" does "in the ear, not conscience ring," Herbert moves from the ear and eye working together to the ear alone. Although preaching is an oral/aural art, the imagery up to this point has been visual as well as auditory. The poem opens with an appeal to the ear, "Lord, how can man *preach* thy eternal *word?*" and then immediately engages the eye with "brittle crazy glass," followed by the image of the window God anneals. But now at the end of the poem we have "speech alone," and the emptiness of speech alone is captured by the final word, "ring." The short *i* followed by the guttural stop of the *g* contrasts with the richness of when the divine life is made to "shine" through the preacher in stanza 2. Say aloud in sequence the words "shine" and "ring," and you will hear the difference in the music of the two words. Shine with its long *i* following by *n* gives a note that hangs in the air, while "ring" dies quickly away. As a poet Herbert knows what Meynell knows: you need to feed the imagination with all the senses, and because the imagination is that creative space where we encounter God, the issue is theological as well as artistic. Even though Herbert realizes that the poet/preacher ultimately depends on God's "grace," he is a master at fashioning what Meynell calls "Beautiful similes, 'fair and flagrant things,' / Enriched, enamouring, raptures, metaphors / Enhancing life." As a poet Herbert depends not on "speech alone" but on language that is musical (the contrast of "shine" and "ring"), visual ("brittle crazy glass"), and vivid even when describing something that is pale ("wat'rish, bleak, and thin"). The word "wat'rish" sounds like what it describes. We can feel the dilution of the preacher's power when the life of God is not shining through.

I have several times referred to Herbert as a poet/preacher. I have done this in part because historically that is true of the man: he preached sermons and wrote poems. But I have also termed him a poet/preacher because I consider "The Windows" to be a poem/sermon for preachers. It is structured like a good sermon: we can follow his line of thought from beginning to end. It has a sound theological anthropology: the human creature is a "brittle crazy glass" but by the grace of God can be a window through whom shines the life of God. It is rooted in a profound knowledge of scripture: God's story is annealed in us. It grows out of a holistic understanding of human life as it brings together "Doctrine and life, colours and light." It honors the "glorious and transcendent" qualities of the God who affords us a place in the temple. It uses vivid, memorable language that is congruent with its theological thought. There is no question about it: this is an excellent sermon.

But it is also an excellent poem. It allows the imagery to carry the thought. It uses the beat of the language to get the accents just where they need to be. It employs the sound of words to express the realities they describe and to suggest a depth of meaning that lies beyond language. And it does all of this in the service of preaching without ever becoming preachy! There is no question about it: it is an excellent poem. If you fuse together an excellent sermon with an excellent poem so that they make one seamless, coherent piece in which homiletical and artistic elements "combine and mingle," then you have one excellent poem/sermon.

I do not conclude from my reading of "The Windows" that every sermon should be a poem, and every poem should be a sermon. What the poem reveals is that the imagination is essential to the practice of faith and the preaching of God's word. Herbert and Meynell both give witness to the inescapable role of the imagination in making our spiritual lives vital, rich with a sense of God's presence. Read side by side, the two poets remind us there are different ways of envisioning the imagination. Herbert's work portrays the imagination as the temple where God affords us the grace to be a window through whom divine life shines, while Meynell's work pictures the imagination as the landscape of the heart through which we make the pilgrimage of faith to the epiphany. We ourselves may have other ways of picturing the imagination. Perhaps we see it as a starry night sky whose points of light we arrange in multiple constellations of meaning. Or perhaps it is an enchanted forest with open glades where the sun breaks through to cast shifting shadows of leaf and cloud upon the grass. Or perhaps it is a vast beach whose shoreline and sands are forever being rearranged by waves arising from the deep. Or perhaps it is a universe of sound that sweeps us along in music that sometimes paints a text in notes and sometimes uses no text at all but still creates in us a sense of something unfolding, sometimes building to a climax and then finding resolution, sometimes rejoicing, sometimes weeping, sometimes pondering, and through all these varied affects awakening an awareness of a world just beyond the sound itself.

Journey or temple or starry night or forest or beach or universe of sound—whatever way we picture the imagination—it is an essential element in the life of faith: "Whether we acknowledge it or not, we have been employing imagination in our religion and in our theology, ever since we first became involved in these practices. It is a question, then, not of whether we employ it or not, but of how good, how irre-proachable we can, by the grace of God, make our employment of it."[28] Rather than neglecting or resisting artists and the beauty that breathes through their work, preachers and the church need to learn from them how to move through the landscape of the heart, how to enter the temple, how to set off on the journey, how to use the imagination cre-atively, energetically and with the discipline that marks the artists' work. To dismiss this need as mere aestheticism is to fail to see that imagina-tion is a gift that God uses for our salvation: "To save sinners, God seizes them by the imagination: the preacher places himself at the service of this saving act by the obedient and lucid engagement of his own imagination."[29] Note that strong verb "seizes." Consider all the ways that the world seizes our imagination to sell something, to stir up our worst demons, to get us rabidly behind some cause. If preachers are going to contend with these forces, then they will indeed have to prac-tice "the obedient and lucid engagement" of their own imaginations. That is what we have seen in all the artists we have considered, from the writers of the spirituals and hymns to the composers of the major choral works to the lyric poets.

To listen attentively to how composers blend melody and rhythm, harmony and dissonance, instruments and voices is to practice prayer. We listen to prepare our imaginations to be seized by God. In recent years the phrase "quality time" has become a part of our common speech. Living lives that are jammed to overflowing with responsibilities and activities, people have less and less time to nurture their intimate relationships with family and friends, and they hunger for quality time, for time to linger over a glass of wine and a sunset or to read a good story to their child. When they do finally manage to eke out a few hours of quality time, it is like water in the desert. Unfortunately, the church's worship sometimes takes on the same jammed character as our over-stuffed daily schedules. Preaching on works of artistic beauty is a way of reclaiming quality time in our worship. Instead of singing through a hymn and being done with it, the preacher creates quality time by con-sidering the depth of meaning that repeated singing of the hymn has buried. Instead of listening to an aria or a choral work as if we were interrupting worship with a concert, the preacher creates quality time by preparing ourselves to absorb the music's treasures so that we can hear anew the Spirit praying through us in sighs too deep for words. Instead of reading quickly through a great lyric poem, the preacher creates quality time by exploring and meditating on its images and its theopoetic glimpses into the mystery of human creatures encountering the divine. Just as quality time in our personal lives restores our closest human relationships, so too quality time in worship restores our relationship to the numinous, to mystery, to the deep dear core of things, to God, to Christ, to the Spirit.

Quality time is holy time because through it we sense a dimension of being unbounded by finitude, a dimension that the Gospel of John terms "eternal life." A common understanding of "eternal life" is that it refers to life beyond the grave. But John writes about eternal life as a reality that we can experience here and now. "And this *is* eternal life, that they may know you, the only true God, and Jesus Christ whom you have sent" (John 17:3). Such knowledge is more than intellectual comprehension. It is knowledge suffused with the experience of a profound relationship to the holy God. It is a kind of sensing and tasting, a kind of apprehending with the sum total of our being, a kind of knowing the truth that is forever beyond our complete knowing, a kind of intuition that comes to us through artistic works of great beauty that are offered to the glory of God. A church in which such knowing is nurtured and honored, a church in which the creative imagination "is the true home of faith,"[30] will be open to all that is beautiful and fills us with wonder and gratitude toward God. The place of beauty in preaching is far, far more than adding ornament or interest to a fundamentally prosaic proclamation of the Gospel. Rather, it lies at the heart of our witness to Christ. It is a way of continually returning to the source, to the well of living water that is life and light, vitality and resilience, generativity and visionary power. We make room in our preaching and worship for beauty so that wonder may be reborn as God is known and experienced anew.

Notes

INTRODUCTION

    1. Mark I. Wallace, *The Second Naiveté: Barth, Ricoeur, and the New Yale Theology,* Mercer University Press, Macon, Ga.: 1990, 123.

CHAPTER 1

    1. Harold C. Schonberg, *The Lives of the Great Composers,* 3rd ed., New York: Norton, 1997, 438.

    2. Ibid., 442.

    3. Langdon B. Gilkey, "Can Art Fill the Vacuum?" in *Art, Creativity, and the Sacred: An Anthology in Religion and Art,* ed. Diane Apostolos-Cappadona, rev. ed., New York: Continuum, 1995, 189.

    4. Patrick Sherry, *Spirit and Beauty: An Introduction to Theological Aesthetics,* 2nd ed., London: SCM Press, 2002, 44.

    5. Aidan Nichols, *The Art of God Incarnate,* London: Darton, Longman, and Todd, 1980, 91.

    6. John Scotus Eriugena, *Periphyseon,* trans. I. P. Sheldon Williams, rev. John J. O'Meara, Montreal, Wash.: Bellarmin, 1987, book 3, 255–56.

    7. Richard Harries, *Art and the Beauty of God,* London: Mowbray, 1996, 47 and 48.

    8. Don E. Saliers, "Liturgical Aesthetics: The Travail of Christian Worship," in *Arts, Theology and the Church: New Intersections,* ed. Kimberly Vrudny and Wilson Yates, Cleveland, Ohio: Pilgrim Press, 2005, 197.

9. Nicholas Wolterstorff, *Art in Action: Toward a Christian Aesthetic*, Carlisle, UK: Solway, 1997, 194.

10. Jacques Maritain, *Art and Scholasticism and the Frontiers of Poetry*, trans. Joseph W. Evans, New York: Scribner's, 1962, 63.

11. Quoted in Patrick N. Findlay, "Handel's Messiah through the Centuries," *Early Music News*, 24, no. 4 (December 1999), http://psg.com/~patf/handel/messiah.html.

12. Sherry, *Spirit and Beauty*, 136. Sherry here is drawing upon the work of David Coffey, in particular Coffey's book *Grace: The Gift of the Holy Spirit*.

13. John W. de Gruchy, *Christianity, Art and Transformation: Theological Aesthetics in the Struggle for Justice*, Cambridge: Cambridge University Press, 2001, 226.

14. Augustine, *Confessions*, trans. Henry Chadwick, Oxford: Oxford University Press, 1998, 210.

15. Harries, *Art and the Beauty of God*, 11.

16. Augustine, *Expositions on the Book of Psalms*, vol. 2, trans. by members of the English Church, a Library of Fathers of the Holy Catholic Church, Oxford: John Henry Parker, F. and J. Rivington, 1848, 230.

17. Eriugena, *Periphyseon*, book 5, 633.

18. De Gruchy, *Christianity*, 122. De Gruchy acknowledges that he is drawing here upon the work of Hans Urs von Balthasar and Karl Barth,

19. Ibid., 73. He is quoting from P. T. Forsyth, *Christ on Parnassus*, London: Hodder and Stoughton, 1911, 42.

20. Harries, *Art and the Beauty of God*, 23.

21. Sherry, *Spirit and Beauty*, 65.

22. Bernard Häring, *Free and Faithful in Christ: Moral Theology for Priests and Laity*, vol. 2, *The Truth Will Set You Free*, New York: Seabury Press, 1979, 103.

23. David Grayson, *Adventures in Contentment*, New York: Grosset and Dunlap, 1907, 123. David Grayson was the pen name of Ray Stannard Baker (1870–1946).

24. Ibid., 126.

25. Ibid., 129, emphasis in original.

26. Ibid., 122.

27. Ibid., 126.

28. Ibid., 131.

29. Ibid., 125.

30. Saliers, "Liturgical Aesthetics," 181.

31. Thomas Aquinas, *Summa Theologiae*, vol. 39, *Religion and Worship* (2a2ae. 80–91), ed. Kevin D. O'Rourke, O.P., London: Blackfriars, 1964, 251.

32. David G. Buttrick, "Side Thoughts on Preaching for Those Who Must Stammer God's Unnamed Name," *Best Advice: Wisdom on Ministry from 30 Leading Pastors and Preachers*, ed. William J. Carl, III, Louisville, Ky.: Westminster John Knox Press, 2009, 35.

33. J. A. Simpson and E. S. C. Weiner, eds., *The Oxford English Dictionary*, 2nd ed., 3, Oxford: Clarendon Press, 1989, vol. 3, 1104.

34. H. Rogers writing in 1840, as quoted in Ibid., vol. 1, 657.

35. Frank Burch Brown, *Religious Aesthetics: A Theological Study of Making and Meaning*, in *Theological Aesthetics: A Reader*, ed. Gesa Elsbeth Thiessen, Grand Rapids, Mich.: Eerdmans, 2005, 267. I am indebted to Thiessen's excellent anthology for reminding me of a number of works on aesthetics and theology that I had forgotten and for leading me to a number of resources I had not previously read.

36. De Gruchy, *Christianity*, 55–56.

37. Alejandro García-Rivera, *The Community of the Beautiful: A Theological Aesthetics*, Collegeville, Minn.: Liturgical Press, 1999, 9.

38. De Gruchy, *Christianity*, 158. He is quoting Bernard J. F. Lonergan, *Insight: A Study of Human Understanding*, New York: Philosophical Library, 1973, 184.

39. De Gruchy, *Christianity*, 8.

40. Charles Wesley, "Jesus, Show Us Thy Salvation" ("Love divine, all loves excelling"), in Erik Routley, *A Panorama of Christian Hymnody*, edited and expanded by Paul A. Richardson, Chicago: GIA Publications, 2005, 67.

41. Sherry, *Spirit and Beauty*, 18–19.

42. Ibid., 21.

43. Ibid., 103.

44. Harries, *Art and the Beauty of God*, 6.

45. De Gruchy, *Christianity*, 199–200.

46. Häring, *Free and Faithful*, 107.

47. Fred B. Craddock, *As One without Authority*, revised and with new sermons, St. Louis, Mo.: Chalice Press, 2001, 72.

48. Häring, *Free and Faithful*, 108.

49. Richard Viladesau, *Theological Aesthetics: God in Imagination, Beauty, and Art*, New York: Oxford University Press, 1999, 212.

50. Keziah Conrad, "Ivo Markovic," a priest and scholar, founder of the interfaith Pontanima choir in Sarajevo: Profile, March 2007, 1. This is an unpublished piece given to us in preparation for a conversation with Markovic, followed by a concert by his choir. I subsequently discovered that the profile is available online at http://crinfo.beyondintractability.org/reflections/peacebuilder_profiles/Ivo_Markovic.jsp?nid=6799.

51. Ibid., 2.

52. Ibid.

53. Ibid., 3.

54. "The Pontanima Choir and Chamber Orchestra," from an unpublished information sheet without an author's name, 2.

55. Sherry, *Spirit and Beauty*, 171.

56. Quoted in De Gruchy, *Christianity*, 87–88.

57. Ibid., 71. He is quoting P. T. Forsyth, *Religion in Recent Art*, London: Hodder and Stoughton, 1905, 7.

58. Craddock, *As One without Authority*, 72.

59. Ibid., 71.

60. Harries, *Art and the Beauty of God*, 1.

61. Craddock, *As One without Authority*, 71.

62. Sherry, *Spirit and Beauty*, 171.

63. Ibid., 170.

64. Brian Wren, *What Language Shall I Borrow? God-Talk in Worship: A Male Response to Feminist Theology*, New York: Crossroad, 1989, 117.

65. Sherry, *Spirit and Beauty*, 60.

66. B. L. Reid as quoted in Helen Gardner, *Religion and Literature,* New York: Oxford University Press, 1983, 60.

67. De Gruchy, *Christianity*, 107.

68. Frank Burch Brown, "How Important Are the Arts, Theologically?" in *Arts, Theology and the Church: New Intersections*, ed. Kimberly Vrudny and Wilson Yates, Cleveland, Ohio: Pilgrim Press, 2005, 33–34.

69. Ibid., 34.

70. April Austin, "Art's Longing for 'Connectedness,'" *Christian Science Monitor*, October 4, 1996, 10, as quoted in Robert Wuthnow, *All in Sync: How Music and Art Are Revitalizing American Religion*, Berkeley: University of California Press, 2006, 17–18.

71. Wuthnow, *All in Sync*, 77.

72. Ibid., 137.

73. Ibid., 245.

74. Yale Institute of Sacred Music: http://www.yale.edu/ism/.

75. De Gruchy, *Christianity*, 239.

76. Wuthnow, *All in Sync*, 210.

77. Thomas H. Troeger, *Imagining a Sermon*, Nashville, Tenn.: Abingdon Press, 1990; Troeger, *Ten Strategies for Preaching in a Multi Media Culture*, Nashville, Tenn.: Abingdon Press, 1996.

78. David Tracy, *The Analogical Imagination: Christian Theology and the Culture of Pluralism*, New York: Crossroad, 1981, 262.

79. Marilynne Robinson, *The Death of Adam: Essays on Modern Thought*, New York: Picador, 2005, 85.

80. Donald Whittle, *Christianity and the Arts*, London: A. R. Mowbray, 1966, 3–4.

81. Brown, *Religious Aesthetics*, 268.

82. Whittle, *Christianity and the Arts*, 5.

83. L. William Countryman, *The Poetic Imagination: An Anglican Spiritual Tradition*, Maryknoll, N.Y.: Orbis Books, 1999, 5.

84. De Gruchy, *Christianity*, 44.

85. Grayson, *Adventures in Contentment*, 125.

86. García-Rivera, *Community of the Beautiful*, 11.

87. Tina Beattie, *The New Atheists: The Twilight of Reason and the War on Religion*, Maryknoll. N.Y.: Orbis Books, 2007, 75.

CHAPTER 2

1. The introductory section of this chapter is a substantial revision of my article "Hymns as Midrashim: Congregational Song as Biblical Interpretation and Theological Reconstruction," *Hymn* 49, no. 3 (July 1998): 13–16.

Readers wanting to pursue hymns as a resource for preaching would do well to join the Hymn Society in the United States and Canada, Boston University School of Theology, 745 Commonwealth Avenue, Boston MA 02215–1401 (800-THE HYMN / 617-353-6493; Fax 617-353-7322; www.thehymnsociety.org). With membership comes a subscription to the organization's lively and informative quarterly journal, the *Hymn*, a gold mine of insights about the theology, poetry, and music of hymnody.

2. Robert Wuthnow, *All in Sync: How Music and Art Are Revitalizing American Religion*, Berkeley: University of California Press, 2006, 30.

3. Ibid., 32.

4. David Curzon, ed., *Modern Poems on the Bible:An Anthology*, Philadelphia: Jewish Publication Society, 1994.

5. Quoted by Gary G. Porton in "Midrash," in *The Anchor Bible Dictionary*, ed. David Noel Freedman, vol. 4, New York: Doubleday, 1992, 818.

6. Richard B. Hays, *Echoes of Scripture in the Letters of Paul*, New Haven, Conn.:Yale University Press, 1989, 14–21.

7. Ibid., 2.

8. For a fuller discussion and a chart that outlines the periods and developing characteristics of postbiblical, rabbinic midrashim, see "Midrash," in *Encyclopaedia Judaica*, ed. Fred Skolnik, 2nd ed., vol. 14, Detroit: Macmillan Reference USA, 2007, 183–85.

9. Curzon, *Modern Poems*, 4, emphasis added.

10. Ibid., 7.

11. Robert Alter, *The World of Biblical Literature*, New York: Basic Books, 1992, 152, as quoted in Curzon, *Modern Poems*, 19.

12. Curzon, *Modern Poems*, 20.

13. Ibid., 4.

14. "Haggadah," in *Harper's Bible Dictionary*, ed. Paul J. Achtemeier, San Francisco: HarperCollins, 1985, 366, emphasis added.

15. See Proverbs 8:22ff.

16. John Hollander, *Rhyme's Reason: A Guide to English Verse*, new, enlarged edition, New Haven, Conn.: Yale University Press, 1989, 19. Hollander uses this line in a sonnet describing the Elizabethan form, but it also succinctly states how an effective hymn works.

17. George Herbert, *The Complete English Poems*, ed. John Tobin, London: Penguin, 1991, 48.

18. "Six Prayers from Tukaram, an Indian Peasant Mystic, 1608–49," in *The Oxford Book of Prayer*, ed. George Appleton, New York: Oxford University Press, 1986, 293.

19. Erik Routley, *Christian Hymns Observed: When in Our Music God Is Glorified*, Princeton, N.J.: Prestige Publications, 1982, 6.

20. Amos Niven Wilder, *Theopoetic: Theology and the Religious Imagination*, Philadelphia: Fortress Press, 1976, 1.

21. Walter J. Ong, S.J., *The Presence of the Word: Some Prolegomena for Cultural and Religious History*, New Haven, Conn.: Yale University Press, 1967, 6. For a much fuller application of the sensorium to preaching and liturgy and not just hymns, see Thomas H. Troeger, *Preaching and Worship*, St. Louis, Mo.: Chalice Press, 2003.

22. Stephen H. Webb, *The Divine Voice: Christian Proclamation and the Theology of Sound*, Grand Rapids, Mich.: Brazos Press, 2004, 32.

23. Wayne A. Meeks, ed., *The HarperCollins Study Bible*, New Revised Standard Version, New York: HarperCollins, 1993, 2212n1.

24. Alexander Jones, ed., *The Jerusalem Bible*, Garden City, N.Y.: Doubleday, 1966, 344–45. Although this version is not my favored translation, I am using it initially because it prints the hymn text in verse form. However, my later citations of the hymn are all from the New Revised Standard Version. There are scholarly debates about the origin of the Colossian hymn and how the strophes ought to be arranged. My primary concern is not to consider these technical matters but to demonstrate that preaching on a hymn text has biblical roots and is characterized by the interfusion of culture and faith that would continue to manifest itself in the writing of new hymns during the centuries to come.

25. Raymond E. Brown, *An Introduction to the New Testament*, New York: Doubleday, 1997, 605.

26. Ibid., 600. "Probably in 1: 15–20 an extant hymn has been adapted."

27. I am often asked: How long ought a sermon to be? The only honest answer is to observe that the length of sermons varies enormously from tradition to tradition, from congregation to congregation, and from occasion to occasion. Because I preach in a wide range of traditions and settings, the length of my sermons varies greatly to meet what is requested. These first two sermons, the longest in the book, were for groups that wanted the preaching to fill most of the service. The other sermons in the book reflect the expectation of greater brevity that characterized the churches in which they were preached.

28. Patrick Miller, "Jeremiah," in David L. Petersen and Gene M. Tucker, eds., *The New Interpreter's Bible*, vol. 6, Nashville, Tenn.: Abingdon Press, 2001, 648.

29. Howard Thurman, *Deep River and the Negro Spiritual Speaks of Life and Death*, Richmond, Ind.: Friends United Press, 1975, 60.

30. Arthur C. Jones, *Wade in the Water: The Wisdom of the Spirituals*, Maryknoll, N.Y.: Orbis Books, 1993, 127.

31. Ibid., 7.

32. Ibid., 10.

33. Ibid.

34. This text is available to be printed at http://www.hymns.me.uk/ christ-the-lord-is-risen-today-hymn.htm.

35. Luke 24:21, NRSV, footnoted alternate translation.

36. Thomas H. Troeger, *Above the Moon Earth Rises: Hymn, Texts, Anthems, and Poems for a New Creation*, New York: Oxford University Press, 2002, 8.

37. Although the words are nearly universally sung to the setting "Easter Hymn," there are many variants of the text. Depending on which hymnal you use, the opening line will be either "Christ the Lord is risen today, Alleluia!" or "Jesus Christ is risen today, Alleluia!" Also, different hymnals employ different stanzas in different order. For a complete version of the original ten stanzas, see the beginning of this sermon.

38. http://www.recmusic.org/lieder/get_text.html?TextId=5060.

39. Carlton R. Young, ed., *Companion to the United Methodist Hymnal*, Nashville, Tenn.: Abingdon Press, 1993, 476.

40. http://www.recmusic.org/lieder/get_text.html?TextId=5060.

41. Young, *Companion to the United Methodist Hymnal*, 476.

42. Erik Routley, ed., as edited and expanded by Paul A. Richardson, *A Panorama of Christian Hymnody*, Chicago: GIA Publications, 2005, 67.

43. Young, *Companion to the United Methodist Hymnal*, 476.

44. Download a review copy of the anthem at http://www.selahpub.com/ Choral/ChoralTitles/420-117-LoveDivine.html.

45. Routley and Richardson, *Panorama of Christian Hymnody*, 147.

46. Colin Gibson in Ibid., 627. Copyright © 1994 Hope Publishing Company, Carol Stream, Illinois. All rights reserved. Used by permission.

47. Ruth Duck, "How Could a God Whose Name Is Love," in Ruth Duck, *Circles of Care: Hymns and Songs*, Cleveland, Ohio: Pilgrim Press, 1998, no. 24.

48. http://nethymnal.org/htm/s/i/singtong.htm.

49. http://nethymnal.org/htm/r/i/rideride.htm.

50. http://nethymnal.org/htm/n/m/nmtmtell.htm.

51. The third and fifth stanzas from a composite translation of the nineteenth century in Routley and Richardson, *Panorama of Christian Hymnody*, 160.

52. Stanzas 1 and 3 in Ibid., 86.

53. Ibid., 44.

54. Stanza 2 from a composite translation of the nineteenth century in Ibid., 160.

55. Ibid., 86.

56. Bryan D. Spinks, *Liturgy in the Age of Reason: Worship and Sacraments in England and Scotland 1662–c. 1800,* Bodmin, Cornwall: Ashgate, 2008, 241. The quotation within the quotation is from J. R. Watson, *The English Hymn: A Critical and Historical Study,* Oxford: Clarendon Press, 1997, 133.

57. Routley and Richardson, *Panorama of Christian Hymnody,* 143. This is part of a composite translation, different from the one cited earlier in note 35.

58. Ibid., 445.

59. Raymond Glover, ed., *The Hymnal 1982 Companion,* vol. 3B, New York: Church Hymnal Corporation, 1064–65.

60. Thomas H. Troeger, *Preaching While the Church Is under Reconstruction: The Visionary Role of Preachers in a Fragmented World,* Nashville, Tenn.: Abingdon Press, 1999, 70.

CHAPTER 3

1. Daniel Levitin, *This Is Your Brain on Music: The Science of a Human Obsession,* New York: Dutton, 2006, 6.

2. Ibid., 188.

3. Martin Jean, "Of New Wine and Old Wine Skins: Can Old Music Mean Anything New Today?," unpublished lecture delivered at the Institute of Sacred Music, as part of a conference entitled "Listening Is Performing," Yale University, March 10, 2009, 12–13. I am indebted to Professor Jean for giving me a copy of his lecture.

4. J. A. Simpson and E. S. C. Weiner, eds., *The Compact Oxford English Dictionary,* 2nd ed., Oxford: Clarendon Press, 1993, 1309. I am also indebted to Professor Richard Ward, a former colleague at the Iliff School of Theology, who combines performance studies and homiletics in his scholarly work and who first drew my attention to the etymology of the word "performance."

5. Editor's introduction to the "Medieval Church" in *Theological Aesthetics: A Reader,* ed. Gesa Elsbeth Thiessen, Grand Rapids, Mich.: Eerdmans, 2005, 61.

6. Emil Brunner, *The Divine Imperative,* Philadelphia: Westminster Press, 1947, 502.

7. Karl Rahner, "Theology and the Arts," in *Thought: Fordham University Quarterly,* Faith and Imagination Issue, 57, no. 224 (March 1982), 25.

8. Quentin Faulkner, *Wiser Than Despair: The Evolution of Ideas in the Relationship of Music and the Christian Church,* Westport, Conn.: Greenwood Press, 1996, 167.

9. Jean, "unpublished lecture," 2. I am drawing substantially from Jean's lecture throughout this section.

10. Ibid., 11.

11. Ibid., 12. He is quoting from Kendall Walton, "Listening with Imagination: Is Music Representational?" *Journal of Aesthetics and Art Criticism* 52, no. 1, (Winter 1994), 47–61.

12. Eugene L. Lowry, *The Sermon: Dancing the Edge of Mystery*, Nashville, Tenn.: Abingdon Press, 1997, 55.

13. Evans E. Crawford, *The Hum: Call and Response in African American Preaching*, Nashville, Tenn.: Abingdon Press, 1995, 16.

14. Stephen H. Webb, *The Divine Voice: Christian Proclamation and the Theology of Sound*, Grand Rapids, Mich.: Brazos Press, 2004, 32.

15. Levitin, *This Is Your Brain on Music*, 250.

16. Amos Niven Wilder, *Theopoetic: Theology and the Religious Imagination*, Philadelphia: Fortress Press, 1976, 2.

17. Robin A. Leaver, *J. S. Bach as Preacher: His Passions and Music in Worship*, St. Louis, Mo.: Concordia, 1984, 7.

18. Thomas H. Troeger, *God, You Made All Things for Singing: Hymn Texts, Anthems and Poems for a New Millennium*, New York: Oxford University Press, 2009, 3.

19. Here is the order of musical compositions on which the sermons that follow will be based: J. S. Bach, Cantata 180, "Schmücke dich, o liebe Seele" (Deck Thyself, O Beloved soul); Gabriel Fauré "Requiem;" individual arias by J. S. Bach: from the Mass in B Minor, "Laudamus te" (We praise thee); from Cantata 27, "Gute Nacht, du Weltgetümmel!" (Good night, you worldly tumult); from Cantata 198, "Der Ewigkeit spahirnes Haus" (Eternity's sapphire house); from Cantata 78, "Wir eilen mit schwachen, doch emsigen Schritten" (We hasten with weak yet eager steps); from Cantata 61, "Öffne dich, mein ganzes Herze" (Open, my whole heart); the spiritual "Swing Low, Sweet Chariot."

20. I have found the following book to be the most thorough and helpful analysis of Bach's cantatas in English: Alfred Durr, *The Cantatas of J. S. Bach: with Their Librettos in German-English Parallel Text*, trans. Richard D. P. Jones, Oxford: Oxford University Press, 2005. A nonspecialist will find the book lucid and readable. It includes a close musical analysis of nearly every movement of all the cantatas. I consulted this volume in preparing all the sermons on Bach's music that are in this book.

21. Ibid., 590. "The anonymous librettist of this chorale cantata bases his text upon Johann Franck's communion hymn of 1649."

22. Carlo Cabalerro, *Fauré and French Musical Aesthetics*, New York: Cambridge University Press, 2001, 184. I am heavily indebted to this book for the historical and musical information on which I base the sermon.

23. The text and translation of all parts of the Requiem are from http://members.macconnect.com/users/j/jimbob/classical/Faure_Requiem.html#faure.

24. Durr, *Cantatas of J. S. Bach*, 554.

25. Ibid., 864.

26. Ibid., 523.

27. Troeger, *God, You Made All Things for Singing*, 36.

28. Durr, *Cantatas of J. S. Bach*, 76. The aria is from Cantata 61, "Nun komm, der Heiden Heiland" (Now Come, Savior of the Gentiles), and it is for soprano and continuo alone so that it does not require a large number of skilled instrumental players.

29. Erik Routley, ed., as edited and expanded by Paul A. Richardson, *A Panorama of Christian Hymnody*, Chicago: GIA Publications, 2005, 338.

CHAPTER 4

1. The remark originally appeared on a book jacket of Stevens's poems, *The Man with the Blue Guitar and Other Poems*, New York: Knopf, 1937, and is cited in Nathan A. Scott Jr., *The Poetics of Belief: Studies in Coleridge, Arnold, Pater, Santayana, Stevens, and Heidegger*, Chapel Hill: University of North Carolina Press, 1985, 1.

2. Edward Hirsch, *How to Read a Poem and Fall in Love with Poetry*, San Diego: Harcourt, 1999, 244.

3. Ibid., 245.

4. Fred B. Craddock, "Foreword" to Eugene L. Lowry, *The Homiletical Plot: The Sermon as Narrative Art Form*, expanded edition, Louisville, Ky.: Westminster John Knox Press, 2001, xiii.

5. Karl Rahner, "Theology and the Arts," in *Thought: Fordham University Quarterly*, Faith and Imagination Issue, Vol. LVII, No. 224 (March 1982), 25.

6. Andrew M. Greeley, *Religion as Poetry,* New Brunswick, N.J.: Transaction, 1996, 24.

7. Ibid., 23.

8. Ibid., 25.

9. Ibid., 32.

10. David Daiches, *God and the Poets*, The Gifford Lectures, 1983, New York: Oxford University Press, 1984, 101.

11. John Hollander, *Rhyme's Reason: A Guide to English Verse*, new, enlarged edition, New Haven, Conn.: Yale University Press, 1989, 4.

12. Timothy Steele, *Missing Measures: Modern Poetry and the Revolt against Meter*, Fayetteville: University of Arkansas Press, 1990, 293.

13. Donald Davie, ed., *The New Oxford Book of Christian Verse*, New York: Oxford University Press, 1981, xx.

14. Hirsch, *How to Read a Poem*, 1.

15. Ibid., 6.

16. Quoted without citation in Ibid., 27.

17. Enda McDonagh, *The Gracing of Society*, Dublin: Gill and Macmillan, 1989, 126.

18. Frederick Buechner, *Telling the Truth: The Gospel as Tragedy, Comedy and Fairy Tale*, New York: HarperCollins, 1977, 21.

19. Greeley, *Religion as Poetry*, 35.

20. David Brown and David Fuller, *Signs of Grace: Sacraments in Poetry and Prose*, Ridgefield, Conn.: Morehouse, 1995, 119.

21. The three Herbert poems that I have chosen are among texts that have been set to music by Ralph Vaughan Williams. Titled "Five Mystical Songs," they are composed for baritone vocal solo, choir, and orchestra or keyboard. I have sometimes preached on these poems, and a performance of Vaughan Williams's music immediately followed. But my emphasis in these sermons is on the poetry, not the music, and therefore the musical performance is optional. Preachers should also note that "The Call" and "Antiphon (I)" have been set as hymns and are available in some more recent denominational hymnals. "The Call" is No. 164 in *The United Methodist Hymnal*, 1989, and No. 487 in *The Hymnal 1982*, Episcopal Church. "Antiphon (I)" is No. 93 in *The United Methodist Hymnal*, 1989, No. 468 in *The Presbyterian Hymnal* (1990), and Nos. 402 and 403 in *The Hymnal 1982*, Episcopal Church.
There have also been some musical settings of Meynell's poems, but I have neither heard them nor been able to secure recordings of them.

22. Davie, *New Oxford Book of Christian Verse*, xxiv. Davie ranks him along with Vaughan, Smart, and Cowper as one of "the masters of the sacred poem in English."

23. George Herbert, *The Complete English Poems*, ed. John Tobin, London: Penguin, 1991. All of George Herbert's work is in the public domain. I am using the following edition because it has clear notes that are helpful in understanding antiquated words and lines whose meaning may elude the modern reader. These are the opening lines of his sonnet "The Holy Scriptures (2)," 52.

24. Hollander, *Rhyme's Reason*, 19.

25. Herbert, *Complete English Poems*, 147.

26. Ibid., 47.

27. Ibid., 178.

28. http://poetry.elcore.net/CatholicPoets/Meynell/index.html.

29. Hirsch, *How to Read a Poem*, 257.

30. Quoted in June Badeni, *The Slender Tree: A Life of Alice Meynell*, Padstow, Cornwall: Tabb House, 1981, xi.

31. Steele, *Missing Measures*, 24.

32. Ibid., 68.

33. Wendell Berry, *Standing by Words: Essays by Wendell Berry*, San Francisco: North Point Press, 1983, 201.

34. Badeni, *Slender Tree*, xi.

35. Pat Alexander and Veronica Zundel, eds., *Eerdmans Book of Christian Poetry*, Grand Rapids, Mich.: Eerdmans, 1984, 73.

36. Badeni, *Slender Tree*, 28.

37. Ibid.

38. Ibid., 77.

39. These are the opening words of Isaiah 45:8: "Drop down dew, ye heavens, from above, and let the clouds rain the just. Let the earth be opened and send forth a Saviour" (Vulgate). "The text is used frequently both at Mass and in the Divine Office during Advent, as it gives exquisite poetical expression to the longings of Patriarchs and Prophets, and symbolically of the Church, for the coming of the Messias. Throughout Advent it occurs daily as the versicle and response at Vespers" (http://www.newadvent.org/cathen/13183b.htm).

CHAPTER 5

1. George Herbert, *The Complete English Poems*, ed. John Tobin, London: Penguin, 1991, not paginated, but the second page of the brief biography of Herbert that serves as the frontispiece.

2. Wendell Berry, *Standing by Words: Essays by Wendell Berry*, San Francisco: North Point Press, 1983, 205.

3. Martin Jean, "Of New Wine and Old Wine Skins: Can Old Music Mean Anything New Today?" unpublished lecture delivered at the Institute of Sacred Music, Yale University, March 10, 2009, 3.

4. William Wordsworth, "Ode: Intimations of Immortality from Recollections of Early Childhood," in *Selected Poetry of William Wordsworth*, ed. Mark Van Doren, New York: Modern Library, 2002, 520.

5. Ibid., 522.

6. Andrew M. Greeley, *Religion as Poetry*, New Brunswick, N.J.: Transaction, 1996, 154.

7. Ibid., 24, emphasis added.

8. John Ruskin from *Modern Painters*, in *Theological Aesthetics: A Reader*, ed. Gesa Elsbeth Thiessen, Grand Rapids, Mich.: Eerdmans, 2005, 185. "The deaf children sitting in the market-place" is an allusion to Luke 7:32: "They are like unto children sitting in the market place, and calling one to another, and saying, We have piped unto you, and ye have not danced; we have mourned to you, and ye have not wept" (KJV).

9. Thomas H. Troeger, *Borrowed Light: Hymn Texts, Prayers and Poems*, New York: Oxford University Press, 1994, 79.

10. Langdon B. Gilkey, "Can Art Fill the Vacuum?" in *Art, Creativity, and the Sacred: An Anthology in Religion and Art*, ed. Diane Apostolos-Cappadona, rev. ed., New York: Continuum, 1995, 263.

11. Bernard Häring, *Free and Faithful in Christ: Moral Theology for Priests and Laity*, vol. 2, *The Truth Will Set You Free*, New York: Seabury Press, 1979, 341.

12. Joan Chittister, "Monastic Wisdom for Seekers of Light," in Thiessen, *Theological Aesthetics*, 366.

13. Tina Beattie, *The New Atheists: The Twilight of Reason and the War on Religion*, Maryknoll, N.Y., Orbis Books, 2007, 163.

14. Chittister, "Monastic Wisdom for Seekers of Light," 367.

15. Beattie, *New Atheists,* 166.

16. Ibid., 163–64.

17. Ibid., 173.

18. David Daiches, *God and the Poets*, The Gifford Lectures, 1983, Oxford: Oxford University Press, 1984, 212–13.

19. Ibid., 212, emphasis in original.

20. Beattie, *New Atheists*, 173.

21. Fred B. Craddock, "Foreword" to Eugene L. Lowry, *The Homiletical Plot: The Sermon as Narrative Art Form*, expanded edition, Louisville, Ky.: Westminster John Knox Press, 2001, xi.

22. Berry, *Standing by Words*, 204.

23. Herbert, *Complete English Poems*, 61.

24. J. A. Simpson and E. S. C. Weiner, eds., *The Compact Oxford English Dictionary*, 2nd ed., Oxford: Clarendon Press, 1993, 359.

25. Herbert, *Complete English Poems*, xvi.

26. *Compact Oxford English Dictionary*, 54.

27. Ibid., 317.

28. John McIntyre, *Faith, Theology and Imagination*, Edinburgh: Handsel Press, 1987, 176.

29. Garrett Green, *Imagining God, Theology and the Religious Imagination*, San Francisco: Harper and Row, 1989, 149.

30. Beattie, *New Atheists*, 173.

Bibliography

Achtemeier, Paul J., ed. *Harper's Bible Dictionary*. San Francisco: HarperCollins, 1985.

Alexander, Pat, and Veronica Zundel, eds. *Eerdmans Book of Christian Poetry*. Grand Rapids, Mich.: Eerdmans, 1984.

Alter, Robert. *The World of Biblical Literature*. New York: Basic Books, 1992.

Apostolos-Cappadona, Diane, ed. *Art, Creativity, and the Sacred: An Anthology in Religion and Art*. Rev. ed. New York: Continuum, 1995.

Appleton, George, ed. *The Oxford Book of Prayer*. New York: Oxford University Press, 1986.

Aquinas, Thomas. *Summa Theologiae*. Vol. 39, *Religion and Worship* (2a2ae. 80–91), ed. Kevin D. O'Rourke, O.P. London: Blackfriars, 1964.

Augustine. *Confessions*. Trans. Henry Chadwick. Oxford: Oxford University Press, 1998.

———. *Expositions on the Book of Psalms*. Vol. 2. Trans. by members of the English Church. A Library of Fathers of the Holy Catholic Church. Oxford: John Henry Parker, F. and J. Rivington, 1848.

Badeni, June. *The Slender Tree: A Life of Alice Meynell*. Padstow, Cornwall: Tabb House, 1981.

Beattie, Tina. *The New Atheists: The Twilight of Reason and the War on Religion*. Maryknoll, N.Y.: Orbis Books, 2007.

Berry, Wendell. *Standing by Words: Essays by Wendell Berry*. San Francisco: North Point Press, 1983.

Brown, David, and David Fuller. *Signs of Grace: Sacraments in Poetry and Prose.* Ridgefield, Conn.: Morehouse, 1995.

Brown, Frank Burch. *Religious Aesthetics: A Theological Study of Making and Meaning.* In *Theological Aesthetics: A Reader,* ed. Gesa Elsbeth Thiessen. Grand Rapids, Mich.: Eerdmans, 2005.

Brown, Raymond E. *An Introduction to the New Testament.* New York: Doubleday, 1997.

Brunner, Emil. *The Divine Imperative.* Philadelphia: Westminster Press, 1947.

Buechner, Frederick. *Telling the Truth: The Gospel as Tragedy, Comedy and Fairy Tale.* New York: HarperCollins, 1977.

Cabalerro, Carlo. *Fauré and French Musical Aesthetics.* New York: Cambridge University Press, 2001.

Carl, William J., III, ed. *Best Advice: Wisdom on Ministry from 30 Leading Pastors and Preachers.* Louisville, Ky.: Westminster John Knox Press, 2009.

Chittister, Joan. "Monastic Wisdom for Seekers of Light." In *Theological Aesthetics: A Reader,* ed. Gesa Elsbeth Thiessen. Grand Rapids, Mich.: Eerdmans, 2005.

Countryman, L. William. *The Poetic Imagination: An Anglican Spiritual Tradition.* Maryknoll, N.Y.: Orbis Books, 1999.

Craddock, Fred B. *As One without Authority.* Rev. ed. . St. Louis, Mo.: Chalice Press, 2001.

Crawford, Evans E. *The Hum: Call and Response in African American Preaching.* Nashville, Tenn.: Abingdon Press, 1995.

Curzon, David, ed. *Modern Poems on the Bible: An Anthology.* Philadelphia: Jewish Publication Society, 1994.

Daiches, David. *God and the Poets.* The Gifford Lectures, 1983. New York: Oxford University Press, 1984.

Davie, Donald, ed. *The New Oxford Book of Christian Verse.* New York: Oxford University Press, 1981.

de Gruchy, John W. *Christianity, Art and Transformation: Theological Aesthetics in the Struggle for Justice.* Cambridge: Cambridge University Press, 2001.

Duck, Ruth. *Circles of Care: Hymns and Songs.* Cleveland, Ohio: Pilgrim Press, 1998.

Durr, Alfred. *The Cantatas of J. S. Bach: with Their Librettos in German-English Parallel Text.* Trans. Richard D. P. Jones. Oxford: Oxford University Press, 2005.

Eriugena, John Scotus. *Periphyseon.* Book 3. Trans. I. P. Sheldon Williams, rev. John J. O'Meara. Montreal, Wash.: Bellarmin, 1987.

Faulkner, Quentin. *Wiser Than Despair: The Evolution of Ideas in the Relationship of Music and the Christian Church.* Westport, Conn.: Greenwood Press, 1996.

Findlay, Patrick N. "Handel's Messiah through the Centuries." *Early Music News* 24, no. 4 (December 1999), http://psg.com/~patf/handel/messiah.html.

Freedman, David Noel, ed. *The Anchor Bible Dictionary*. Vol. 4. New York: Doubleday, 1992.

García-Rivera, Alejandro. *The Community of the Beautiful: A Theological Aesthetics*. Collegeville, Minn.: Liturgical Press, 1999.

Gardner, Helen. *Religion and Literature*. New York: Oxford University Press, 1983.

Glover, Raymond, ed. *The Hymnal 1982 Companion*. Vol. 3B. New York: Church Hymnal Corporation, 1982.

Grayson, David. *Adventures in Contentment*. New York: Grosset and Dunlap, 1907.

Greeley, Andrew M. *Religion as Poetry*. New Brunswick, N.J.: Transaction, 1996.

Green, Garrett. *Imagining God, Theology and the Religious Imagination*. San Francisco: Harper and Row, 1989.

Häring, Bernard. *Free and Faithful in Christ: Moral Theology for Priests and Laity*. Vol. 2, *The Truth Will Set You Free*. New York: Seabury Press, 1979.

Harries, Richard. *Art and the Beauty of God*. London: Mowbray, 1996.

Hays, Richard B. *Echoes of Scripture in the Letters of Paul*. New Haven, Conn.: Yale University Press, 1989.

Herbert, George. *The Complete English Poems*. Ed. John Tobin. London: Penguin, 1991.

Hirsch, Edward. *How to Read a Poem and Fall in Love with Poetry*. San Diego: Harcourt, 1999.

Hollander, John. *Rhyme's Reason: A Guide to English Verse*. New, enlarged edition. New Haven, Conn.: Yale University Press, 1989.

Jones, Alexander, ed. *The Jerusalem Bible*. Garden City, N.Y.: Doubleday, 1966.

Jones, Arthur C. *Wade in the Water: The Wisdom of the Spirituals*. Maryknoll, N.Y.: Orbis Books, 1993.

Leaver, Robin A. *J. S. Bach as Preacher: His Passions and Music in Worship*. St. Louis, Mo.: Concordia, 1984.

Levitin, Daniel. *This Is Your Brain on Music: The Science of a Human Obsession*. New York: Dutton, 2006.

Lowry, Eugene L. *The Homiletical Plot: The Sermon as Narrative Art Form*. Expanded edition. Louisville, Ky.: Westminster John Knox Press, 2001.

———. *The Sermon: Dancing the Edge of Mystery*. Nashville, Tenn.: Abingdon Press, 1997.

Maritain, Jacques. *Art and Scholasticism and the Frontiers of Poetry*. Trans. Joseph W. Evans. New York: Scribner's, 1962.

McDonagh, Enda. *The Gracing of Society*. Dublin: Gill and Macmillan, 1989.

McIntyre, John. *Faith, Theology and Imagination*. Edinburgh: Handsel Press, 1987.

Meeks, Wayne A., ed. *The HarperCollins Study Bible*. New Revised Standard Version. New York: HarperCollins, 1993.

Nichols, Aidan. *The Art of God Incarnate*. London: Darton, Longman, and Todd, 1980.

Ong, Walter J., S.J. *The Presence of the Word: Some Prolegomena for Cultural and Religious History*. New Haven, Conn.: Yale University Press, 1967.

Petersen, David L., and Gene M. Tucker, eds. *The New Interpreter's Bible*. Vol. 6. Nashville, Tenn.: Abingdon Press, 2001.

Rahner, Karl. "Theology and the Arts." In *Thought: Fordham University Quarterly*, Faith and Imagination Issue, vol. LVII, no. 224 (March 1982).

Robinson, Marilynne. *The Death of Adam: Essays on Modern Thought*. New York: Picador, 2005.

Routley, Erik. *Christian Hymns Observed: When in Our Music God Is Glorified*. Princeton, N.J.: Prestige Publications, 1982.

Routley, Erik, ed., as edited and expanded by Paul A. Richardson. *A Panorama of Christian Hymnody*. Chicago: GIA Publications, 2005.

Ruskin, John. *Modern Painters*. In *Theological Aesthetics: A Reader*, ed. Gesa Elsbeth Thiessen. Grand Rapids, Mich.: Eerdmans, 2005.

Schonberg, Harold C. *The Lives of the Great Composers*. 3rd ed. New York: Norton, 1997.

Scott, Nathan A., Jr. *The Poetics of Belief: Studies in Coleridge, Arnold, Pater, Santayana, Stevens and Heidegger*. Chapel Hill: University of North Carolina Press, 1985.

Sherry, Patrick. *Spirit and Beauty: An Introduction to Theological Aesthetics*. 2nd ed. London: SCM Press, 2002.

Simpson, J. A., and E. S. C. Weiner, eds. *The Compact Oxford English Dictionary*. 2nd ed. Oxford: Clarendon Press, 1993.

———. *The Oxford English Dictionary*. 2nd ed. Vol. 3. Oxford: Clarendon Press, 1989.

Spinks, Bryan D. *Liturgy in the Age of Reason: Worship and Sacraments in England and Scotland 1662–c. 1800*. Bodmin, Cornwall: Ashgate, 2008.

Steele, Timothy. *Missing Measures: Modern Poetry and the Revolt against Meter*. Fayetteville: University of Arkansas Press, 1990.

Stevens, Wallace. *The Man with the Blue Guitar and Other Poems*. New York: Knopf, 1937.

Thiessen, Gesa Elsbeth, ed. *Theological Aesthetics: A Reader*. Grand Rapids, Mich.: Eerdmans, 2005.

Thurman, Howard. *Deep River and the Negro Spiritual Speaks of Life and Death*. Richmond, Ind.: Friends United Press, 1975.

Tracy, David. *The Analogical Imagination: Christian Theology and the Culture of Pluralism*. New York: Crossroad, 1981.

Troeger, Thomas H. *Above the Moon Earth Rises: Hymn Texts, Anthems, and Poems for a New Creation*. New York: Oxford University Press, 2002.

———. *Borrowed Light: Hymn Texts, Prayers and Poems*. New York: Oxford University Press, 1994.

———. *God, You Made All Things for Singing: Hymn . Texts, Anthems and Poems for a New Millennium*. New York: Oxford University Press, 2009.

———. *Imagining a Sermon*. Nashville, Tenn.: Abingdon Press, 1990.

———. *Preaching and Worship*. St. Louis, Mo.: Chalice Press, 2003.

———. *Preaching While the Church Is under Reconstruction: The Visionary Role of Preachers in a Fragmented World*. Nashville, Tenn.: Abingdon Press, 1999.

———. *Ten Strategies for Preaching in a Multi Media Culture*. Nashville, Tenn.: Abingdon Press, 1996.

Viladesau, Richard. *Theological Aesthetics: God in Imagination, Beauty, and Art*. New York: Oxford University Press, 1999.

Vrudny, Kimberly, and Wilson Yates, ed. *Arts, Theology and the Church: New Intersections*. Cleveland, Ohio: Pilgrim Press, 2005.

Wallace, Mark I. *The Second Naiveté: Barth, Ricoeur, and the New Yale Theology*. Macon, Ga.: Mercer University Press, 1990.

Watson, J. R. *The English Hymn: A Critical and Historical Study*. Oxford: Clarendon Press, 1997.

Webb, Stephen H. *The Divine Voice: Christian Proclamation and the Theology of Sound*. Grand Rapids, Mich.: Brazos Press, 2004.

Wesley, Charles. "Jesus, Show Us Thy Salvation" ("Love divine, all loves excelling"). In *A Panorama of Christian Hymnody*, ed. Erik Routley, ed. and expanded by Paul A. Richardson. Chicago: GIA Publications, 2005.

Whittle, Donald. *Christianity and the Arts*. London: A. R. Mowbray, 1966.

Wilder, Amos Niven. *Theopoetic: Theology and the Religious Imagination*. Philadelphia: Fortress Press, 1976.

Wolterstorff, Nicholas. *Art in Action: Toward a Christian Aesthetic*, Carlisle, UK: Solway, 1997.

Wordsworth, William. "Ode: Intimations of Immortality from Recollections of Early Childhood." In *Selected Poetry of William Wordsworth*, ed. Mark Van Doren. New York: Modern Library, 2002.

Wren, Brian. *What Language Shall I Borrow? God-Talk in Worship: A Male Response to Feminist Theology*. New York: Crossroad, 1989.

Wuthnow, Robert. *All in Sync: How Music and Art Are Revitalizing American Religion*. Berkeley: University of California Press, 2006.

Young, Carlton R., ed. *Companion to the United Methodist Hymnal*. Nashville, Tenn.: Abingdon Press, 1993.

Index